NEW PLAYWRIGHTS
The Best Plays of 2005

SMITH AND KRAUS PUBLISHERS
Contemporary Playwrights / Full-Length Play Anthologies

Humana Festival: 20 One-Act Plays 1976–1996
Humana Festival 1993: The Complete Plays
Humana Festival 1994: The Complete Plays
Humana Festival 1995: The Complete Plays
Humana Festival 1996: The Complete Plays
Humana Festival 1997: The Complete Plays
Humana Festival 1998: The Complete Plays
Humana Festival 1999: The Complete Plays
Humana Festival 2000: The Complete Plays
Humana Festival 2001: The Complete Plays
Humana Festival 2002: The Complete Plays
Humana Festival 2003: The Complete Plays
Humana Festival 2004: The Complete Plays
Humana Festival 2005: The Complete Plays

New Playwrights: The Best Plays of 1998
New Playwrights: The Best Plays of 1999
New Playwrights: The Best Plays of 2000
New Playwrights: The Best Plays of 2001
New Playwrights: The Best Plays of 2002
New Playwrights: The Best Plays of 2003
New Playwrights: The Best Plays of 2004
New Playwrights: The Best Plays of 2005

Women Playwrights: The Best Plays of 1995
Women Playwrights: The Best Plays of 1996
Women Playwrights: The Best Plays of 1997
Women Playwrights: The Best Plays of 1998
Women Playwrights: The Best Plays of 1999
Women Playwrights: The Best Plays of 2000
Women Playwrights: The Best Plays of 2001
Women Playwrights: The Best Plays of 2002
Women Playwrights: The Best Plays of 2003

If you would like information about forthcoming Smith and Kraus books, you may receive our annual catalogue, free of charge, by sending your name and address to *Smith and Kraus Catalogue, PO Box 127, Lyme, NH 03768.* Or call us at (888) 282-2881, fax (603) 643-1831. www.SmithandKraus.com

NEW PLAYWRIGHTS

The Best Plays
of 2005

CONTEMPORARY PLAYWRIGHTS
SERIES

SK
A Smith and Kraus Book

A Smith and Kraus Book
Published by Smith and Kraus, Inc.
177 Lyme Road, Hanover, NH 03755
www.SmithandKraus.com

Manufactured in the United States of America
Cover and text design by Julia Gignoux, Freedom Hill Design, Reading, Vermont

First Edition: June 2006
10 9 8 7 6 5 4 3 2 1

The Library of Congress Cataloging-In-Publication Data

New Playwrights: the best plays of 2005. —1st ed.
p. cm. — (Contemporary playwrights series)

ISBN 1-57525-446-8
1. American drama—20th century. I. Series.
PS634.N416 2000
812'.5408—dc21   00-029707

CONTENTS

FOREWORD

This, the sixth in Smith and Kraus' New Playwrights series that I have had the honor to edit, is the best yet. I know, I say that every year, but I mean it this time.

Two words in the title of this volume need some clarification. They are "new" and "best." What is a "new playwright"? Someone who never wrote a play before? Someone who's not yet won the Pulitzer Prize? In the pecking order of American playwrights there are, let's face it, a select group whom pretty much everyone who knows plays would have to agree are definitely on the A Team — writers such as Horton Foote, Edward Albee, Terrence Mc-Nally, Donald Margulies, and so on. When these folks write a new play, their agents don't have to work very hard, I would think, to arrange a significant premiere production. There is a far vaster list of B Team writers — wonderful playwrights all, but not exactly drama aficionado household names. These writers sometimes struggle to get productions of their work, or are just coming up in the ranks. Time will tell how far their careers take them. For the purposes of this volume, a "new playwright" comes from this list.

As for "best," *any* "best" list can seem rather eccentric and subjective. There are, after all, more plays then you could imagine that are truly worthy of consideration for this series; but I had to pick six. I freely admit, my choices are eccentric and completely subjective. I don't just go "eeny, meeny, minee, mo," though. I try, in my eccentric, subjective way, to pick plays that are ethically and genderly (is that a word?) diverse, and that also represent the diversity of styles in which American playwrights are currently working, including good ol' linear realism, which many these days hold in disdain. Not me. I like a well-constructed realistic play, such as Jan Buttram's *Texas Homos,* which wins my vote as this year's funniest title. But I also can get into plays that do not attempt to realistically portray the world in which we live, that take us on a surreal (to varying degrees) journey, such as Adam Bock's *Swimming in the Shallows* and Mark Schultz's *Everything Will Be Different,* as long as I can care about the characters and follow the story, which is not often the case with these sorts of plays, let's be frank. Usually, I don't much care for narration in lieu of drama, but Michele Lowe's wonderfully funny and poignant *String of Pearls* manages to make narration brilliantly theatrical. *Comfort Women,* by Chungmi Kim, and *Learning Curve,* by Rogelio Martinez, are both fundamentally realistic plays, though both depart in wonderfully theatrically ways from the conventions of realism.

I think the plays in this volume represent the "best" and the "new." I hope you enjoy them.

— *D. L. Lepidus*

INTRODUCTION

If a playwright types alone in the forest and no one hears him, does he make a sound? Or she. I wonder, especially when the work is not going well, or when submitted, it disappears into ether. In order to will myself through these minefields, I step back and ask myself, Why do I write plays in the first place? There are two reasons, really: 1) foremost, to express myself through a singular and collaborative art form, by telling a story through dialogue; and 2) the conceit that what I write will be of interest to others. Of course, there's a third reason, also a conceit: to be rich and famous and to reap all that goes along with it. But, as the playwright Robert Anderson famously said, "You can make a killing in the theater but you can't make a living." Still, playwrights are eternally optimistic. We have to be. Perseverance is *everything* for "success," such as it is, is often incremental. I was fortunate to have my play, *Adult Fiction*, published by Smith and Kraus in *New Playwrights: The Best Plays of 2000*. Smith and Kraus has given many playwrights the gift of seeing their words in print. For that, we are grateful; and if wealth and fame are still, perhaps, elusive, then being published by Smith and Kraus shows that 1) and 2) are within reach. Whatever obstacles there are along the way — and there are many (oh, so many!) — let's be clear: the journey is worth the struggle.

— *Brian Mori*

SWIMMING IN THE SHALLOWS

Adam Bock

PLAYWRIGHT'S BIOGRAPHY

Adam Bock's plays include *The Shaker Chair* (Humana Festival), *Swimming in the Shallows* (Second Stage), *The Thugs, Five Flights* (Rattlestick), and *The Typographer's Dream* (Encore Theater, San Francisco). *Five Flights* won the 2002 Will Glickman Award for best new play produced in the Bay Area, four Dean Goodman awards, and it was nominated for the American Theater Critics, the Osborn, and two BATCC awards. It was named in the *San Francisco Chronicle* and *The Oakland Tribune's* Top Ten Theatrical Events and the *Chronicle's* Top Ten Cultural Events for 2002. Shotgun Player's production of *Swimming in the Shallows* won the 2000 BATCC awards for best production, best ensemble, and best original script. It was a Clauder Competition award-winner, and it has been produced in New York City, Los Angeles, Boston, London, Toronto, Key West, Ithaca, Santa Cruz, and the Edinburgh Fringe. *The Typographer's Dream* has been produced in New York City, San Francisco and at the Edinburgh Fringe. He is the resident playwright at Encore Theater, a Shotgun Players Artistic Associate, and a member of the MCC Playwrights' Coalition. Adam Bock is a NEA and CASH grantee, was a resident at Yaddo, and was a member of the Soho Rep Writer/Director Lab. Adam's plays are published by Dramatists Play Service and Playscripts Inc. Adam is represented by The William Morris Agency.

ORIGINAL PRODUCTION

The World Premiere of *Swimming in the Shallows* was produced by Coyote Theater/Theatrics! in May 1999 in Boston, and it was directed by Betsy Carpenter. The cast was as follows:

BARB	Sophie Parker
BOB	Gary Bisantz
DONNA	Leslie Arnott
CARLA CARLA	Lizza Reilly
NICK	Daniel J. Kells
THE SHARK	Nick Park

The West Coast Premiere was produced by Shotgun Players in San Francisco/Berkeley in September 1999, and it was directed by Kent Nicholson. The cast was as follows:

BARB	Mary Eaton Fairfield
BOB	Gene Thompson
DONNA	Katie Bales
CARLA CARLA	Dawn-Elin Fraser
NICK	Liam Vincent
THE SHARK	John Flanagan

The New York City Premiere was produced by Second Stage Theatre in June and July of 2005, and it was directed by Trip Cullman. The cast was as follows:

BARB . . . . .Mary Shultz
BOB . . . . .Murphy Guyer
DONNA . . . . .Rosemarie DeWitt
CARLA CARLA . . . . .Susan Pourfar
NICK . . . . .Michael Arden
THE SHARK . . . . Logan Marshall-Green

CHARACTERS

BARB: late forties. A nurse.

CARLA CARLA: early forties. A nurse. Best friends with Barb.

DONNA: mid thirties. Carla Carla's girlfriend. Works at the Twig, Rhode Island Aquarium.

NICK: mid thirties. Spotty employment history.

THE SHARK: a mako shark in the Twig, Rhode Island Aquarium.

BOB: Barb's husband.

TIME AND PLACE

The present. Twig, Rhode Island.

STAGING NOTES

I would like to see *Swimming* performed on a long narrow horizontal stage. Perhaps five or seven feet deep. With two long benches. A runway along the back for the SHARK. A slide screen above it. Painted blue. The shark tank. Project the How To titles here. An alternative is to have the actors announce the titles. Either works for me. I'd avoid an elaborate set.

I like it when the Shark has a fin.

The action should be pressed flat. Like a screen. The actors' physical work should be vertical and horizontal rather than three-dimensionally horizontal. I like physical experimentation.

No blackouts except where noted.

Swimming in the Shallows

PART ONE

Barb and Carla Carla are in nurses' uniforms. They are soaking their feet. They are on a break.

BARB: Did you know there're Buddhist monks who only own eight things.

CARLA CARLA: Really?

BARB: From Thailand.

CARLA CARLA: Not including clothes.

BARB: No. Including clothes.

CARLA CARLA: What do they wear? A robe?

BARB: And sandals.

CARLA CARLA: The sandals count as one pair or two things?

BARB: I don't know two I guess I don't know.

CARLA CARLA: If I was the Buddhist monk I'd count'm as one pair.

BARB: And then they maybe have eyeglasses. Or a belt. Or an umbrella. Maybe a bag.

CARLA CARLA: Why would they have a bag?

BARB: So they can carry things.

CARLA CARLA: What? Your one other Buddhist-monk thing?

BARB: So I thought I bet I've got eight pens right here in my purse. I looked. I had nine! Nine pens. What do I need nine pens for?

CARLA CARLA: I bet they borrow everything.

BARB: Who?

CARLA CARLA: Those monks.

BARB: I bet I have eight hundred probably eight thousand things just in my kitchen.

CARLA CARLA: I bet Thailand people say Oh hide the stuff here comes that Buddhist monk again. He's going to want to borrow something.

BARB: Forks knives spoons and glasses wine glasses milk glasses water glasses cocktail glasses and plates coffee cups I have coffee cups Carla Carla

CARLA CARLA: I know.

BARB: I don't even know how many coffee cups I have.

CARLA CARLA: I do. A lot.

BARB: I have. A lot.

CARLA CARLA: Buddhist monk could borrow a coffee cup or two from you.

BARB: mixing bowls pots pans pie plates

CARLA CARLA: Yeah but sure everybody has all that stuff

BARB: cake pans can-opener bottle-opener garlic roaster toaster toaster-oven microwave-oven oven-oven dishwasher fridge my blender my waffle iron my mixer Bob's electric carving knife the cutting boards all my Tupperware I've got tons of Tupperware

CARLA CARLA: Everybody has Tupperware Barb.

BARB: At Peggy's Tupperware party I got forty-eight new pieces alone the other night forty-eight that's enough for six monks that's six Buddhist monks worth of Tupperware at one shot in one night Carla Carla

CARLA CARLA: That's a lot.

BARB: I read this and I got a very upset very unnerved feeling.

So I told Bob about it.

CARLA CARLA: What'd he say?

BARB: He said Lucky we don't live in Thailand. Lucky we live in Twig Rhode Island U.S.A. I was gonna say No Bob that's all they want. But he was going (blah blah blah).

Same time I was looking around the room counting things. I passed two hundred I stopped. And we were only in the den. And I thought to myself Maybe I only want eight things.

I think maybe that was a very important moment. For me.

CARLA CARLA: Hmm. *(Pause. Gives Barb a gift.)* So anyway Happy Birthday.

BARB: Oh Carla Carla you shouldn't have.

CARLA CARLA: Yeah well.

BARB: Isn't this

CARLA CARLA: Oh just open it.

BARB: Thank you so much. Oh what is

CARLA CARLA: It's a cat bowl a bowl for your cat Barb.

BARB: Oh I love it it's cute she'll love it

CARLA CARLA: I know you already have one but I saw this one and I liked it and I wanted you to have it. Do you like it?

BARB: I do I like it.

CARLA CARLA: 'Cause I have the receipt. And I wouldn't mind.

BARB: Well

CARLA CARLA: You don't like it?

BARB: No I do.

CARLA CARLA: You want something else.

BARB: No I don't

CARLA CARLA: Here's the receipt. Since you don't like it.

BARB: No I have so much stuff I feel heavy. I love this bowl. I have so much stuff.

(Pause.)

CARLA CARLA: Nick has a new boyfriend.

BARB: Another one?

CARLA CARLA: Yup.

BARB: He keeping the old one too?

CARLA CARLA: I don't think so.

BARB: Oh I liked him. What was his name?

CARLA CARLA: Rick.

BARB: Rick? Was it Rick?

CARLA CARLA: Yeah Rick. Right?

BARB: It was Rick? Rick.

CARLA CARLA: Rick.

BARB: Jack.

CARLA CARLA: Right Jack. No it was Rick.

BARB: No it was Jim.

CARLA CARLA: Rick was before Jack?

BARB: Yeah it was Rick then Jack

CARLA CARLA: Then Jim.

BARB: Yeah.

CARLA CARLA: Rick Jack Jim.

BARB: Where does he find them?

CARLA CARLA: Outside. He walks outside he finds a new boyfriend. This one sells ballpark hot dogs. Nick went to a Pawsox game. Now he's in love. This new guy's name is Lance. You keeping the cat bowl? 'Cause if you don't want it I'll give it to Donna.

BARB: This Lance like him back?

CARLA CARLA: Look do you want it or not? I won't be upset.

BARB: You think Donna'd want it?

CARLA CARLA: Give it here. I swear I don't get you sometimes Barb.

BARB: Are you mad?

CARLA CARLA: No.

BARB: You seem mad.

CARLA CARLA: It's a birthday present.

BARB: Give it back.

CARLA CARLA: *(She doesn't.)*

This the beginning of another craze?

BARB: No.

CARLA CARLA: Because if it is I want fair warning.

BARB: Bob said the same thing.

CARLA CARLA: Because if this is the same as the needlework and the acupuncture and the running through the woods with the compass with the needle spinning and all of it being connected 'cause of the needles and how everywhere you look there are needles filled with meaning in barometers and porcupine needle art and the Seattle Space Needle I don't know if I can take it again or even if I want to.

BARB: If you're mad just be mad. Don't be nasty. Don't make fun of me.

CARLA CARLA: So I might be a little mad.

BARB: I feel heavy. Do you want our dishwasher?

CARLA CARLA: No.

BARB: I'm going to wash our dishes by hand.

CARLA CARLA: We don't want your dishwasher.

BARB: How about the microwave?

CARLA CARLA: The dishwasher and the microwave?

BARB: Either. Or. Both.

CARLA CARLA: Did you talk to Bob about this?

BARB: I have too much stuff. I feel heavy. I don't like it.

CARLA CARLA: So I went home and I said to Donna
      Donna Barb is thinking of giving away all her stuff.

DONNA: What'd she give us?

CARLA CARLA: She wants to give us her dishwasher. And the microwave.

DONNA: Hey lucky us!

CARLA CARLA: I didn't say we'd take them.

DONNA: Take the dishwasher. But not the microwave. Leave it I don't trust them.

CARLA CARLA: Don't you think it's weird that she wants to give away all her stuff?

DONNA: Did you tell her?

CARLA CARLA: Tell her what?

DONNA: What we talked about last night?

CARLA CARLA: No.

DONNA: So did you think about it?

CARLA CARLA: Yeah.

DONNA: So what do you think?

CARLA CARLA: I don't know yet.

DONNA: Why didn't you talk to Barb about it?

CARLA CARLA: I don't know.

DONNA: Are you going to talk to her about it?

CARLA CARLA: I don't know.

DONNA: When are you going to know?

CARLA CARLA: She didn't want the cat bowl.

DONNA: She didn't want the cat bowl?

CARLA CARLA: She only wants eight things. In her whole life. You want it?

DONNA: No. Thanks.

CARLA CARLA: You want this?

NICK: What is it.

CARLA CARLA: It's a cat bowl a bowl for your cat. I got it for Barb. For her birthday.

NICK: So why you giving it to me?

CARLA CARLA: She didn't want it.

NICK: Oh 'cause of the Buddhists.

CARLA CARLA: She wants to give us their dishwasher.

NICK: She's giving you the dishwasher?

CARLA CARLA: I don't want their dishwasher.

NICK: I'll take it.

CARLA CARLA: She offered it to me.

NICK: Maybe since you don't want it I can have it.

CARLA CARLA: To me and Donna.

NICK: You guys get everything.

CARLA CARLA: Nobody seems to think it's weird she wants to give it away.

NICK: She feels heavy.

CARLA CARLA: So you don't want this either.

NICK: Hey guess what I met someone new yesterday.

CARLA CARLA: What about Lance?

NICK: Lance? Lance. Oh.

CARLA CARLA: Here you can sell this too.

BARB: (*Barb is carrying yard-sale stuff from offstage left to offstage right.*) Donna didn't want it?

CARLA CARLA: I don't want to talk about it.

> Donna wants me to tell you yes to the dishwasher and she wants us to get married. Nick says yes definitely take the dishwasher and says maybe could he have the microwave if you want to give it away but only if you really want to give it away because he has a really nice friend who wants one but doesn't have any money and that he doesn't love Lance anymore but he met a really really cute guy at the Home Depot when he was re-caulking his bathroom.

BARB: Bob doesn't want me to give away the dishwasher.

CARLA CARLA: Oh.

BARB: Bob suggested I should have this yard sale instead. See if maybe if I get rid of some stuff I'll feel better.

CARLA CARLA: This's a good idea.

BARB: I said Bob I don't think that's going to work but I figure What the heck can't hurt.

NICK: Barb. You've got some great stuff here.

BARB: Nick you take whatever you want.

NICK: How about the dishwasher?

CARLA CARLA: Bob has a problem with her giving away appliances. You're selling your Hummels?

BARB: If I only want eight things I'm not keeping my Hummels.

NICK: What're Hummels?

CARLA CARLA: These're Hummels. They're collectibles very difficult-to-find collectibles.

NICK: Is this Hummel Heidi?

CARLA CARLA: You're selling Heidi?

NICK: Look she's yodeling. On her little tiny Alp.

CARLA CARLA: It took so long to find her.

NICK: You don't want your yodeling Heidi?

BARB: No.

CARLA CARLA: Yodeling Heidi is one of the hardest Hummels to find.

NICK: You sure you want to sell this?

BARB: Look you keep her.

CARLA: CARLA: Stop giving me things.

BARB: Nick you take yodeling Heidi.

NICK: I don't want her.

BARB: See? Nobody wants this stuff.

NICK: I know how collecting works. I start with little yodeling Heidi I end up with a whole bunch of you know special edition plates of the pope the pope in India the pope in Brazil the pope in Denver I'll take the dishwasher.

CARLA CARLA: Bob doesn't want her giving away the dishwasher.

(Barb goes offstage.)

Can I help you?

NICK: HEY THAT'S NOT FOR SALE! That's my bike!

CARLA CARLA: That your knapsack?

NICK: THAT'S NOT FOR SALE EITHER! NONE OF THAT'S FOR SALE! NONE OF THAT WHOLE PILE!

BARB: (*Enters.*) People are weird.

CARLA CARLA: These are yard-sale people Barb.

BARB: It says fifty cents on it so they come and ask me if they can have it for twenty-five. I say Sure! Then they look disappointed 'cause I say Sure! — maybe I'm too happy? They're thinking Oh I should offered a dime!

NICK: My bike's worth more than fifteen bucks Barb.

BARB: Look at it. Donna wants to get married?

NICK: Donna wants you two to get married?

CARLA CARLA: Yeah.

NICK: You knew. How come she knew and I didn't know?

CARLA CARLA: I just told her.

NICK: When?

BARB: I'm throwing you a bridal shower.

CARLA CARLA: I don't know.

BARB: You are going to get some beautiful things.

CARLA CARLA: Don't give me stuff from your house.

NICK: Like a real marriage? In a church?

CARLA CARLA: We didn't talk about that.

NICK: So?

CARLA CARLA: What?

NICK: So

CARLA CARLA: So what.

NICK: So I'm your best man? Right?

BARB: I don't think so. She's having a matron of honor.

NICK: Oh no she is not.

BARB: If I throw the bridal shower

NICK: Bridal showers are for sissies.

BARB: and since I have dibs on the bridal shower I get to be the matron

NICK: She's having a stag party.

CARLA CARLA: I don't know.

NICK: Come on it'll be a blast. Girls popping out of cakes.

CARLA CARLA: I don't know.

NICK: Girls popping out of lots of cakes.

CARLA CARLA: Girls huh.

NICK: And cake. You love cake.

CARLA CARLA: I don't know if I want to marry her.

BARB: Oh.

(Pause.)

NICK: Why not.

BARB: Nick.

NICK: Well why not?

CARLA CARLA: I don't know.

NICK: What do you mean I don't know. I mean you love her don't you Don't you love her

CARLA CARLA: I LOVE HER I JUST DON'T KNOW AND EVERY TIME I SAY I DON'T KNOW SOMEONE GIVES ME A FRIGGING HARD TIME AND ALL I KNOW IS I DON'T FRIGGING KNOW I DON'T KNOW I DON'T KNOW

NICK: OK OK OK OK!

BARB: OK Carla Carla

NICK: OK.

CARLA CARLA: *(To audience.)*

(Pause.)

I'm ambivalent about marriage.

(Pause.)

So. How'd the yard sale go?

BARB: We made a lot of money.

CARLA CARLA: That's good.

BARB: But everyone brought me stuff to sell.

CARLA CARLA: Yeah?

BARB: So they left anything that didn't sell So I counted and now I've got more than when I started. I'm taking it to the dump.

CARLA CARLA: Hey have another sale.

BARB: That's what Bob said too. I like the dump. You just dump it.

Bob he's full of suggestions. Have a yard sale he says. Have another yard sale he says. For every new thing we get we get rid of two old things he says. So he took the yard-sale money and bought a new Lazyboy and now I have to figure out what to get rid of.

CARLA CARLA: Is something wrong?

BARB: No I mean I think it's fine. I'm just not sure he gets it.

Here.

CARLA CARLA: What's this.

BARB: Cat bowl. Didn't sell.

BARB: The dump.

(Music.)

(To audience.)

I packed the back of the Buick. Bob helped at first. But then he was taking things in as fast as I was bringing them out so I sent him over to the neighbor's kiddie pool to cool down and I got into the Buick and drove right to the dump halfway between Twig and Bristol.

I had a picture of the dump in my head. It was going to be a beautiful dump. With old dumped cars and old dumped stuff and old dumped fridges with no doors so the little drug kids can't get stuck inside them and suffocate. Sort of orderly but chaotic. Like a big Sears jumble sale but bigger.

And as I drove I thought Maybe seagulls! Maybe rats. Probably trees probably a little river certainly mud broken glass cans. Maybe wildflowers!

I got there.

It was a dump. It was a real dump.

I dumped my junk and left.

And as I drove away I thought

I thought this dumping was going to make me feel better and I'm not I'm feeling a sense of kind of despair. But now I think Maybe this is like water aerobics and it's going to hurt at first until I get used to it.

(Pause.)

I went to the dump.

CARLA CARLA: And?

BARB: I've got to stop for a while.

CARLA CARLA: Why?

BARB: Bob's angry. I dumped the *National Geographics*. He kind of hit the roof.

THE SHARK

It is dark blue. In the aquarium. The Shark is swimming.

THE SHARK: swim swim swim swim swim swim swim swim swim OH GLASS GLASS WATCH OUT FOR THE GLASS swim swim swim swim swim swim swim swim swim OH GLASS GLASS WATCH OUT FOR THE GLASS swim swim swim swim swim swim swim swim swim OH GLASS GLASS WATCH OUT FOR THE GLASS swim swim swim

HOW TO QUIT SMOKING

DONNA: Is it because I smoke?

NICK: I don't know.

DONNA: Did she mention smoking?

NICK: I don't think so.

DONNA: It's so stupid. She won't marry me because I smoke.

NICK: Maybe it's not the smoking.

DONNA: It's not like I smoke a lot.

NICK: Oh yeah Donna.

DONNA: I don't.

NICK: You do.

DONNA: I don't.

NICK: So quit then.

DONNA: Yeah right I don't want to.

NICK: Since you don't smoke a lot.

DONNA: I like smoking.

NICK: Want to get married? Stop.

DONNA: You stop.

NICK: Stop what?

DONNA: Picking up guys.

NICK: Why would I do that?

DONNA: You want to get married too right.

NICK: I don't know. Marriage. It's kind of a commitment.

DONNA: You want a relationship.

NICK: Yeah.

DONNA: Longer than three weeks.

NICK: Yeah.

DONNA: You want to see his apartment.

NICK: I've seen their apartments.

DONNA: During the day. Maybe find out his last name.

NICK: Aw Donna come on. I don't do that

DONNA: All you guys do it.

NICK: Not always.

DONNA: You Frankie George Peter Alex you all come to me saying Oh I'm in love

NICK: I never say that.

DONNA: You always say that. I'm in love with fill in the name He's really supercute He's supernice

NICK: I would never say supernice.

DONNA: I just met him last night

NICK: I would never use that word. Supernice. It's queer.

DONNA: We talked

NICK: Yeah yeah.

DONNA: and talked and talked

NICK: Yeah yeah yeah.

DONNA: We had fun We had sex He didn't call.

NICK: Frankie George Peter and Alex maybe do that.

DONNA: But not you.

NICK: My boys call me back.

DONNA: So what happened to Lance?

NICK: Which Lance?

DONNA: Uh huh.

NICK: Last-week Lance? I saw Lance's apartment. During the day.

DONNA: Lance have a last name?

NICK: He wasn't a boyfriend he was a fling.

DONNA: A fling.

NICK: What's wrong with flings? You flung every woman in Rhode Island. Cecily Sunshine Nancy Rose Marcy Venus Shosanna Solstice

DONNA: Nick.

NICK: Tonya Sonya Linda Lyn Lynny Jolynn

DONNA: I just think it'd be nice if me and Carla Carla were married and you and whoever with a last name were married and we could go camping. All four of us.

NICK: I'm not going camping.

DONNA: And in order for that to happen clearly I have to quit smoking and you have to go out with someone for more than three weeks.

NICK: If I have a relationship I have to go camping?

DONNA: You get to go camping.

NICK: I don't like camping.

DONNA: Camping's great.

NICK: I hate camping.

DONNA: I know what I'm going to do. I'm going to quit smoking. And I'm finding you a boyfriend.

NICK: I can find my own boyfriends.

DONNA: Carla Carla will marry me. I'm going to be so irritable.

NICK: Later that week.

DONNA: OK. I asked everyone I know How to quit smoking and here's the list. Hypnosis. Smokenders. The patch the gum. Tried'm tried'm. Willpower ha. Eat carrots because if you don't you'll blow up like a whale. That's from Sandy who's kinda *("Chubby" gesture.)* but at least she doesn't smoke. Read up about lung cancer. Thank you. Pray to Jesus. Exercise. Put Carla Carla's picture on the cigarette pack with a rubber band. Just keep saying I'm going to quit smoking!

So.

Today I'm going to a hypnotherapist.

Here's David's number. He's cute single meeting you tonight 7:00 P.M. at Twig Beach watch the sunset OK?

I'm going to quit smoking!

NICK: Tuesday.

DONNA: The hypnotherapist. What a creep. Doctor William White.

NICK: Oh.

DONNA: Call me Bill.

NICK: Oh.

DONNA: You're getting sleepy.

NICK: Ew.

DONNA: He put his hand on my arm. A lot. I don't think so. I got home. Smoked my brains out.

How'd it go with David?

NICK: Good.

DONNA: You slept with him. You weren't supposed to sleep with him. It was a date.

NICK: I'm not dating him. He kissed me and then he went

(Makes gun hand/wink/clicking gesture. Makes gesture again.)

DONNA: Oh.

OK so tonight I go to my Stop Smoking Breathfree class. Here's Jason's address. You pick him up at eight. Coffee Exchange.

I'm going to quit smoking!

NICK: Wednesday.

DONNA: My class. Excellent. OK so we were all smokers mostly still smoking and some of us were a little irritable even though we're still smoking but our instructor Janice says That is very normal and me and this guy Marty I met sat in the back of the room and laughed and then had a quick cig together in the bathroom. Class number two tonight.

Jason?

NICK: Artist. Cute artist.

DONNA: You didn't.

NICK: Cute cute artist.

DONNA: We had a deal.

NICK: I had to. He's working on not blocking his impulses.

DONNA: Nick!

NICK: He's calling me.

DONNA: He is?

NICK: I had such a great time. We talked for like three hours about his family and my family and all that stuff and how we came out and how it hurt and he got so quiet and what he wants to do as an artist and art and then more about art and just on and on about. Everything. This was different. This was something it felt. New for me. We're going out again. Tonight.

DONNA: Pretty successful night last night for us!

NICK: I really like him. I really.

DONNA: I'm going to quit smoking!

NICK: Thursday.

DONNA: Stop Smoking Breathfree class was FUN last night. Sondra she's French from France well She Cracked and She Smoked. In class. Janice had to ask her to leave. Me and Marty met her in the women's room and she was crying and we were going oh oh oh and then we each had one of her French cigarettes from France and just sat together quietly smoking. It was very spiritual which is something Janice is talking about all the time so all in all I think it was a very good night. How'd it go with Jason.

NICK: We didn't get to go out.

DONNA: You going out tonight instead?

NICK: Maybe.

DONNA: He call?

NICK: No.

DONNA: Probably busy. OK. Stop Smoking Breathfree for me tonight Call from Jason for you. I'm going to quit smoking!

NICK: Friday.

DONNA: Janice split me and Marty up and she won't let us go to the bathroom together anymore. I hate her.

Jason call?

NICK: No.

Saturday.

DONNA: That guy call?

NICK: No.

DONNA: OK so Marty's not smoking anymore. Janice told him smoking screws up the capillaries in your dick. You can't get enough blood in the right place. It's a leading 'cause of impotence. Marty gets very quiet and suddenly he doesn't need to go to the bathroom. I asked Janice if the same thing was happening to my clitoris but she changed the subject. I smoke alone in the bathroom now which is no fun.

I brought you Marty's number.

NICK: No thanks.

DONNA: He's a chiropractor.

NICK: I want to see Jason again.

DONNA: Don't you get it?

NICK: What?

DONNA: Jason's not calling you.

NICK: Yeah he is.

DONNA: He said he'd call Wednesday.

NICK: So.

DONNA: It's Saturday.

NICK: Yeah well you're still smoking!

DONNA: Yeah so?

NICK: Yeah so maybe you don't know everything!

DONNA: Right this is the one who's going to call.

NICK: Maybe!

DONNA: Like any of the others did.

NICK: Maybe.

DONNA: He's not calling and the next one you sleep with too fast with isn't going to call and neither will the one after that and you won't ever get married.

NICK: Yeah well you can cover your whole body with one big nicotine patch and you'll still smoke and you'll never get married either! And besides you don't have to get married to go camping. You just have to get a stinky old tent and a couple of stinky old sleeping bags that who knows who slept in last wearing who knows what and a crappy old Bunsen burner and tin plate thing and that crappy food and some toilet paper and dump the whole crappy kit and caboodle near some stinky old swamp and suffer!

DONNA: Well you don't have to go camping!

NICK: Well I'm not going to go camping!

(Pause.)

DONNA: I'm going to have a cigarette out on the porch. Want to come?

NICK: Sure.

Sunday.

You're going to church?

DONNA: It's nondenominational. Unitarians. They barely believe in God.

NICK: Going to pray huh.

DONNA: No. I'm checking out the hall. For the commitment ceremony.

NICK: I'm not dating anymore.

DONNA: Didn't call huh.

NICK: Alex saw him with another guy last night.

DONNA: Lots of cute boys go to church.

NICK: Yeah?

DONNA: A whole section of them sit upstairs and look at each other the whole time. Coming?

NICK: Let me get my coat.

DONNA: I'm going to quit smoking!

CARLA CARLA: She's cheating.

BARB: She is?

CARLA CARLA: She's sneaking. She's cheating she's sneaking she's lying and she's smoking.

BARB: Oh!

CARLA CARLA: Why would I want to marry a liar a cheat a sneak?

BARB: What makes you think she's cheating?

CARLA CARLA: Oh I know. I know. Officially she has only one pack of cigarettes Marlboro Lights with a photo of me and a cutout gown from *Bride* magazine glued on top of me this whole little bridal dream–collage rubber-banded to her pack of cigarettes. I'm not sure how I feel about that but she's quitting her disgusting filthy habit so OK fine I ignore it.

BARB: That's a very cute that's a cute idea.

CARLA CARLA: Every night she comes home and she says Oh Carla look I only smoked two today Oh Carla look I only smoked one today and she shows me and I say Honey! and I kiss her congratulations.

BARB: She's down to two a day?

CARLA CARLA: But

BARB: But that's good that's very good!

CARLA CARLA: But yesterday she's in the shower and I look on her dresser and she has three packs of matches going. Two of them are almost empty.

BARB: So?

CARLA CARLA: They were full two days ago!

BARB: Oh!

CARLA CARLA: And we today we went to lunch at Downcity Diner and the host Tom looked at her and said Smoking section again today for you?

BARB: Oh!

CARLA CARLA: And today she comes home what do I smell?

BARB: What?

CARLA CARLA: Menthol!

BARB: No!

CARLA CARLA: Yes! Menthol!

BARB: Oh!

CARLA CARLA: But I don't know where she's getting them. The house is clean I checked all her hiding spots. I checked her purse. I checked her car. I checked her locker at work.

BARB: Carla Carla!

CARLA CARLA: I'm not marrying a sneaky lying cheater.

BARB: Still.

CARLA CARLA: Someone is sneaking her cigarettes.

BARB: Oh!

CARLA CARLA: She has a sneaky partner.

BARB: Who?

CARLA CARLA: And I am going to catch them.

THE SHARK 2

Donna is leading an aquarium tour.

DONNA: We're real proud of this fella here at the Twig Rhode Island Aquarium. This is Isurus oxyrinchus Rafinesque 1810. The mako shark. This fella's known to jump fifteen twenty feet in the air when he's hooked. In order to jump that high he'd have to be swimming 22 mph through the water. That's fast. You're looking at what is probably the most graceful most beautifully proportioned fastest meanest-looking animal on earth. The word *mako* is Maori
Nick! Over here.
(Nick enters.)
HI Will you all excuse me for one moment You got them?
(Nick gives her the cigarettes.)
They need me in the office Huh! You'll all have to excuse me for just another short moment Talk'm through this part of the tour OK Nick The word *mako* is Maori etc etc etc I'll be right back
(Donna exits.)

NICK: Um Donna? Um

(Pause.)

Well Um Huh

This is a shark. Um. A mako. Um. The word *mako* is Maori from New Zealand although we don't know what it means. These big guys are Um big and Oh Um scary and really Um Something huh?

THE SHARK: swim swim swim swim swim swim swim swim swim OH GLASS GLASS WATCH OUT FOR THE GLASS swim swim swim swim swim swim swim swim swim OH GLASS GLASS WATCH OUT FOR THE GLASS swim swim swim swim

DONNA: Well. Well well well OK let's move on Thanks Nick. To the jellyfish exhibit on your left.

NICK: Donna!

DONNA: Yeah?

NICK: Carla Carla knows.

DONNA: How?

NICK: The matches.

DONNA: Rats!

NICK: And Barb said Carla Carla said she smelled menthol.

DONNA: Rats!

NICK: I'm not bringing you anymore.

DONNA: Nick! Come on.

NICK: She'll catch us and then I'm going to get it.

DONNA: I'll use a lighter!

NICK: Nope.

DONNA: I won't touch another menthol anything.

NICK: I can't.

DONNA: I promise!

NICK: NO.

DONNA: Great friend you are.

NICK: Oh yeah great friend you are too. She'll go ballistic on me. Not you.

DONNA: She's not going to catch us.

NICK: Barb isn't bringing you anymore either.

DONNA: Oh great.

NICK: She thinks we're helping you not stop.

DONNA: You're both abandoning me?

NICK: We want you to get married.

DONNA: I have abandonment issues. You both know that!

NICK: You have smoking issues.

DONNA: *(To tour.)* I'LL BE WITH YOU IN A MINUTE!

NICK: Don't be mad. Huh?
DONNA: Thanks.
NICK: That's a cool shark huh.
DONNA: Thanks a lot. Great.

HOW TO COOK A RABBIT

Barb is showing Carla Carla her empty room.

BARB: What do you think?
CARLA CARLA: Where is everything?
BARB: Isn't it beautiful?
CARLA CARLA: It's an empty room Barb.
BARB: Exactly!
CARLA CARLA: Where's your sewing machine?
BARB: Salvation Army.
CARLA CARLA: You gave it to the Salvation Army?
BARB: Yeah.
　　See the cushion that's where I sit and I put a candle here or a flower.
CARLA CARLA: Did you give them all your sewing stuff?
BARB: They know me down there now. They say Hey here comes Barb! Then
　　I hear Hey Barb! Hey Barb! Hey Barb! and I say Hey Joe Hey Pablo Hey
　　Randy except when one of them's gotten drunk the night before and then
　　I say Where's Randy or Joe or whoever? and they go He got drunk This
　　is the new guy Larry Hey Larry this is Barb.
CARLA CARLA: You give them your rocking chair?
BARB: Bob Jr. wanted it so I gave it to him. You know how to cook a rabbit?
CARLA CARLA: A rabbit.
BARB: Hm?
CARLA CARLA: Where'd you get a rabbit?
BARB: Bob got it.
CARLA CARLA: Where'd Bob get rabbit?
BARB: He went hunting.
CARLA CARLA: Bob shot it?
BARB: He hit it with the car. On the highway. On his way home from hunting.
CARLA CARLA: He hit it?
BARB: He says he swerved to hit it so it counts. It's his trophy rabbit. He wants
　　me to cook it. I'm not cooking it.

CARLA CARLA: What a jerk. I can't believe he hit a rabbit.

BARB: He just brought it home and said Barb will you get a load of this!

And I look and he's standing there Bob with his new hunting hat and pants and hunting boots and bag and gun.

He bought the whole outfit for this one hunting trip Carla Carla.

CARLA CARLA: He has the rabbit just

BARB: He's got a whole another outfit for when we ride our bikes!

CARLA CARLA: So?

BARB: And one for jogging!

CARLA CARLA: I think you're being kind of hard on him.

BARB: I don't want to cook the rabbit. I'd have to skin it.

CARLA CARLA: Loads of people have lots of clothes.

You have a new way of seeing things now right. But Bob doesn't get it. You want him to get it. But he doesn't.

BARB: We have three TVs.

CARLA CARLA: So?

BARB: Since Bob Junior moved to Boston there are only the two of us at home and we have three TVs. I told Bob that.

CARLA CARLA: He doesn't get it.

BARB: What could be more simple. Three TVs two people.

He thinks I miss Bob Junior. Which I do. That's not the point. I got this room cleared. He wanted to fill it. He drags me to the Big Boys store. Let's buy in bulk and stuff that we don't need now But Barb we might need it it's on sale and

I was crying

In the aisle I was

I couldn't stand it. He didn't even notice.

CARLA CARLA: That's well That's just Bob.

Bob's always been like that.

And you two always used to shop at Big Boys.

BARB: I don't want to anymore.

CARLA CARLA: You sure you're making the

I mean You're changing a lot.

BARB: I don't know how to explain it I just

I feel lighter.

CARLA CARLA: 'Cause sometimes I get worried too. But if it's working Maybe I shouldn't worry.

BARB: I'm feeling much much better.

CARLA CARLA: You look better. It's just scary to see someone change so

BARB: I like how I feel.

CARLA CARLA: As long as you feel OK.

BARB: I do.

CARLA CARLA: You do.

BARB: I do.

CARLA CARLA: OK.

BARB: I'm in here. Cushion candle shoes dress sweater underwear bra eight things. In this room I only own eight things Carla Carla. And suddenly a lot of things seem possible.

HOW TO FALL IN LOVE

NICK: I'm in love.

BARB: Yeah yeah.

NICK: No I am.

BARB: How long's it been?

NICK: Three days.

BARB: You're not in love. You're infatuated. It goes You're infatuated You are getting to know someone You're spending a lot of time together You have someone special then after six months to a year or so you might feel the first stirrings of love.

NICK: I'm in love.

BARB: Where'd you meet him?

NICK: The aquarium.

BARB: He works with Donna?

NICK: Not exactly.

BARB: What's his name?

NICK: I don't know.

BARB: Oh you're definitely not in love then You haven't met him. That's a crush. That's even before infatuation.

NICK: I'm in love.

DONNA: Great.

NICK: Yeah.

DONNA: I'm in love too.

NICK: Great huh?

DONNA: Yeah.

NICK: I'm in love.

CARLA CARLA: She's cheating isn't she.

NICK: What?

CARLA CARLA: Donna.

NICK: Why?

CARLA CARLA: Don't play stupid.

NICK: I don't think she's been

CARLA CARLA: She's been sneaking.

NICK: I don't think she's

CARLA CARLA: She's been smoking.

NICK: I

CARLA CARLA: A lot.

NICK: I don't

CARLA CARLA: You've been helping her.

NICK: Oh.

CARLA CARLA: Are you all right?

NICK: Oh.

CARLA CARLA: You look sick.

NICK: I feel a little sick.

CARLA CARLA: Have you been eating?

NICK: I haven't been eating. I'm in love.

CARLA CARLA: HOW COULD YOU HELP HER SMOKE!

NICK: She asked me.

CARLA CARLA: SHE ASKED ME. SHE ASKED ME.

NICK: Don't go off on me. DON'T you go off on me.

CARLA CARLA: Why shouldn't I?

NICK: Because I'm not your girlfriend.
> *(Pause.)*

CARLA CARLA: I'm going to go off on both of you.
> *(Pause.)*
> She's lying.
> *(Pause.)*

NICK: She's scared you won't marry her.

CARLA CARLA: She should be. Lying.

NICK: She's scared.
> *(Pause.)*
> Kind of hard. Ask someone to marry you. They say Maybe Except you do this one thing I don't like.
> *(Pause.)*

CARLA CARLA: You saying I should?

NICK: Marry her? You want to?

CARLA CARLA: I do I don't. What if the smoking's telling me more about her than just smoking?

NICK: Like what?

CARLA CARLA: Maybe she doesn't like herself so much.

NICK: Maybe.

CARLA CARLA: Well there you are.

NICK: Maybe that's not so important.

CARLA CARLA: It is.

NICK: Maybe it's taking her time to learn how to.

CARLA CARLA: Maybe.

NICK: She's trying to stop.

CARLA CARLA: But she hasn't has she.

NICK: Look at Barb though. Right? She's trying to do something new and she's asking Bob for help and he buys a Lazyboy.

CARLA CARLA: Yeah but.

NICK: At least Donna's listening to you.

CARLA CARLA: Yeah but.

NICK: I remember when you and Donna first started following each other around.

You were God you were Nick Donna said this

CARLA CARLA: OK

NICK: and Nick Donna does

CARLA CARLA: OK

NICK: that and Oh Donna Donna Nick Donna Donna and

CARLA CARLA: OK OK

NICK: laughing and Nick how wild it is to be in love and I've been waiting I've been waiting so long

CARLA CARLA: Yeah yeah yeah.

NICK: And I'm so lucky I'm so lucky and

CARLA CARLA: OK.

NICK: Yeah and I think maybe you're forgetting it's hard to find love.

CARLA CARLA: I'm not forgetting that.

NICK: It's not so easy.

CARLA CARLA: You're always in love.

NICK: How many times they been in love with me?

CARLA CARLA: Huh.

NICK: Yeah huh. They ever stay in love with me?

CARLA CARLA: So I went home and I said to Donna
Donna I'm thinking I might say yes to you.

DONNA: What

CARLA CARLA: I think we should.

DONNA: OH!

    I'm still smoking.

CARLA CARLA: I know.

DONNA: More than I've been telling you though.

CARLA CARLA: I know.

DONNA: I know you were spying on me.

    (Pause.)

    I want to quit.

CARLA CARLA: I know you will.

NICK: I'm in love.

CARLA CARLA: I said yes.

DONNA: We're getting married!

BARB: I'm moving out of our house.

ALL: Oh. Oh. Oh. Oh.

CARLA CARLA: Why?

BARB: Bob bought me a car.

DONNA & NICK & CARLA CARLA: Huh.

    (Pause.)

NICK: So?

BARB: He won't stop buying me things.

    (Pause.)

    So I'm leaving him.

CARLA CARLA: You sure?

BARB: Hm.

CARLA CARLA: You thought it over?

BARB: Hm.

CARLA CARLA: What'd Bob say?

NICK: Bob.

DONNA: Bob.

BOB

    Overhead is projected "Bob." Or Bob carries a sign saying Bob. Bob enters.
    BOB stands. Bob exits.

BARB: Bob

    Well Bob's not too happy.

BOB: (*Bob is offstage.*) THAT'S RIGHT I'M NOT TOO HAPPY.

BARB: He thinks I'm ungrateful.

BOB: THAT'S RIGHT Barb!

BARB: and selfish

BOB: UH HUH!

BARB: and stubborn

BOB: UH HUH!

BARB: and maybe crazy.

BOB: BRAND-NEW BUICK PARK AVENUE. DUAL AIRBAGS. ANTI-LOCK BRAKES. 3.8 LITER V-6 SFI ENGINE. AIR CONDITION-ING-ELECTRONIC CLIMATE CONTROL. POWER ANTENNA. KEYS IN THE IGNITION BARB!

BARB: I DON'T WANT A NEW CAR BOB!

(*Bob enters.*)

BOB: It's a Buick Barb!

BARB: I didn't ask for it. You didn't ask me. I don't want it.

BOB: Well I bought it Barb.

BARB: Well bring it back Bob.

BOB: What's bought is bought Barb.

BARB: Where's my Buick Bob?

BOB: This is a Buick Barb a brand-new Buick.

BARB: Where's my old Buick Bob.

BOB: I traded it in.

BARB: You traded it in for that? BOB!

BOB: Come on honey.

BARB: Don't come on honey me Bob.

BOB: I can't believe you're getting all bent out of shape over a new car Barb.

(*Bob exits.*)

DONNA: Sounds like a nice car.

NICK: Yeah.

BARB: Aren't you even listening to me? At all? Isn't anyone?

CARLA CARLA: Seems like you're over-reacting. A little.

BARB: I don't want a new car. I didn't want my old one.

CARLA CARLA: How'd you get to work?

BARB: Bus bike walk get a ride carpool. I have a car. I have to put gas in it. I have to clean it. I have to wash it. I have to get the oil changed. I have to get it tuned up. I have to get new tires. I have to get it fixed. I have to register it. I have to insure it. I have to have a license. I have to pay for tolls. I have to pay for parking. I have to pay for meters. I have to pay for tickets. I have a job partly to pay for the car. So I can save time driving to work. But have you ever thought Maybe the time I save with the car is less than the time I have to work to pay for the car? This is what is spinning around all day every day in my head. I have more and more stuff every day and every day more and more stuff has me. And all I want to do is stop and be quiet and see whether I want it.

(Pause.)

NICK: I'm in love with a shark.

(The Shark crosses the stage.)

CARLA CARLA: You are?

BARB: You are?

DONNA: Naw.

CARLA CARLA: You're in love with a shark.

NICK: Um hum.

CARLA CARLA: A shark.

DONNA: Naw.

BARB: A shark?

CARLA CARLA: Any particular shark or just any shark?

NICK: Not just any shark. The mako shark You know Donna the shark at the aquarium.

DONNA: My shark.

NICK: You know.

DONNA: He's in love with my shark.

CARLA CARLA: You know the shark?

DONNA: Well not well.

CARLA CARLA: Is it cute?

DONNA: Well

NICK: Well what?

DONNA: I don't know.

BARB: Is it?

DONNA: It's a shark.

NICK: It's the shark I'm in love with.

BARB: You're not in love with that shark.

NICK: I am too.

BARB: You have a crush on it.

CARLA CARLA: This shark you love have a name?

BARB: He hasn't met it yet. He hasn't met it yet it's just a crush. It goes crush THEN infatuation THEN like. Love takes time.

CARLA CARLA: Why haven't you met?

NICK: I'm shy.

BARB: You're shy?

CARLA CARLA: Since when are you shy?

NICK: Since now I guess.

CARLA CARLA: Get Donna to introduce you.

DONNA: I can't.

CARLA CARLA: Why not?

DONNA: I barely know him.

NICK: Barely is better than nothing.

BARB: The shark doesn't know you're alive?

NICK: No.

BARB: Then it's a one-sided crush.

DONNA: This isn't good.

NICK: What's not good.

DONNA: You make me introduce you and you go out fall in love then break up and then you don't want to ever come by and see me at work anymore because you're afraid you'll bump into the shark.

BARB: They're divorced. She's divorcing them already. He hasn't met the shark yet. They're still in the CRUSH stage. Divorce comes way after LOVE.

DONNA: I don't want him to get hurt.

CARLA CARLA: Him him or the shark him?

BARB: Nick's boyfriends do end up hurt.

NICK: Hey!

BARB: Well they do don't they?

CARLA CARLA: You've said it yourself.

NICK: Hey!

BARB: Is the shark sensitive?

DONNA: I don't know.

BARB: 'Cause if it is maybe you should warn him about Nick.

NICK: Hey!

CARLA CARLA: Maybe the shark's a shark.

NICK: Can't anyone be happy for me?

(Pause.)

DONNA: It's a nice-looking shark.

CARLA CARLA: Nice-looking cute or nice-looking nice?

DONNA: Both.

CARLA CARLA: There you go.

BARB: I'm sure you'll be really happy.

CARLA CARLA: Course he's going to be happy.

BARB: Once you meet it.

CARLA CARLA: You are planning on meeting the shark I guess huh?

BARB: Or maybe it'll be love from afar?

CARLA CARLA: Love from afar with a shark might be good.

BARB: Love from afar is romantic.

DONNA: This isn't good.

NICK: Why not?

DONNA: You're never going to meet It's going to be love from afar and you are going to slowly pine away saying If only I'd met the shark If only I'd met the shark.

NICK: I'm going to meet the shark. You're going to introduce us.

DONNA: I am?

NICK: You'd do that for me.

DONNA: I barely know him. Oh OK I will I will.

NICK: Good.

    (The next week was a whoosh of preparation.)

    (Carla Carla and Donna planning their commitment ceremony.)

DONNA: Purple.

CARLA CARLA: Purple?

DONNA: Definitely purple.

CARLA CARLA: OK fine. Purple.

    (Pause.)

    I don't like purple. How about green?

DONNA: No.

CARLA CARLA: I like green.

NICK: Barb wanting to tell Bob she's moving out.

BARB: Bob

    (Long pause.)

NICK: Me thinking about the shark shark shark shark shark shark shark shark shark shark shark

    It was exhausting.

ALL: I'm going to take a nap.

    (Carla Carla, Donna, and Nick exit.)

3 DREAM SEQUENCES

Dream # 1

BARB: My dream sequence.

I dream:

I'm in the cereal aisle at the Twig Super Stop N Buy looking for Quaker Oats. Bob laughs at me because I'm intimidated by the cereal aisle. Barb it's cereal he says. People aren't scared of cereal Barb he says. People love cereal. It's part of a balanced breakfast. Here I am in my dream I'm surrounded by cereal. I don't know where Bob is. Normally I go to the dairy section cheese butter milk and Bob buys the cereal. But here I am boxes and boxes of cereal. Cereal and cereal and cereal. A whole long long aisle of cereal. Bran Flakes. Bran Flakes and Raisin Bran. And Bran Raisin Flake Nuts and Honey Nuts and Bran. And Honey Nut Raisin Fruit Bran. With Nuts. Without Nuts. With Nuts and Fruit. And Nuts. Fruit Nut Raisin Flake Nut Flake Raisin Raisin Flake Nut Honey Nut Stuff with BRAN BRAN

and I think Barb.

Leave the shopping cart.

Walk. Out.

Just get to the car. Drive away.

I think Tomorrow I'll eat toast.

Now in my dream I'm in the car and I'm driving.

And now I'm in a parking lot.

And now I'm in an alleyway. There's a door and I open it. And I walk down steps and through a door and into a room. With a brown red floor and a circle of chairs. And people in the chairs. They're sitting. One person is talking quietly and no one. Is buying. Anything.

I sit down.

I don't see Bob anywhere.

Dream #2

Carla Carla and Donna cross the stage. The Wedding March. Slightly sped up. They are wearing white T-shirts. Blue jeans. Big black belts. Construction boots. And wedding veils, which are starched to look windblown back. They are running in slow motion. Carla Carla is hopping. Trying to put on one of her boots. They are late.

Dream #3

Music. Something with a upbeat. Club music.
The Shark is dancing.
Nick enters. He is wearing a bathing suit. A life jacket and goggles. Or water
wings.

   The Shark and Nick swim/dance. Underwater courtship dance. Flirt.
Make love. Should be a subtle and slow shift from funny to sexy. Wet. The life
jacket the goggles come off. Perhaps projections of National Geographic
shark closeups. Blood in water. Shark attack. Not dancey. More muscular.
Water eddying. Swirls. Music slows.
Lights fade.
To black.

BOB: Barb!
   (Lights up.)
BARB: Hm Bob?
BOB: Where are the keys to the lawn mower?
BARB: Bob?
BOB: You seen them?
BARB: I'm thinking of getting an apartment.
BOB: What?
BARB: An apartment.
BOB: Why?
BARB: To live in.
BOB: Why would you want to do that?
BARB: I want to live alone for a while.
BOB: Hm.
BARB: For a while. To
   I'm not so happy.
   (Pause.)
   I don't like having
   (Pause.)
   I'm not so happy.
BOB: You seen the keys?
BARB: No I haven't I
   I think I've found one.
   (Pause.)
   An apartment. Downtown.

BOB: You've already found one.

BARB: It's small.

BOB: What do you want an apartment for? We've got everything here Barb.

BARB: Well that's exactly

I don't want all this

BOB: Don't start with all that *Buddhist monk* stuff.

BARB: What

BOB: Is that what all this is about I'm not even listening 'cause I am sick of that stuff.

BARB: I'll pay for it myself.

(Bob smiles.)

BARB: I figured it out My job'll be enough for the rent and

BOB: You signed a lease?

BARB: I like it. It's small.

BOB: You didn't ask me You just signed it?

BARB: I didn't know I'd have to ask you.

BOB: Is this about the car?

BARB: It's more

BOB: 'Cause the car's just a car Barb.

BARB: This isn't just

It didn't just happen. Partly the car. Other things.

I wanted to talk to you about it.

BOB: Why didn't you?

BARB: I am. Right now.

BOB: This isn't talking.

BARB: I've been trying all along to

BOB: Talking is Bob I'm unhappy. Oh no Barb what's the matter? What can I do? Not Bob I'm thinking of leaving you. And if it is then I say if we're talking No Barb really Don't. And you say Why not? 'Cause we're married I don't want you to. And then you don't. Or on and on from there. That's talking. I get to say something.

BARB: Um

BOB: Aw HELL Barb.

BARB: Bob

BOB: This is BAD Barb. This is BAD This is lousy It's BAD.

BARB: I wanted to talk to you.

BOB: Yeah right you did. The HELL you did So why didn't you

BARB: Not only you talk to me.

BOB: WHAT.

BARB: Um
BOB: OK. Talk.
BARB: Um.
> (Pause.)
> It's the stuff.
BOB: Not that. Barb.
BARB: But Bob
BOB: Not that.
BARB: But that's it.
BOB: Barb. Not that.
BARB: It is. So if you want me to talk
BOB: Talking isn't you deciding everything either.
BARB: No I haven't
BOB: You already have an apartment.
BARB: Don't get upset.
BOB: Don't go then.
BARB: No I have to
> I have
> I have to
> Hmm.
BOB: Wait a while. We keep the apartment. We talk. Barb. We can talk about giving back the new car getting your old car back.
BARB: Bob.
BOB: I don't want you to. We'll talk about this later.
BARB: No.
> I guess I didn't want to talk to you. I just wanted to tell you.

HOW TO GET A MAN

Donna and Nick go to the aquarium.

NICK: Act casual.
DONNA: OK.
NICK: Like I just happened to drop by.
DONNA: OK.
NICK: Coincidentally.
DONNA: OK.
NICK: Like Oh Hey Look who's here!

DONNA: What a coincidence.

NICK: Right!

DONNA: OK.

NICK: Or Hey How've you been Nick!

DONNA: Nick.

NICK: Only don't call me Nick in front of him.

DONNA: OK.

NICK: OK? Call me Nicholas. Not Nick OK.

DONNA: OK.

NICK: 'Cause Nick sounds unsophisticated.

DONNA: OK.

NICK: OK?

DONNA: OK.

Um. This is my friend Nicholas.

THE SHARK: swim swim swim swim swim swim swim swim

NICK: Hi.

(Pause.)

THE SHARK: swim OH GLASS GLASS WATCH OUT FOR THE GLASS
swim swim swim swim swim swim

(The Shark exits.)

(Pause.)

NICK: Well that went well.

DONNA: I guess.

NICK: I think it went well What do you think I think he liked me.

DONNA: Uh huh?

NICK: I'm taking it slow.

DONNA: Oh you are.

NICK: After Jason my therapist said maybe I sleep with people too fast sometimes.

DONNA: Oh really.

NICK: Uh huh. My therapist said that maybe maybe I sleep with people before I am totally emotionally prepared. Physically I'm ready fast and so I
sleep with them fast but then I wake up and I'm freaked 'cause who the
hell is this guy? see I'm slower emotionally. And so then I push them
away and then get sad 'cause I'm all alone again.

DONNA: Huh.

NICK: Unless I just want to have sex which is OK my therapist says. But. If I
want to develop something then I have to develop it. Which is slow.
Weird huh.

DONNA: Your therapist said that?

NICK: Think he maybe might be right?

DONNA: I TOLD YOU THAT TWO YEARS AGO.

NICK: Well yeah.

DONNA: I'VE BEEN TELLING YOU THAT EVERY DAY SINCE.

NICK: Well yeah.

DONNA: AND YOU'RE GOING TO LISTEN TO HIM?

NICK: He's my therapist.

> *(Pause.)*
>
> Do you think he liked me?

DONNA: She wants to invite my mother.

NICK: To the commitment ceremony?

DONNA: My mom won't come.

NICK: Maybe she will.

DONNA: She didn't come to our house-blessing ceremony. She won't come to this.

NICK: Is Carla Carla's dad coming?

DONNA: And her stepmother. And her mom.

NICK: I thought you weren't having too many people.

DONNA: I just wanted you and Barb and our friends and a few other people like our massage therapist and the guy at the Super Stop and Buy who always saves us the good mangoes. Small.

NICK: Your backyard won't hold that many people.

DONNA: She wants it big.

CARLA CARLA: I do I want it big.

DONNA: How big?

CARLA CARLA: Real big. If I'm getting married I want it big. I want bells and rings and cake and dancing. I want lots and lots of dancing. Lots of dancing and the whole shebang. And lots of white everywhere.

DONNA: Well

CARLA CARLA: So we better get cracking.

HOW TO AGREE ON A MINISTER

DONNA: She's not really a minister. She's more a crystal worker who specializes in partner/partner blessing ceremonies drawing from all kinds of ethnic traditions Judaism Tantric Balinese rainbow light therapy Buddhism

CARLA CARLA: Barb'll be pleased.

DONNA: Yeah I thought
   Anyhow she used to be a Wiccan priestess.
CARLA CARLA: How'd you find her?
DONNA: She's someone I used to know. Wanna meet her? Her name's Solstice.
CARLA CARLA: Sure.
DONNA: Great.

HOW TO PICK A RING

Donna and Carla Carla look at rings.

BOTH: That one.
   (Pause.)
   Really?

HOW TO CHOOSE A CATERER

CARLA CARLA: You said you wanted Southwestern food.
DONNA: Not Texan food. Southwestern food.
CARLA CARLA: Texas is in the Southwest.
DONNA: It's practically Midwestern. My mom won't eat Texan food.
CARLA CARLA: You said you didn't want to ask your mom.
DONNA: If I ask her and if she says yes she won't eat Texan food.
CARLA CARLA: You said your mom won't come even if you ask her.
DONNA: I was thinking more New Mexican food.
CARLA CARLA: Your mom would eat New Mexican food?
DONNA: You know my mom's not coming!
CARLA CARLA: Donna.
DONNA: Why are you making this so difficult?
CARLA CARLA: What am I doing?
DONNA: If you don't want to get married just say it instead of all this making
   it difficult and bringing up my mom. She's not coming.
CARLA CARLA: Donna.
DONNA: Because it just makes me really. I don't even
   (Pause.)
CARLA CARLA: When'd I say I don't want to get married?
DONNA: You might as well have.

CARLA CARLA: I want to get married.

DONNA: You want a big wedding. You don't want to get married. You just want a big splash wedding thing with this and this and this.

CARLA CARLA: You know I want to get married

DONNA: Maybe you think you have to now we told everyone. But you don't.

CARLA CARLA: I know I don't.

DONNA: Fine. We'll just call it off. It's off. Fine it's off.

(Pause.)

CARLA CARLA: It's not off.

(Pause.)

DONNA: It is. It's off.

CARLA CARLA: Donna.

DONNA: Call and cancel.

CARLA CARLA: Donna.

DONNA: You just keep making problems.

CARLA CARLA: I make problems?

DONNA: Yeah

CARLA CARLA: I make problems.

DONNA: Um hm.

CARLA CARLA: I don't make problems.

DONNA: You do.

CARLA CARLA: Hey. I didn't ask my ex-girlfriend the High Witch Priestess who is still in love with me to be our minister. "I want you to think long and hard about this Donna I'm looking I'm looking I don't see a very good future for you and Carla Carla."

DONNA: I said sorry about her.

CARLA CARLA: I'm not the one making problems.

You know I want your mom to come.

DONNA: Then why do you think we should have Texan food?

CARLA CARLA: We won't. We won't. We won't have it.

DONNA: No the wedding's off.

CARLA CARLA: Donna.

DONNA: It's off.

My mom said I'd never get married.

HOW TO ARRANGE FLOWERS

NICK: The wedding is on again. I will be doing the flowers.
   (Pause.)
   That was easy wasn't it.

HOW TO FIND A DJ

BOB: *(Enters. Interrupting.)* Um Carla Carla?
CARLA CARLA: Bob? Hi Bob.
DONNA: Hey Bob.
NICK: Hey Bob.
BOB: Donna. Hey. Nick. Um. You seen Barb?
CARLA CARLA: Today?
DONNA: No.
CARLA CARLA: No.
NICK: She's at that thing.
CARLA CARLA: What thing?
BOB: I drove by that
   by her apartment and I didn't see the Buick
NICK: She's at that thing. That thing at the museum where those monks are
   making a picture out of sand. In Providence. You know the Buddhist
   thing.
BOB: Oh. So
   (Pause.)
   How you doing?
NICK: They're fighting over a DJ.
DONNA: We're not fighting.
CARLA CARLA: We're discussing.
NICK: You're fighting.
CARLA CARLA: We're not fighting.
DONNA: We're discussing. A lot.
BOB: For a party?
DONNA: We're planning our commitment ceremony.
BOB: Your what?
CARLA CARLA: Our ceremony.
NICK: Their wedding.
BOB: You two. Hey! Congratulations!

DONNA: Thanks.

BOB: Married huh. Barb didn't tell me.

CARLA CARLA: It's going to be small.

BOB: That's great.

DONNA: A small ceremony. But with lots of dancing.

BOB: No that's great. OK so.

(Pause.)

If you see Barb

CARLA CARLA: You OK Bob?

BOB: Me? Yeah.

(Pause.)

Well. It's been rough. But

(Pause.)

OK.

(Pause.)

OK.

(Pause.)

She doesn't have any furniture. At that at her apartment. She doesn't have a bed. She has a big cushion. A futon. It's called.

(Pause.)

OK.

(Exits.)

(Pause.)

NICK: He looks crappy.

DONNA: Um.

NICK: He should of listened to Barb He should have tried to change and do a little of what

(The Shark enters.)

DONNA: Shut up. Look.

CARLA CARLA: That the shark?

DONNA: Um.

CARLA CARLA: We'll

DONNA: Yeah.

NICK: Yeah.

CARLA CARLA: Yeah.

NICK: Quick.

(They're gone.)

Excuse me I

You're the

THE SHARK: (*Pause. Smiles.*)

NICK: I met you the other day With Donna
    She was just here.

THE SHARK: I remember.
    (*Pause.*)
    You're Nicholas.

NICK: You can call me Nick Some people call me Nicholas Some people Nick
    They used to call me Fatboy

THE SHARK: Really? Fatboy?
    Why?

NICK: I used to be
    I spent a couple of summers in front of a fryolator at Twig Beach. I ate a
    lot of French fries. I was kind of
    So you're a real swimmer huh?

THE SHARK: Yup.

NICK: You like it?

THE SHARK: What?

NICK: Swimming?

THE SHARK: Oh yeah I do.
    Which is lucky 'cause I do it all day long.

NICK: Yeah.

THE SHARK: Swim. You know. And swim.
    (*Pause.*)
    I love the beach.

NICK: Want to go?

THE SHARK: Where?

NICK: Want to go to the beach?

THE SHARK: With you?

NICK: Yeah?

THE SHARK: Now?

NICK: Yeah?

THE SHARK: Sure.

NICK: You do?

THE SHARK: Sure.

NICK: Great.
    (*Nick throws sand on stage. They are at Twig Beach.*)

THE SHARK: Umm.
    Gosh. The water's so blue.

NICK: See over there? Just past where that house

THE SHARK: The grey one?

NICK: Yeah That's where Donna lives. They're having their commitment ceremony If they have it in their backyard so the procession goes up the beach and through the street and then into their backyard for the service. Beautiful huh?

THE SHARK: Yeah.

NICK: And over there? That was where my fryolator.

THE SHARK: Nice.

(Pause.)

The water is so blue.

NICK: Want to sit down?

THE SHARK: It's so blue. I forgot. At the aquarium it's either the glass or something they put in it but the water's green it's not blue.

NICK: You like the aquarium?

THE SHARK: It's OK It's a job. It's kind of boring. People stare a lot.

NICK: Well

THE SHARK: Yeah I guess that's

Before that I used to sell Avon. Skin So Soft. Door to door up on Federal Hill.

NICK: Oh I love Skin So Soft.

THE SHARK: It's a good product.

NICK: Does it really repel blackflies?

THE SHARK: Yup.

NICK: Chemistry huh?

(Pause.)

I once sold paintings door to door.

THE SHARK: You did?

NICK: Horrible.

THE SHARK: Bad?

NICK: Unbearable.

THE SHARK: Grotesque?

NICK: The paintings. They were landscapes. And one completely ugly clown painting I still

You know Sad clown sad eyes big white mouth head tilted ugh

(Pause.)

Me and my friend Shao Mei we were totally broke so we answered an ad Do you want a Career in Art? And since she's a macrame artist and I'm well I'm artistic too

THE SHARK: You are?

NICK: I don't do art but I love art Van Gogh Picasso Michelangelo that guy
that paints the sunflowers you know what's his name

THE SHARK: Van Gogh

NICK: Oh yeah Van Gogh so we thought We're perfect. So we go to the place
this was outside of Boston and the guy running it piles me and Shao Mei
and ten other people in a van and drives us for miles and then when we
get there he gives us each a portfolio of ten different paintings Oh they
were so ugly The clown Moon over palm trees Moon over waterfall
Moon over fir trees Moon over a circus So they're all signed Blunt so I
have to pretend I'm Nicholas Blunt 'cause you know Nick Blunt? that
sounds stupid so me and Shao Mei Blunt and ten other Blunts walk
around this neighborhood pretending we're poor art school students listen to me I'm just talking and talking and talking

I'm nervous I'm nervous

THE SHARK: I was watching your mouth move.

NICK: Oh.

(Pause.)

I had to stop because the clown painting was so ugly it gave me a
headache. Plus I walked into a house and they already had one of my
paintings. Moon over the mountains right over the sofa.

Horrible.

What'd you do before Avon?

THE SHARK: Before that

Used to be I was. Out there.

NICK: Here?

THE SHARK: I used to come here.

NICK: To Twig Beach?

THE SHARK: I liked this beach.

NICK: I wonder if I ever saw you.

THE SHARK: I'd swim and I'd see the beach and the people on the beach pink
people and brown people and white. And I'd stare at them.

Scoot in.

NICK: You'd swim in?

THE SHARK: I liked swimming in the shallows. I liked being near people in the
water. I liked feeling the blood vibrating in their bodies. I liked the heat.
I liked the thrash.

And I remember thinking

(Makes biting gesture.)

Course I didn't.

Would of ruined a good day at the beach for someone. Kind of.

That scare you?

NICK: No.

THE SHARK: Donna think you should be here with me?

NICK: Huh?

THE SHARK: Go out with a shark you going to get bitten. Or shark today gone tomorrow. Or I knew a guy who dated a shark he's got one leg and a big chunk missing out of him.

(Pause.)

That scare you?

NICK: No.

THE SHARK: I'm talking too much. I got a big mouth.

That scare you?

NICK: No.

THE SHARK: No?

NICK: I have a crush on you.

THE SHARK: You do?

NICK: That's what my friend Barb says.

THE SHARK: She does?

NICK: It comes before infatuation which she says is around the corner if we keep talking which I think I might be feeling.

THE SHARK: I like Barb.

(Kisses Nick.)

NICK: I like Barb too.

THE SHARK: I like Barb a lot.

(Kisses Nick.)

NICK: Oh a lot me too.

THE SHARK: A lot.

(Kisses Nick.)

NICK: Hm.

THE SHARK: Sometimes I'd swim way far out there.

Late at night Empty and I'd get lonely and that blue and blue forever and then a swimmer and

we'd circle each other looking at each other and he'd look back and I'd follow him and I'd feel that

(Pause.)

and after I'd swim again. Looking. And I'd be lonely again.

(Kisses Nick. Kisses Nick and touches his chest. Kisses Nick and touches his leg. Kisses Nick and moves his hand up Nick's leg.)

NICK: Can we
   Um
   wait on this?
THE SHARK: Huh?
NICK: Just for awhile?
THE SHARK: Sorry. Yeah. Forget it.
NICK: I'd rather just
THE SHARK: Yeah sorry OK.
NICK: 'Cause I like it but
   Don't you like kissing?
THE SHARK: No I do.
NICK: Me too. I could kiss
   See I'm not supposed to go too fast. I mean I want to But everyone's say-
   ing Not too fast Not too fast
   I usually jump too fast.
THE SHARK: Me too.
   I think I shouldn't.
   But then I forget.
NICK: Me too. Let's forget it. I can forget it.
THE SHARK: Naw.
NICK: Yeah lets. My therapist says I'm fast. So what I sleep with people too
   fast. I want to. Let's sleep together now and next date let's wait.
THE SHARK: No.
NICK: I changed my mind. I want to.
THE SHARK: No.
NICK: I do I want to.
THE SHARK: No.
   (Pause.)
NICK: We could Maybe Maybe we could go out to Would you want to maybe
   go to the wedding with me To Donna's commitment?
THE SHARK: *(Pause.)* Can I call you?
NICK: Oh.
   (Long pause.)
   Sure. Yeah.
THE SHARK: OK I'll call you.
NICK: Yeah.
THE SHARK: OK.
   (The Shark exits.)
NICK: I'm so stupid I'm so stupid I'm so stupid I'm so stupid.

DONNA: He'll call.

NICK: He won't call.

DONNA: He'll call.

NICK: I like him. We had fun. He won't call. I'm so stupid.

>*(Barb sees something offstage. She goes and gets it. She brings it onstage. It is a soaking wet dufflebag. It is dripping water. She sits. Stares at the duffle bag.)*

BARB: I found this floating in our pool.

CARLA CARLA: What's in it?

BARB: All my shoes.

>I wasn't going to throw them away.

CARLA CARLA: Did Bob throw them in the pool?

BARB: Bob threw everything in the pool. Our living room set's in the pool.

CARLA CARLA: He did not.

BARB: Our dining room table is in the pool.

CARLA CARLA: He did not.

BARB: Our lawn mower's in the pool. Our orientals our paintings our plants. My winter clothes. My linens. The china. The vacuum cleaner. The pool table. Is in the pool.

>*(Pause.)*

>Bob. *(Pause.)* Is sad.

CARLA CARLA: Hm.

BARB: He must be really sad.

>*(Pause.)*

>I saw it. I got so sad. I got so sad I went out and walked and walked and walked

CARLA CARLA: He shouldn't have done that Barb

BARB: I made him so sad

CARLA CARLA: Hey You've got to be allowed to learn something new. That wasn't OK he did this Barb.

BARB: That wasn't OK you did that Bob.

BOB: What?

BARB: I found

>*(Pause.)*

BOB: You

>I was going to pull the pool cover over it.

BARB: Um.

BOB: I'm

>*(Pause.)*

BARB: I know you are.

BOB: You've got to come home Barb

BARB: No Bob

BOB: The house is empty. It almost is. Our bedroom is. I emptied it I gave it all to the Salvation Army. I only kept some of my clothes the bed. A few small things. Like you want.

BARB: You should do what you want Bob.

BOB: I want to have you home Barb.

BARB: I'm not sure you

BOB: It's part of life to have stuff Barb. It's part of life to want stuff. It's part of life to get attached. But if you don't want anything well OK. OK with me.

BARB: It's All the shopping At the
   I don't want

BOB: You're so stubborn.

BARB: I'm not stubborn.

BOB: You don't you don't even listen.

BARB: I'm trying to be

BOB: You get an idea in your head and that's
   Doesn't matter that someone else

BARB: Bob. I'm trying to be truthful.

BOB: Doesn't matter that I
   Doesn't matter Anything else Anything that doesn't fit Pfft
   And Barb's
   Well I'm not
   I'm just caught. Caught. Caught.

BARB: I'm just trying. Bob.
   And if that means
   if it takes time then it just takes time
   and you have to wait.

BOB: Much longer Barb?

BARB: Or if you don't want to

BOB: Much longer Barb?

BARB: I get to decide Bob.

BOB: 'Cause I'm tired of waiting. I'm doing what you want. Getting rid of everything. But I'm tired of waiting.
   (Pause.)

BARB: Is that a new shirt Bob?

BOB: Barb

(Pause.)

BARB: I think we should take a real break from each other for a while.

NICK: HE CALLED!

CARLA CARLA: SHH.

NICK: he called I knew he would

DONNA: when

NICK: he's coming to the wedding

DONNA: wedding's off Nick

NICK: wedding is ON Donna

CARLA CARLA: Nick. Then what'd he say?

BARB: He said

BOB: OK.

> *(Pause.)*

> OK. Whatever you want.

CARLA CARLA: And what did you say?

BARB: Nothing. I mean What could I say What

CARLA CARLA: *(Carla Carla is dressing for the commitment ceremony.)* Wedding's off again

BARB: Uh huh.

CARLA CARLA: She's not convinced I know what I am doing.

BARB: Uh huh.

CARLA CARLA: She doesn't think I know why I want to marry her. Which made me think Why do I want to marry her. Which is one of the things I like about her.

BARB: Sure.

CARLA CARLA: She said it's alright to be happy Carla Carla. It's alright to be happy Carla Carla. And I thought I am. That's what I am. I'm happy with her.

BARB: She's happy with you.

CARLA CARLA: It's just simple.

BARB: You're lucky.

CARLA CARLA: Of course then she called the wedding off again.

BARB: Well.

> Ready?

CARLA CARLA: Yup.

> *(Superfast Wedding March music.)*

BARB: I stand here as witness to the love of my friend Carla Carla for Donna.

NICK: I stand here as witness to the love of my friend Donna for Carla Carla.

BARB & NICK: As witnesses we stand by them and Will stand by them and Promise to stand by their union.

BARB: Carla Carla do you take Donna to have and to hold To cherish and love for ever more and always?

CARLA CARLA: I do.

NICK: And Donna do you take Carla Carla to have and to hold To cherish and love for ever more and always?

DONNA: Totally. I do.

BARB: Carla Carla the ring.

CARLA CARLA: Donna. With this ring I promise to love you always To hold onto you To consider you To love you always To push you forward and To pull you into me To talk to you To walk with you To sing with you and To laugh forever and ever and To love you always I promise.

NICK: Donna the ring.

DONNA: Carla Carla with this ring I love you.

(Pause.)

(Whispered.)

I only smoked one today.

(They kiss.)

BARB & NICK: Youmaykissthebride.

(Music. Rice. Slow motion. Donna tosses the bouquet. Nick catches it.)

(Carla Carla Donna Barb Nick and the Shark at the commitment ceremony. They do the dances at the commitment ceremony. Freeze frame after freeze frame. Like too many photos. They do the Frug. The Twist. The Bump. The Chicken.)

(Barb and Nick are on the beach. Nick picks up a stone and throws it into the ocean.)

BARB: Your shark looks nice.

NICK: Um.

BARB: Looks like he might be in love.

NICK: Not yet. It's a little early for

He called. And he showed up. So far so good.

BARB: He's a good dancer.

NICK: I feel sick at work. I go to work and I put my head on my desk and just leave it there.

BARB: That's normal.

NICK: It is?

BARB: I had that with Bob.

NICK: You did?

BARB: I was lovesick.

NICK: Oh that's what it is.

> (Pause.)

> Donna's mom didn't make it.

BARB: No.

> (Pause.)

> I don't think I'm going to be able to only own eight things. I have things of my grandmother's

> I'm having

NICK: I bet that's not the point huh. Only having eight things.

BARB: No.

NICK: Is it interesting?

BARB: What?

NICK: What you're doing?

BARB: Oh it is. It is. I'm seeing

> (Pause.)

> I'm

> (Pause.)

> It is.

> (Pause.)

NICK: That's good then.

BARB: It is.

> (Pause.)

> I am down to 147 things.

NICK: Huh.

> (She takes off her shoes. She leaves them on the beach. She looks at Nick.)

NICK: 146.

BARB: 145.

> I'm going to eat some cake.

> (Blackout.)

END OF PLAY

COMFORT WOMEN

Chungmi Kim

For all "comfort women"

PLAYWRIGHT'S BIOGRAPHY

Chungmi Kim, originally from South Korea, earned an M.A. in Theater Arts from UCLA and has participated in the Warner Brothers Minority Writers Program for Television, WGA Open Door Writing Program for screenwriting, USC Professional Writing Program, and the Mark Taper Mentor Playwrights Program in Los Angeles.

Awards she has received include the first-place Open Door Writing Award for her screenplay, *The Dandelion,* from the Writers Guild Foundation, West; Harry Kurnitz Creative Writing Award for her one-act play, *I Beg Your Pardon*; Grand Prize at the 1995 USC One-Act Play Festival for *The Comfort Women* (completed with the Jerome Lawrence Playwright Award from the USC Professional Writing Program), which was also a finalist of the O'Neill Playwrights Conference. Its full-length version, *Hanako,* had a world premiere at East West Players in Los Angeles in 1999. (Ms. Kim was featured as one of the "Faces to Watch" in the *Los Angeles Times*.) Its revised version, *Comfort Women,* had a New York premiere at Urban Stages in the fall of 2004. In 2005, *Comfort Women* translated into Korean and titled *Nabi* was presented at the Seoul Theater Festival by Arirang Theater Company and had an extended run at other theaters in Korea.

Her television credits include writing and producing *The Koreans in L.A.* and *Poets in Profile* for KCET-TV. As a co-producer of a one-hour news documentary, *Korea: The New Power in the Pacific,* and a twenty-three-part news mini documentary series, *Korea,* for KCBS-TV, she received a Certificate of Merit from the Associated Press and Emmy nominations.

She is the author of *Chungmi — Selected Poems* and *Glacier Lily,* her latest poetry book published by Red Hen Press. Her poetry has appeared in many anthologies, magazines, journals, books, and on a spoken CD. She was one of the poets chosen for the Poetry Society of America's Poetry in Motion L.A.'98–'99 Project. Ms. Kim will be featured in Bob Bryan's forthcoming documentary on contemporary literary poets as part of his *Graffiti Verité* documentary series.

She is a member of PEN USA, Pacific Asian American Women Writers-West, and the Dramatists Guild.

ORIGINAL PRODUCTION

Urban Stages in New York City — Off-Broadway production — October 28, 2004, to November 28, 2004. Directed by Frances W. Hill with the following cast:

GRANDMA . . . . .Tina Chen
MOTHER . . . . .Haerry Kim
JINA . . . . .Ji-young Kim
SOONJA PARK . . . . .Jade Wu
BOKHI LEE . . . . Jo Yang
JAPANESE OFFICER . . . . .Jade Wu
FUMIKO . . . . Jo Yang
HANAKO . . . . .Ji-young Kim
Set/Lighting Design . . . . Roman J. Tatarowicz
Costume Design . . . . Heesoo Kim
Sound Design . . . . Jane Shaw
Stage Manager . . . . .Mimi Craig

Hanako, an earlier version of *Comfort Women*, made its world premiere at East West Players in Los Angeles in April 1999, directed by Tzi Ma, featuring Marilyn Tokuda, Dian Kobayashi, June Angela, and Christina Ma. This play was originated from *The Comfort Women*, a one-act play, which received the Grand Prize at the USC One-Act Festival in 1995. In May 2005, *Comfort Women*, translated into Korean and titled *Nabi* was presented at the Seoul Theater Festival and had an extended run at other theaters in Korea through September by Arirang Theater Company, directed by Eunmi Bang.

TIME
Summer, 1994

PLACE
Queens, New York

CHARACTERS
GRANDMA, a sixty-eight-year-old Korean-American woman
JINA, her granddaughter, a twenty-one-year-old Korean-American woman
SOONJA PARK, a seventy-year-old Korean woman
BOHKI LEE, a sixty-nine-year-old Korean woman

MEMORY SCENES CHARACTERS
MOTHER
HANAKO (JINA)
JAPANESE OFFICER (SOONJA PARK)
FUMIKO (BOKHI LEE)

FROM THE PLAYWRIGHT

My journey for this play started in Los Angeles in 1994 when I was given a book of testimonies by the surviving "comfort women." Until then I never knew about them even though I was born and raised in Korea. Reading their horrifying experiences as forced sex slaves for the Japanese military during World War II shocked and enraged me.

Between 1937 and 1945, about 200,000 young women and girls, as young as eleven, were conscripted or abducted from Asian countries. Eighty percent of them, mostly teenagers, were Korean. After the war, the survivors kept silent, living in shame, isolation, and poverty for decades. In 1991, the first woman broke the silence. Since then, other survivors have come forward, demanding justice and reparations from the Japanese government. There are only a little over a hundred survivors in South Korea, and many passed away in recent years.

I wanted to honor all the "comfort women"; those who broke the silence and those who have not. And I wanted to give them a voice with dignity in hopes that the world would listen to them and do something to prevent the recurrence of such horrific human-rights violations. After all, the comfort women issue is more than just to condemn such war crimes by Japan. It has to do with injustice and violence against fundamental human rights. And it is not just the story of the past. Look at what's happening in the world today, especially to women and children. Similar war crimes have occurred and still are happening.

Inspired by the testimonies I read, I wrote a one-act play, *The Comfort Women*, with a fellowship from the USC Professional Writing Program. Then I went to meet the survivors in Korea. Meeting them made a deeper emotional impact on me. Afterwards, I developed the one-act into a full-length play, *Hanako*, which was produced at East West Players in Los Angeles in 1999. Its revised version, *Comfort Women*, was produced at Urban Stages in New York in the fall of 2004.

In May 2005, *Comfort Women* translated into Korean and titled *Nabi* was presented at the Seoul Theater Festival and other theaters afterwards by Arirang Theater Company in Korea. Some of the survivors came to see the play. When they thanked me and the others involved for writing and presenting their stories, all of us were deeply moved. It was one of the most gratifying moments in my life. "Please let the world know the truth" was their plea.

Special thanks to Frances Hill of Urban Stages, Tina Chen, and Peggy Chane whose support and dedication made the New York premiere at Urban Stages possible. Thanks also to all those who have helped me bring this play to life, especially Dr. James Ragan of the USC Professional Writing Program, Tim Dang of East West Players, and Tzi Ma. Thanks to the Korean Council for Women Drafted for Military Sexual Slavery, Professor Hyo-jae Lee, Professor Chung-Ok Yun, Eunmi Bang of Arirang Theater Company in Korea, and all the actors and crews involved in the productions and readings. And thanks to my friends and family whose love and support nurtured me through difficult times along my journey, especially Ronnie Golden, Inja Kim, my brother Jong Sang Kim, and my husband Sung M. Lee. Most importantly, I dedicate this play to all "comfort women."

Comfort Women

Setting: A small detached guest room in the back of a house in Queens, New York. Upstage center, a single bed (a foam mattress on a low platform) is set against a wall, covered with a comforter. A few clean undergarments are strewn on the bed. Next to its right is an end table with two framed pictures (Grandma's mother and brother) in front of an incense burner. Above the bed, curtains are drawn over a window. A bathroom door upstage right is half open. Downstage, a floor lamp stoops over a round table and two chairs. On the table a basketful of silk flowers brightens this cocoon-like hideout. Downstage left, a closet door is closed. A footstool sits in the middle of the room under a dangling ceiling lamp, which throws warm light in a circle. Downstage right, the entrance door is locked. Outside the door, a stool sits under a tree in a garden path, which leads to the stairway upstairs. Upstage on a platform, memory scenes happen behind a scrim. (Note: A simple and suggestive set is recommended rather than a realistic one.)

At Rise: Stage lights come up slowly on Grandma, a sixty-eight-year-old Korean-American woman with glasses, perched on the footstool under the light. Making a silk flower, she is humming a tune. She wears a long skirt, a short blouse, and an old Korean-style hairdo with a bun. Charming and elegant, she is a woman of many layered emotion and extremely fastidious manner. Grandma stops humming, reminisces. She hears the voice of Mother, singing.

VOICE OF MOTHER: Doraji, doraji — doraji — ee
    sheem sheem saan choneh, dora — ji —
GRANDMA: Oh, Mother. You sing so well —
    (Mother, a young Korean woman in her early thirties, appears behind the scrim.)
MOTHER: *(Waving at Grandma.)* Dance with me, Yuniya—
    (Grandma takes off her glasses. As Grandma sings and dances, her face radiates a childlike smile.)
GRANDMA/MOTHER: *(Singing.)* Doraji—doraji—dora—ji—ee
    Sheem sheem saan choneh, doraji—
    Hahn doo ppoori mahan, kayer—er—do-oh-oh—
    daebagunieh—chori cherl cherl, numb noo woo nah—
    eheiyo-eheiyo—eeheei—yo—oh—

(Twirling and laughing, Grandma dances along. Suddenly Grandma trips on the stool and stumbles. Mother behind the scrim disappears.)

GRANDMA: *(Panting.)* Oh, how clumsy you are — old woman! Lucky — you are indeed — very lucky that — you did not break your bones!
(Grandma bends down and rubs her leg.)

GRANDMA: Damn you. I should throw you away. You are so old and worn out — *(Chuckles.)* Well — Like me.
(A crow caws. Grandma frowns, listening.)

GRANDMA: A crow? *(Beat.)* Just like in my dream!
(Behind the scrim, Mother in a white Korean traditional dress appears, holding a white candle as in a dream. A crow caws.)

GRANDMA: Do you hear that crow cawing, Mother?

MOTHER: A blue bird. My beautiful blue bird —

GRANDMA: That is a crow, Mother. A bad omen!
(A crow caws in the distance.)

MOTHER: A blue bird, my son. He sings like a bird, flying in limbo. Soon he will fly into my nest. *(Beat.)* I pray for him. You pray for him
(Sound of a bird.)

MOTHER: How I pray to Buddha to protect my children —
(Sings, walking away.)
Sae ya, sae ya, parang sae ya
nokdoo bateh anhchi marah
nokdoo kkochi tter rher jimyun
chungpo jangsoo woolgo gandah—
(Mother behind the scrim disappears.)

GRANDMA: *(Shaking her head.)* O mother, you come to my dream, always reminding me of my brother — *(Glances at the photos.)* You do not need to worry, Mother. I have been praying for Brother Insung every day. For you, too. I am making new flowers for his memorial—
(A crow caws.)

GRANDMA: Is it possible — he became a bird? *(Beat.)* I get confused — cannot tell sometimes — from a dream to reality.
(Grandma resumes making flowers, humming "Sae ya, sae ya". Outside, Jina, Grandma's twenty-one-year-old granddaughter appears, carrying a brown bag. She wears jeans and long frizzy hair. Her pretty face is full of curiosity and naïveté. Playful but determined. Grandma stops humming, sighs.)

GRANDMA: Another day is passing by — like a flower petal that falls off.

(Beat.) Brother Insung, you would be seventy — what — ah, seventy-one now if you were still —

(Jina knocks. Grandma is startled.)

JINA: Halmoni —

(Jina tries to open the locked door.)

JINA: Grandma, would you please open the door? It's Jina.

GRANDMA: Jina? Oh, Jina —

(Grandma gets up, sees her undergarments.)

GRANDMA: Uh-oh. *(Loudly.)* Wait one minute —

(Grandma frantically removes her undergarments from the bed and hides them under the comforter. Jina puts down her brown bag, loosely braids her hair.)

JINA: *(Knocking.)* Grandma — !

GRANDMA: I am coming —

(Mutters to herself.)

— cannot do things fast anymore —

(Jina picks up the brown bag and knocks again.)

JINA: Grandma. Open the door, please. This is me.

GRANDMA: Coming — !

(Grandma opens the door.)

GRANDMA: *(Shaking her head.)* How impatient you are —

(Jina breezes in.)

GRANDMA: Your — your shoes —

(Jina kicks off her shoes.)

GRANDMA: *(Pointing at Jina's shoes.)* Ah-ah.

(Jina places her shoes by the door. Grandma closes the door, arranges the shoes neatly. Jina goes to the table, puts down the brown bag on the chair.)

JINA: I called you earlier. Where were you, Grandma?

GRANDMA: When? You know I go nowhere.

JINA: Where's the phone? Did you hide it again?

GRANDMA: You know I hate the sound of the telephone. Every time I hear that telephone ring, I almost have a heart attack.

JINA: How am I supposed to reach you then?

(Grandma smoothes out the bed.)

GRANDMA: Did your mother send you here to get the flowers?

JINA: No. I don't think she sold all those flowers you made last week. *(Showing the candles.)* Here, I brought you the candles you wanted.

GRANDMA: Oh good.

(Grandma takes the bag of candles, walks toward the end table. Jina takes out a "chamoe," a Korean melon, from the brown bag.)

JINA: *(Playing like a magician.)* And — heeee — errrrrrrrr — re — s the CHAMOE! The most delicious melon from the land of morning calm —Korea!

(Grandma laughs, puts down the bag of candles on the end table, walks over to Jina and takes the melon from her.)

GRANDMA: Oh, your great uncle will appreciate this. Chamoe was his favorite melon. Your great grandma's, too.

JINA: That is for you, Grandma. Not for the dead.

GRANDMA: *(Clicks her tongue, whispers.)* Hush. Their spirits are around, you know.

JINA: Where?

GRANDMA: Everywhere. Trust me. I know.

(Grandma looks into the brown bag and happily smiles. She drops the chamoe into the bag, takes it to the closet.)

JINA: Grandma. Why do you put everything away in the closet?

GRANDMA: Do you see any other room around here?

JINA: The melons may get rotten in there and stink up the room.

(Jina playfully stretches out on the bed. Grandma rushes to the bed, picks up her undergarments, and puts them in the closet.)

JINA: What is that?

GRANDMA: Nothing.

JINA: Grandma. I have big news. Dad decided to run for president of the New York Korean American Association!

GRANDMA: Your mother told me that last night. I do not understand why he has to spend lots of money for that sort of a thing.

JINA: He can do many good things in that position if he's elected.

GRANDMA: Your mother alone cannot manage the store. And she'll never give up her church activities.

JINA: Don't worry, Grandma. Mom is really excited —

GRANDMA: Jina. You did not tell your mother, did you?

JINA: About what?

GRANDMA: About tomorrow night.

JINA: Our memorial service for Great Uncle? *(Teasing.)* I did. She said she is going to invite her minister to conduct the service in this room.

GRANDMA: What? No, no! I will not have a Christian service here.

JINA: Shall we invite your temple priest as well? We can have a Buddhist "jesah" ceremony afterwards.

GRANDMA: Jina, what are you talking about?

JINA: I'm teasing you, Grandma. I didn't tell her anything.

> *(Grandma reacts with a hand gesture dismissing her.)*

JINA: *(Looking at the flowers.)* Oh you made white peonies. For the memorial?

GRANDMA: Yes. Your great grandmother used to make them for your great uncle's memorial every year after he died. *(Beat.)* She loved making lotus flowers for her Buddhist temple as well — especially for Buddha's birthday celebration.

JINA: I remember you did, too.

GRANDMA: *(Reminisces.)* One day I got upset with my mother — do not remember why. I could not play outside because it was raining. So I walked around inside the temple and found a small corner room. When I opened it, I could not believe my eyes! The room was filled with white and pink lotus paper flowers from floor to the ceiling! Oh, it was —

JINA: Breathtaking!

GRANDMA: It was — the most beautiful sight! *(Beat.)* I stepped in, carefully pushing them away not to crush. I curled up in a small cave-like space, surrounded by thousands of flowers. It was like a dream!

JINA: And nobody knew where you were, right?

GRANDMA: Nobody. Sometime later I heard my mother calling my name — looking for me. I did not answer, hiding in my flower cave.

JINA: And you fell asleep.

> *(Grandma nods, chuckling.)*

GRANDMA: Yes. When I woke up, it was dark. I was scared. When your great grandmother found me, she was so furious. She spanked me hard.

JINA: Whenever Mom scolded me, I hid in your attic — you know, in your flower shop in Seoul.

GRANDMA: Yes. And I had to keep my mouth shut.

JINA: *(Laughs.)* You used to call me "my little monkey." Mom didn't know our secret.

> *(Grandma rearranges the flowers.)*

JINA: Since Mom brought you to live with us in America, you've been a recluse, cooped up in this room. I hate to see your talent wasted.

GRANDMA: I can hardly keep up with your mother's demand.

JINA: Wait until I graduate and get a job. I'll take good care of you, Grandma. I'll take you on trips, first to Korea and then Europe — and any other places you like.

GRANDMA: My, how you have grown — Jina, you are the reason I am enjoying my old age.

JINA: Even if I'm silly and spoiled rotten?

(Grandma pinches Jina's cheek with affection.)

GRANDMA: Yes, my little monkey.

(Jina giggles like a little girl. She takes Grandma's hand and holds it with both hands.)

JINA: Grandma. I have a surprise for you.

GRANDMA: Surprise?

JINA: Yes. *(Beat.)* Grandma. Would you like to meet two very special elderly women from Korea?

GRANDMA: Two old women from Korea? You know I never like to meet strangers.

JINA: I know. But I told them —

GRANDMA: What?

JINA: I told them I have a grandma who loves to show off her talent, making flowers out of silk worms.

(Grandma reacts with a frown. Jina titters, goes behind Grandma and starts lightly massaging her shoulders.)

JINA: No, I didn't say that, Grandma. I said you've suffered so much because your brother, my great uncle, was drafted into the Japanese Army and got killed during World War II. They were very sympathetic and wanted to talk to you.

(Grandma hears the faint sound of wailing. Mother briefly appears behind the scrim, wailing "aigo".)

GRANDMA: Jina. *(Beat.)* You should not have told them about my brother.

JINA: Why not?

GRANDMA: It is a personal matter, and I do not want to talk about him to anyone.

JINA: They have some information on what you should do as a victim's family. I don't exactly know. I thought you'd want to find out —

GRANDMA: Who are these women? Government investigators?

JINA: No. Park Soonja and Lee Bokhi halmonies were comfort women. They know those things —

GRANDMA: Comfort women?

JINA: Yes. Did you know about them? I mean "the military comfort women" — I didn't know anything about them until now! What happened was that I was asked by my professor to help —

GRANDMA: Comfort women! Oh, Jina, how did you get mixed up with them? You did not even tell me what you were up to —

JINA: That's what I was calling you about earlier but you didn't answer.

(Beat.)

I only met them today for the first time. They're very nice. You see, Park halmoni and Lee halmoni were invited to participate in the protest rally —

GRANDMA: What protest rally?

JINA: At the UN. Japanese emperor Akihito is giving a speech today, and there's been a big rally to protest against the Japanese war crimes.

GRANDMA: So, what does it have to do with you? You stay out of it.

JINA: Aren't you even curious to find out what they have to say? About your brother — some kind of reparation, maybe. You've been telling me all these years how much you and Great Grandma suffered because of his tragic death.

GRANDMA: I have no interest in getting any reparation — he is long gone. Tell them I appreciate their concern.

JINA: I told them you'd be happy to meet them. Grandma, please — they're waiting in the house.

GRANDMA: In our house? *(Yells.)* You left the strangers in our house all by themselves, and you have been chattering here?

JINA: They wanted to rest. Jet lag, you know. They just came from Korea last night.

GRANDMA: If your mother knows that you left them alone in the house, she would be very upset. Go back to them now.

(Grandma walks toward the door, waits for Jina to leave.)

JINA: Grandma, what's happened to your good old Korean hospitality? These halmonies are all the way from Korea. *(Teasing.)* I was hoping you'd invite them to stay with you tonight.

GRANDMA: Stay with me? Are you out of your mind? I never — never sleep with strangers! You should know that.

JINA: *(Titters.)* Just a wishful thinking. *(Beat.)* Grandma. The truth is that — I was hoping you'd talk to them for me as well as for Great Uncle's sake. You see, I'm supposed to write about them for the school paper. So I tried to interview them but it was — a little difficult. Park halmoni talked a lot but the other — Lee halmoni — spoke so little. I hardly got anything out of her. I think she's shy — uncomfortable with me. She may be more open to you. They're both about your age.

GRANDMA: Do not waste your time. They are ignorant women.

JINA: Grandma. How would you feel if someone despised you the way you despise them now? You always said that I should never look down on anyone, especially the poor and underprivileged.

(Grandma holds a moment, hearing a bird chatter.)

JINA: Grandma, you're not listening —

GRANDMA: You hear that, Jina? The bird —

JINA: What bird?

GRANDMA: It is not a crow, is it? *(Beat.)* — must be a blue bird. I had a dream of it.

(Behind the scrim, Mother briefly appears in a dim light like in a dream. Grandma smiles.)

JINA: Grandma.

GRANDMA: *(Beat.)* Huh — flew away.

JINA: Did you know anyone — among your friends in your school who was taken away by the Japanese? They say that thousands of young girls were forced —

GRANDMA: Young girls?

JINA: Yes.

GRANDMA: Not the school girls. Some peasant girls were sold for money.

JINA: Sold for money? Grandma, they were abducted!

GRANDMA: That is what they say. *(Beat.)* My mother was so protective of me. She married me off to your grandfather because the Japanese did not bother married women. *(Beat, mutters.)* To a good-for-nothing husband!

JINA: You never told me that. Why was he good for nothing?

GRANDMA: Ask your mother.

JINA: Mom doesn't remember him at all. He died when she was a baby, didn't he?

(Grandma doesn't answer.)

JINA: Grandma?

(Grandma hums a tune. Mother briefly appears behind the scrim, humming.)

GRANDMA: When I was little and having tantrums, my mother would hum this tune to calm me down.

JINA: Please listen to me, Grandma. I'm really compelled to write about them —"the military comfort women." Not just for the school paper but — I'm thinking of writing a book because it is a very important story people should know about.

GRANDMA: A book? Does your mother know about it?

JINA: I'm mad at Mom. I was talking to her about these halmonies this morning. You know what she said? She said it wasn't even worth discussing. And she told me to stay away from "those comfort women."

GRANDMA: You see, it will embarrass your mother and father if you get involved with them.

JINA: You and Mom are always concerned about "chemyon," keeping up the good image! She worries about what her friends and the church people will say. And you worry about what Mom is concerned about. I don't care. Let them criticize!

GRANDMA: Now your father is running for a public office, you should be more discreet —

JINA: Grandma. What I'm doing for school has nothing to do with Dad's campaign.

GRANDMA: Do not defy your mother and grandmother, Jina. You go now. Tell those women that I am sick. I feel really sick. I had no sleep last night — *(Coughing and rubbing her neck, Grandma walks toward the closet.)*

JINA: Grandma, please —

GRANDMA: *(Mutters to herself.)* Huh, I cannot remember what I am coming here for. What did I need — ? *(Grandma walks back to the table, trying to recall.)*

JINA: Aren't you proud that I get involved in working for a good cause?

GRANDMA: Ah, the candles — . *(Jina looks around, picks up the bag of candles from the end table and hands it to Grandma. Grandma turns toward the closet. Jina is determined to get her attention.)*

JINA: You know I cried a lot when we first came to America. I had no friend, didn't speak English — And I hated going to school. *(Grandma walks back to Jina.)*

GRANDMA: I know.

JINA: That kid at school, a pansy little kid — always following me around and yelling at me, "Hey, slant-eyed gook, go back to your country!" And other kids would laugh. I felt so ashamed to be Korean! *(Beat.)* When I came home, you were waiting for me as always. I cried. And you cried, too. You said, "You should be proud of your Korean heritage and do something worthwhile. Nobody will make fun of you then." *(Beat.)* Grandma, I never told you this before — Ever since then, those words stayed in my heart. You taught me to value my Korean heritage and do something worthwhile. *(Grandma puts down the bag of candles on the table, affectionately strokes Jina's head.)*

GRANDMA: Oh, Jina. You know I am very proud of you. But this is different. Not worthwhile as you think. How can I explain — *(Beat.)* Those women — are not the kind of people Koreans are proud of. They are shaming our country.

JINA: That is ridiculous!

(*Grandma turns away.*)

GRANDMA: (*Mutters to herself.*) Why am I so confused today?

JINA: Do you know what will happen if I fail to write a good story on them? I may "flunk" out of NYU!

GRANDMA: "Fulung"? What is that?

JINA: No graduation. No diploma!

(*Dismayed, Grandma sits on the chair, looks into Jina's eyes.*)

JINA: I'm serious, Grandma. Please help me. You know I hardly ever ask you a favor like this.

GRANDMA: No diploma?

(*Jina nods. Grandma sighs.*)

GRANDMA: (*After a pause.*) All right. I will do it just for you, my little monkey. I will properly greet them —

JINA: Oh thank you, Grandma!

(*Jina hugs Grandma from behind.*)

GRANDMA: You must not tell your mother and father about this.

JINA: I won't. I'll keep it our secret.

(*Grandma breaks away from her, stands confused.*)

GRANDMA: But — my room is too messy. (*Picks up lint.*) Look at this. What am I going to do?

JINA: Your room is never messy, Grandma. Would you rather meet them upstairs?

GRANDMA: That may be better.

(*Jina rushes to the door.*)

GRANDMA: Wait, Jina.

(*Jina stops by the door.*)

GRANDMA: I am not properly dressed —

JINA: You look just fine, Grandma. You can change if you want.

GRANDMA: I think I should.

(*Beat.*) Where is — ? Oh, there.

(*Grandma picks up the bag of candles from the table and walks toward the closet. Soonja Park, a seventy-year-old Korean woman, appears outside the door. She is an awkward country woman with the solemn look of a woman warrior, who is overly zealous about her activism. She wears a white traditional Korean dress.*)

JINA: I'll go tell them. Take your time. OK, Grandma?

(*Soonja Park knocks on the door. Grandma turns.*)

GRANDMA: (*Startled.*) Who is that?

JINA: It must be those two halmonies.

GRANDMA: *(Panic.)* Do not open the door! I cannot see them like this, you understand?

JINA: What should I — ?

GRANDMA: Tell them I am sick. Leave with them! Go!

(Grandma rushes to the bed.)

JINA: Grandma! Can't you at least say hello?

GRANDMA: I am sick — really sick —

(Grandma gets in under the comforter trying to hide. Soonja Park knocks harder. Jina opens the door.)

SOONJA PARK: The telephone kept ringing and ringing. I picked up the phone because Lee halmoni was sleeping —

JINA: I'm sorry I didn't mean to leave you alone so long —

SOONJA PARK: I said "hallo," and some woman spoke Engrish. I said, "No Enrish," and she said something and your name. I said, "OK." Now you go and talk to her. *(Beat.)* Is your grandmother here?

JINA: *(Awkward.)* She's — not feeling well today. I'm not sure if she can —

(Grandma coughs in bed.)

JINA: *(Beat.)* Grandma —?

(Grandma reluctantly gets out of the bed. Combing her hair with her fingers, she walks to the door like a feeble, sick woman. Nevertheless, she puts on a façade to play the gracious hostess.)

JINA: This is my Grandma.

SOONJA PARK: How do you do?

GRANDMA: I was just lying down, feeling — sick. My heart is failing —

SOONJA PARK: Oh — I'm sorry if I disturbed you. *(Pause.)* Your granddaughter has been a great help to Lee halmoni and me today. She is a very cheerful and well-mannered young lady.

GRANDMA: Young lady? She is still a baby.

(Grandma gives Jina a pleading look of "please take her away." Ignoring her, Jina jumps in her shoes.)

JINA: I have a call, Grandma. I'll be right back.

(Jina exits. Grandma meets Soonja Park's eyes and awkwardly smiles.)

GRANDMA: What about — your companion?

SOONJA PARK: Lee halmoni lay down on the sofa. Tired from the trip. It was a long flight from Korea, you know.

(Soonja Park cranes her neck, curious to see the room.)

GRANDMA: *(Reluctantly after a pause.)* Would you like to come in? It is not much of a place —

(Soonja Park enters, taking off her shoes by the door. She limps slightly as she walks. Grandma notices it, bends down and arranges the shoes neatly.)

SOONJA PARK: I'm used to a small room myself. *(Looking around.)* Very nice. Very neat.

(Soonja Park goes to the table and looks at the flowers. Grandma rushes to the bed, folds the comforter and pushes it against the wall.)

GRANDMA: Such a mess here. I did not expect anyone to visit me.

SOONJA PARK: Please don't bother for my sake. It looks to me as clean as a monk's room.

(Soonja Park walks about, picks up a flower.)

SOONJA PARK: Silk peonies — You like artificial flowers?

GRANDMA: Fresh ones do not last. They get easily crushed.

SOONJA PARK: But a short blooming life is better than a long miserable life. Don't you think so?

GRANDMA: I would not know.

(Grandma sees that Soonja Park is already sitting on the chair.)

GRANDMA: *(A little spiteful.)* Please have a seat.

SOONJA PARK: *(Smiles, beat.)* Do you like living in America?

(Grandma takes the flower from Soonja Park and puts it back in the basket. Grandma sits on the footstool.)

GRANDMA: I do not know — Everybody is busy working, you know. My son-in-law has a large produce store with a gift shop. He works from six in the morning till eleven at night, seven days a week.

SOONJA PARK: Your granddaughter told me it's a family business.

GRANDMA: Yes. So, everybody is gone. My daughter is hardly home, working at the store or for her church. My granddaughter is busy with school. The house sits empty, and I am here all by myself until late evening. *(Beat.)* But I do not mind being left alone.

SOONJA PARK: At least you have a family to wait for.

GRANDMA: What about you? Do you have a family to visit in America?

SOONJA PARK: No.

GRANDMA: What made you come?

SOONJA PARK: A women's group in New York invited us — Lee Bokhi halmoni and me — to give talks about military comfort women. You know what that is about, don't you?

GRANDMA: Well — not really.

SOONJA PARK: Unfortunately, most Koreans don't know. Even those who survived the Japanese oppression don't know about "Jeong-shin-dae." You know what it means, don't you?

(Grandma clears her throat, arranges the flowers.)

SOONJA PARK: It means Women's Patriotic Service Corps. That was just a cover-up for the Military Comfort Women. It was a shameful secret for many decades. That's why I —

GRANDMA: So, you do not have a family?

SOONJA PARK: No, I never had a chance.

GRANDMA: Maybe, you will in your next life. If you believe in karma —

SOONJA PARK: Yes, I do. When I am reborn, I pray I'll be blessed with a good husband and many children. At my old age, not having children is most unfortunate. I am alone. Don't even have close relatives. Being alone — is like drifting in a vast ocean. You know what I mean?

GRANDMA: No. I would not know.

SOONJA PARK: *(Chuckles.)* Right. How would you know? You have a happy family life. *(Beat.)* Is your husband still with you?

GRANDMA: No.

SOONJA PARK: But you have children. How many do you have?

GRANDMA: I only have one daughter.

SOONJA PARK: How lucky you are to have a daughter who takes care of you at your old age. How old is she?

GRANDMA: *(Irritated.)* Why did you not marry if you wanted children so badly?

SOONJA PARK: *(Beat, a deep sigh.)* What kind of a Korean man — or any man — would marry a woman like me, who was raped by the Japanese soldiers thousands and thousands of times? I could not marry any man. *(Chuckling.)* I cannot even drink milk. Reminds me of semen.

GRANDMA: *(Beat.)* Well, who wants to drink milk anyway?

(They look at each other and chuckle. Pause. Soonja Park looks around the room, points at the photo of Grandma's brother.)

SOONJA PARK: Is that your husband?

GRANDMA: No. My brother.

SOONJA PARK: Ah. Your granddaughter told me that he was conscripted into the Japanese Imperial Army and got killed. Do you know where he died?

GRANDMA: Why do you ask?

SOONJA PARK: Have you ever received any reparation for him?

GRANDMA: I am sorry I do not want to discuss that with you — or anyone.

SOONJA PARK: Oh, I only meant to help you.

GRANDMA: My family never pursued any reparation. No amount of money can bring him back.

SOONJA PARK: You see, an organization in Tokyo is collecting the data for those who were drafted into the Japanese Imperial Army during World War II. There's a good chance that you will —

GRANDMA: Please, I am not interested in it.

SOONJA PARK: He died fighting for Japan, didn't he?

GRANDMA: No. At home.

SOONJA PARK: At home? Then he was not conscripted — ?

GRANDMA: Yes, he was. He was stationed in Hiroshima.

SOONJA PARK: Hiroshima? Was he there when the atomic bomb dropped?

(*Grandma pauses, slightly nodding. She hears the faint sound of wailing like a train whistle. Behind the scrim, Mother briefly appears, wailing "aigo, aigo".*)

SOONJA PARK: Good heavens! How horrible that must've been! I know thousands of Koreans died there, not just Japanese.

GRANDMA: He died after he returned home.

(*Grandma is touched by Soonja Park's sympathetic reaction and talks about her brother, as if she's found someone who understands her sorrow.*)

GRANDMA: My brother Insung returned home very ill. We did not know what was wrong with him. One day, his ribs crumbled — just crumbled into pieces — as small as teeth! (*Beat.*) My mother never got over grieving his death. She died of grief —

(*Grandma takes out her handkerchief out of her skirt pocket, quickly wipes her tears and puts it back.*)

SOONJA PARK: You never got over grieving his death, either, did you?

GRANDMA: Well — You see, my brother was very special to me. He sacrificed so much for me. I loved to draw, and with his allowance he would buy me crayons and papers. He believed in my talent. He said he would support me to become an artist. (*Choked.*) Even when he was dying, he worried about me —

(*Grandma wipes her tears again. Realizing that she has talked too much, she controls her emotion and regains her composure, slightly smiling.*)

SOONJA PARK: I'm sorry. (*Beat.*) I wanted to become a singer. What a foolish dream that was! I could barely feed myself. You know, a woman with my past had no place to stand in our country.

GRANDMA: I can imagine.

SOONJA PARK: If you give me the information on your brother, I can find out what you can do to get the —

GRANDMA: Oh, I do not want to trouble you.

SOONJA PARK: No trouble at all. I'd be happy to — as a matter of fact, we should all work together, you know. After all, we're all victims of that war.

GRANDMA: My brother was. But he is long gone — so what is the use?
(*Changing the subject.*)
Where are you from?

SOONJA PARK: I'm from Jinju. What about you?

GRANDMA: I was born in a small town in Choong Chung Province.
(*Soonja Park searches for cigarettes.*)

SOONJA PARK: Do you have a cigarette? I left my bag with Lee halmoni.

GRANDMA: No. I used to be a chain-smoker. (*Beat.*) Smoking is bad for your health.

SOONJA PARK: I know. But I can't endure my life without the pleasure of smoking.

GRANDMA: Well, I might find a cigarette somewhere hidden —
(*Grandma walks about the room, looking in the corners and under the comforter.*)

SOONJA PARK: Please don't bother.

GRANDMA: I probably have it in the closet. If it is in the closet, I would not know where. It is a real mess in there. I am ashamed to show it to anyone.

SOONJA PARK: I'll go get my bag.
(*Soonja Park walks to the door. Grandma perks up, relieved. Jina appears outside the door, wearing a white sleeveless smock and carrying Soonja Park's large bag. She is followed by Bokhi Lee, a sixty-nine-year-old frail Korean woman with glasses, whose face reminds us of a mask of tragedy. A little hunched, Bokhi Lee carries the weight of her pain in every punctuating step, clutching a purse to her chest. When she speaks, her voice quivers. Bokhi Lee also wears a white Korean dress.*)

GRANDMA: Oh, would you tell my granddaughter that I will come in shortly, too?
(*As Soonja Park opens the door, Jina breezes in. Jina hands the bag to Soonja Park.*)

JINA: Here's your bag you left upstairs.

SOONJA PARK: Aren't you smart! How did you know I needed my cigarettes?
(*Soonja Park walks over to the table. Grandma quickly goes to Jina, grabs her arm and turns her around.*)

GRANDMA: (*Disappointed, whispers.*) She was coming to get it! (*Looking down at Jina's shoes.*) Your shoes.
(*Jina kicks off her shoes and joins Soonja Park at the table. Soonja Park reaches into her bag and takes out a bundle of petitions.*)

GRANDMA: You have a huge bag — like a peddler.

SOONJA PARK: I have everything I need in this bag. I travel so much nowadays.
(Grandma picks up Jina's shoes, walks toward the door. Grandma sees Bokhi Lee standing outside the door. They look at each other in awkward silence.)
SOONJA PARK: *(To Jina.)* Is Lee halmoni still — ?
(Soonja Park and Jina see Grandma facing Bokhi Lee. Jina dashes to them.)
JINA: I'm sorry — Grandma, this is Lee Bokhi halmoni from Korea.
GRANDMA: *(Simultaneously.)* From Korea, I know.
JINA: And this is my Grandma.
(Grandma and Bokhi Lee greet each other with a slight bow.)
SOONJA PARK: Lee halmoni, I left you alone to get some rest. Do you feel better now?
(Bokhi Lee shrugs and looks at Grandma, as if waiting for Grandma to invite her in.)
GRANDMA: So, you are all going to the rally. This is so unexpected — Perhaps, next time my granddaughter will tell me in advance.
SOONJA PARK: We thought perhaps you might join us —
GRANDMA: Oh, but I cannot go out. I do not feel well. *(To Jina.)* I know you are in a hurry. Your professor must be waiting for you.
(Grandma hands Jina her shoes, which she's been holding; a gesture saying that she wants them to leave. Jina takes her shoes, puts them down among other shoes.)
JINA: We have time, Grandma. Since this is the first day for these halmonies, I was told not to rush them. And I have something to finish before we go.
(Jina gives Grandma a pleading look of "please be nice to them.")
GRANDMA: Well — I have nothing to offer you here. No food, no drink —
SOONJA PARK: Your granddaughter already treated us to a nice breakfast.
(Jina motions for Bokhi Lee to enter. Bokhi Lee reluctantly takes off her shoes.)
GRANDMA: She never cooks. What did she serve you? Kimchi and uncooked rice?
JINA: No, Grandma. We stopped by a Korean restaurant on the way. Shall I bring some cold drinks?
SOONJA PARK: No, no. We don't need anything. It only makes you go to the bathroom too often, isn't that right, Lee halmoni?
(Bokhi Lee nods, embarrassed. Soonja Park sits at the table. Grandma is agitated but tries not to show it.)
BOKHI LEE: I hope we are not intruding — *(To Soonja Park.)* It's embarrassing we haven't brought any gift for them.

SOONJA PARK: Oh, you're right. *(To Grandma and Jina.)* We're sorry we visit you with no gift. We didn't know —

JINA: Oh, no, you mustn't feel that way.

GRANDMA: If you did, it would only burden me since I have nothing to offer you.

(Bokhi Lee stands, looking around the room. Jina offers a chair to her. Bokhi Lee sits at the edge of the chair. Grandma notices Jina's white smock for the first time.)

GRANDMA: Why are you wearing an apron?

JINA: This is my smock to wear at the rally. I want to write a slogan in Korean on this. Front and back. Grandma, would you help me?

GRANDMA: No.

JINA: Why not?

GRANDMA: My hands — shaky.

SOONJA PARK: *(To Jina.)* You speak Korean so well. When did you come to America? At what age?

JINA: 1983. I was ten years old.

SOONJA PARK: Many Korean American children I met in Korea couldn't speak the language at all. I'm proud of you.

JINA: My Grandma helped me keep up. But I can't write well.

SOONJA PARK: Ask Lee halmoni. She knows that — what do you call it — brush writing? — you know.

JINA: Oh, great. Would you help me, Lee halmoni?

(Bokhi Lee gets up, clutching onto her purse.)

JINA: No, not now.

BOKHI LEE: *(Embarrassed.)* I need to go to the bathroom.

JINA: Oh, right there.

(Jina leads Bokhi Lee toward the bathroom.)

SOONJA PARK: She's got a damaged bladder.

(Bokhi Lee stops and gives Soonja Park a look. Soonja Park pauses momentarily and continues as soon as Bokhi Lee exits.)

SOONJA PARK: She's got a damaged bladder. She's got a lot of problems. Poor Lee halmoni. You wouldn't believe what she went through.

GRANDMA: If she can travel to this far end of the world, she must be all right.

SOONJA PARK: You don't understand. The pain will not stop us to do our mission. Even if we drop dead tomorrow, we will go anywhere on earth to testify.

GRANDMA: I suppose she does not have a family, either.

SOONJA PARK: No, she does not. *(Beat.)* But she has her siblings in North Korea.

GRANDMA: Oh, she is from North Korea? That is tragic.

SOONJA PARK: Very tragic. She sacrificed for her brother.

JINA: She wasn't abducted?

SOONJA PARK: She was forced, of course. The Japs wanted to draft her brother who was a "sam dae dok ja".

JINA: What does it mean?

GRANDMA: It means —

(Soonja Park cuts in. Grandma sulks, gets up, mumbling to herself.)

SOONJA PARK: The only male heir in three generations. Anyhow, her father offered all his assets in an effort to save the son. That wasn't enough. The Japs wanted his unmarried daughter in his son's place. Lee halmoni. Only sixteen years old. The Japs lied that she would get a factory job in Japan. She didn't know what she was getting into. None of us did.

JINA: So, her father sacrificed the daughter to save the son? That is unbelievable.

SOONJA PARK: You know how precious that is to be the only male heir in three generations of the family lineage. You can't blame them. Blame the Japs. She said her father tried to stop them and got beaten half to death.

JINA: Oh how could they be so inhuman! *(Seizes a copy of the petition from the table.)* I'll definitely work on this petition drive. Grandma, you should sign this petition, too. It's important not only for the comfort women but all the —

(Pretending that she has not heard Jina, Grandma takes the phone out of the flower basket, puts it on the table in front of Jina and points at it.)

GRANDMA: Call your mother.

JINA: What for?

GRANDMA: See if she is all right. *(To Soonja Park.)* In America, it is dangerous to have a store. One can get robbed and shot to death any time, you know.

SOONJA PARK: Oh I heard that!

JINA: Don't worry, Grandma. I just called Mom a little while ago. I couldn't find her sewing kit that I needed and —

GRANDMA: You go help her. Your father is out, I'm sure.

(To Soonja Park.)

My son-in-law is very busy with campaigning. He is running for president of Korean Peoples's — What is it, Jina?

JINA: Korean American Association in New York. He hasn't started campaigning yet.

SOONJA PARK: Ah, he must be a prominent man.

GRANDMA: Yes, he is.

JINA: Grandma, please sign this petition.

(Not wanting to answer, Grandma busies herself, picking up lint and dusting the door. Bokhi Lee re-enters, drying her hand with her large white handkerchief.)

SOONJA PARK: *(To Bokhi Lee.)* A headache again?

(Bokhi Lee nods, sighing. She perches on the footstool. Her torso bent, she rocks back and forth, clutching her purse as always. Grandma intensely watches her for a moment. Soonja Park takes out a cigarette and a match.)

JINA: *(Holding up the petition.)* Shall I do it for you, Grandma?

GRANDMA: No!

(Grandma snatches the petition from Jina, crumples it up, and throws it away. Bokhi Lee looks up, startled.)

GRANDMA: *(Grunts.)* Useless —

JINA: Grandma, there's no danger in signing that.

SOONJA PARK: We need your support. *(Beat.)* If you understand what the Japanese Army did to countless innocent women —

GRANDMA: *(Exasperated.)* Why are you all bothering me? I told you I am sick!

JINA: Grandma! What's the matter with you?

GRANDMA: What is the matter with YOU? I have no time for this.

(Grandma picks up the crumpled petition and drops it in the wastebasket. Bokhi Lee frowns, getting nervous.)

SOONJA PARK: Is there any particular reason why you don't want to sign the petition?

GRANDMA: Koreans have been quiet about it for more than fifty years. Why do you have to stir up the past now?

SOONJA PARK: *(Offensive, firmly.)* So that the past will not repeat itself!

GRANDMA: Sometimes it is better to bury the past. Harboring the pain makes you sick. You should forgive and forget.

SOONJA PARK: I can never forget! *(Rising.)* Every night for the past fifty years, I've had nightmares. I was only thirteen years old when the Japs abducted me from the playground. For nine years I was a sex slave! I will never forgive!

(Bokhi Lee shudders, upset and uncomfortable.)

SOONJA PARK: Do you know what happened to Lee halmoni? Ask her if she can forget and forgive!

BOKHI LEE: *(Whispers.)* Park halmoni. Please — *(Louder.)* Get hold of yourself.

(Soonja Park sits down, tries to control her emotion.)

JINA: I'm sorry — my Grandma didn't mean to offend you. She doesn't really know —

SOONJA PARK: Because of damned ignorant people, we've been condemned and ignored in our own country. For so long, we lived in shame, in silence, as if we were guilty. Guilty of what? But no more. We will bring justice!

GRANDMA: *(With a sneer.)* Justice? If there could be justice in this world, it would not have happened. That part of history is water over the dam.

SOONJA PARK: *(Rising.)* Yeah, even the history ignored us! But we won't let it forget us. We'll speak the truth to the whole world.

GRANDMA: Who is going to listen to you? Do you think the world cares about a few Korean women who cry out? Even the Koreans do not care —

SOONJA PARK: You're right! Even the Koreans, my own people, my own country don't give a damn! The way they treated us — they're worse than the enemies!

GRANDMA: If you know what people think of you, you would not behave like this.

JINA: Grandma! Park Halmoni. Please stop —

SOONJA PARK: I know what people speak of us. Oh, yeah, Japs say we were whores. And people like you believe it.

(Soonja Park confronts Grandma.)

BOKHI LEE: Park halmoni, please — *(Getting up.)* We must leave. We'd better leave.

(With growing anger, Soonja Park speaks with such passion as if testifying before the public.)

SOONJA PARK: We were not whores! We were innocent girls — abducted by the Japs. Forced to become sex slaves. We were marked as military supplies and transported from one station to another in the battlefields. Ha! We had no human identity. Just military supplies. Emperor's gifts for his Imperial Army!

JINA: Emperor's gifts?

SOONJA PARK: And the damn Japanese government denied that it ever happened. Only after we raised hell — and the growing publicity forced them to admit it. But Japan still refuses to give an official apology!

BOKHI LEE: Please — listen to me!

(Bokhi Lee holds Soonja Park by the arm. Soonja Park pushes her away. Hurt, Bokhi Lee leans against the chair.)

SOONJA PARK: "Chosenppi, Korean whore!" That's what the Japs called us. "Public toilet." My body was nothing but a portable public toilet — trampled by twenty to forty men a day. I tell you, those damn barbarians used me like a toilet to discharge their piss and semen!

JINA: My God, twenty to forty men a day?

GRANDMA: Jina, you should not hear this.

SOONJA PARK: Why not? She should know the truth.

GRANDMA: Do not rant about your pain to me and my granddaughter! Go kill the Japanese emperor!

JINA: Grandma, please —

BOKHI LEE: Park halmoni. We'd better leave. Please — Let's go!

(Soonja Park sees Bokhi Lee trembling and pets her on the back, nodding.)

SOONJA PARK: All right, let's go. I know we are not welcome here.

(Beat.)

But I refuse to be misunderstood and mistreated by anyone anymore.

BOKHI LEE: This is not a place for us to talk about it.

SOONJA PARK: *(To Grandma.)* I'm sure you got the education and good fortune that Lee halmoni and I never had. That doesn't make you superior to look down on us. *(Beat.)* I don't believe your story about your brother. If he indeed died because of the Japs, you can't be so ignorant and selfish!

(Soonja Park takes her bag to leave.)

GRANDMA: *(Hateful and angry.)* You have no business to come to my home and insult me. My brother's death has nothing to do with you — comfort women! *(Beat.)* Hirohito was the evil demigod responsible for all your misery! You should have killed him. What is the use of condemning a dead man now?

SOONJA PARK: This is not about just condemning Hirohito. It's about condemning human violence and injustice committed by Japan!

GRANDMA: And begging for money?

(Bokhi Lee bites her lips, staring at Grandma. She pulls Soonja Park to leave. Fuming, Soonja Park turns to Grandma.)

BOKHI LEE: *(Tearful.)* I can't stand this! I can't —

(Bokhi Lee plops down on the chair, clutches onto her purse, trembling.)

JINA: Grandma, you don't understand. They're not begging for money. They want reparations and apologies which will at least set the record straight.

SOONJA PARK: Do you think money can bring back my youth, my life? *(Pause.)* What would you do, if you were in my place?

GRANDMA: Nothing.

(*Grandma turns away.*)

BOKHI LEE: Park halmoni. Let's go!

SOONJA PARK: No! I will not leave. She owes us an apology. We will not leave!

GRANDMA: My apology? Huh! You owe me an apology!

JINA: Oh, my god — What's happening?

SOONJA PARK: We are not beggars! We were not whores! We were the patriots who saved the rest of the Korean women like yourself. You should thank us!

(*Soonja Park sits down. Resigned, Bokhi Lee walks out of the room, leaving the door halfway open. The sunlight shoots in. Grandma goes to the door and slams it.*)

GRANDMA: Patriots? Huh! Water over the dam. There is nothing you can do about it.

(*Outside, Bokhi Lee sits on the stool under the tree. She wipes her tears with her handkerchief.*)

JINA: Yes, there is, Grandma. We're appealing to the UN Commission on Human Rights. At the rally today, there will be not only Koreans but other Asian Americans of all ages shouting for justice together in one voice. Please, Grandma, try to understand. And this is a chance for you, too, to do something for your brother.

(*Grandma bends down and arranges the shoes in a perfect line. Jina goes to Soonja Park.*)

JINA: Please don't be upset with my grandma. Please help her understand. I would like you to give her that information — you know, for her brother —

SOONJA PARK: I tried. Her mind is closed like a clam. It's a pity.

GRANDMA: Do not pity me. Pity yourself.

SOONJA PARK: (*To Jina.*) It's a pity that the victim's family like her will not work together with us. If we petition together, it will be a stronger case.

(*Soonja Park lights a cigarette.*)

JINA: Yes, we should petition together. I can do —

GRANDMA: Do your study, Jina. This does not concern you.

JINA: Yes, it does! What Japan did to these halmonies should never be forgotten! Japan — to this day — won't take responsibility for what they did. (*Beat.*) What happened more than fifty years ago is still happening today, Grandma. Look what's happened to the Cambodians, the Bosnians, and Serbs — War crimes continue, victimizing innocent people. We must do something about human injustice no matter what!

SOONJA PARK: Yes. The younger generation is our hope. We hope they'll carry on our mission even after we all die. Some of us have died. We lost several survivors last year.

GRANDMA: Jina, you should have gotten your guest an ashtray.

(*Soonja Park takes a copy of the petition and drops the ashes on it. Grandma immediately picks it up and goes to the bathroom to dispose of it. Outside, Bokhi Lee gets up from the stool, exits to the garden path.*)

SOONJA PARK: Some people never want to see the truth.

JINA: I'm sorry. (*Beat.*) Please understand my grandma. She's kind of difficult. But she has a good heart. Grandma sometimes says things that hurt but doesn't mean to. She gets nervous around strangers. And she's not used to this kind of confrontation.

SOONJA PARK: We should not have come.

(*Soonja Park gets up, picking up her bag.*)

JINA: No, that's not what I meant. I meant — she has a big heart but — not sociable.

SOONJA PARK: You really love your grandmother, don't you?

JINA: Yes. And I respect her.

SOONJA PARK: I didn't mean to upset her, you know. (*Beat.*) I suppose she can't understand what she didn't experience.

JINA: I'm sure in time she'll come to understand it. I think your stories are so shocking, it's hard for anyone, any woman, to take it. Don't you think?

(*Soonja Park responds with a slow nod.*)

JINA: Park halmoni, I'm so glad I've met you. I really want to do something to help this cause.

SOONJA PARK: Your support means a lot to us.

(*Soonja Park turns, walks toward the door. Jina attempts to stop her.*)

JINA: Park halmoni. I really admire your courage.

(*Soonja Park turns back.*)

JINA: I heard that you spat at the Japanese consul in Seoul. Is it true?

(*Soonja Park proudly grins, nodding.*)

JINA: What happened?

SOONJA PARK: You really wanna know?

JINA: Yes.

(*Soonja Park widely grins, puts down the bag, and sits down on the chair.*)

SOONJA PARK: I gave a testimony at a special hearing in Seoul —

(*Speaks softly, looking toward the bathroom.*)

Well, a Japanese consul was present. He didn't believe me. He said, "Can you sing a Dokodai song?"

JINA: What's Dokodai?

(Soonja Park mimics an airplane plunging.)

JINA: Oh, kamikaze — suicide-bombing airplane?

SOONJA PARK: Right. Anyhow, my heart wrenched with vengeance, I said, "Oh, you want proof? Heaven knows I am the living witness of the unspeakable crimes your country committed! A song? I'll sing you fifty songs!" And I sang as loud as thunder.

(Soonja Park stands tall and sings a Japanese Army song.)

SOONJA PARK: *(Singing in Japanese.)*

Waa-kai chee-shi-oh-no, yo-ka-re-ehn-noh

na-na-tsu ko-ta-ung-wah, sa-ku-ra-ni ee-kah-ri

kyo-doh doh-ku-doh-oh-ku, kas-ning-wah woo-rah-yah—

deh-kai ki-bo-oh-nyo, ku-bong wa-ah-koo—!

(Hearing the song, Grandma re-enters. With a wet rag, she starts wiping the table top. Outside, Bokhi Lee re-enters from the main house, still clutching onto her purse. She walks to the door, pauses to listen. Shaking her head, she goes to the stool and sits.)

SOONJA PARK: Then I spat in his face. "My rage will not subside even if I grind your bones and drink it. You damn savages!" I cursed and shouted, speaking in perfect Japanese for the first time in fifty years. "I'll show you the proof! Look at this scar — and this — and this! For nine years I was kept as a sex slave, beaten up and tortured! What more proof do you want, you sons of bitches!" I didn't even cry. The fire of my rage dried up all my tears!

(While talking, Soonja Park gets carried away, beating her chest, showing the scars on her legs, arms, and on the back of her shoulders.)

JINA: Oh, God — !

(Grandma angrily pushes the chair against the table. Jina looks at Grandma. Soonja Park takes a cigarette and lights it.)

JINA: Grandma, did you see her scars? How horrible — !

GRANDMA: Jina, go get an ashtray.

JINA: I will. In a minute —

GRANDMA: NOW!

JINA: *(Pause, hurt.)* Gee — I'm not deaf, Grandma.

GRANDMA: I cannot stand anyone smoking in my room!

SOONJA PARK: I'm sorry. I'll put it out.

(Soonja Park puts out the cigarette by crushing it between her fingers.)

SOONJA PARK: May I use your bathroom?

GRANDMA: Yes. Flush your cigarette butt down the toilet.

(Telephone rings. Grandma picks it up.)

GRANDMA: *(Without listening, high strung.)* I cannot talk to you now! I am busy.

(Grandma slams the receiver down. Soonja Park stands for a moment, gaping at her and goes into the bathroom.)

JINA: Grandma! Why did you hang up like that? That was probably Mom calling you.

GRANDMA: I told you to get an ashtray.

(Grandma busies herself, putting things in order. She drops Soonja Park's bag by the door.)

JINA: You don't need to shout at me. What's the matter with you, Grandma?

GRANDMA: You have to ask me that? You and that loudmouth gang up on me — !

JINA: She was just trying to make you understand — wanted to help you.

GRANDMA: Help me? That woman wants to use me to get what they want.

JINA: Please don't be so paranoid, Grandma!

GRANDMA: I want both of you to leave me alone! You take that woman out of my room! She knows no shame. Smoking and singing in a stranger's room — she has no manners!

JINA: Grandma! She's not a bad person. It's just that —

GRANDMA: Why did you bring them here? To aggravate me?

JINA: Why are you so rude? What's wrong?

GRANDMA: You should ask HER that! What are they trying to get out of me?

JINA: Nothing! I told you they wanted to meet you because of your brother. You've cried about him all your life, and I wanted you to do something about it. But you don't care. I asked you to talk to them for me — but you don't care. You don't care about anyone!

GRANDMA: Watch your tongue!

(Grandma busies herself with silk flowers.)

JINA: I always worry about you being alone with no friends, I thought you might enjoy meeting them.

GRANDMA: Are these women my friends?

JINA: NO!

(Jina grabs flowers and throws them to the floor.)

JINA: But you're treating them like dirt! Why? *(In tears.)* Sorry I brought them here. I am ashamed of you, Grandma!

(Crying, Jina runs out of the room, slamming the door. Grandma is stunned.)

GRANDMA: *(Deeply hurt, mutters.)* Ashamed of me? *(Beat.)* Ashamed — !

(Grandma sits, petrified. She hears the faint sound of wailing. Behind the scrim, Mother appears.)

MOTHER: My daughter. How you are hurting — ! *(Beat.)* Do not be so harsh — . Trust the heart, not the words spoken out of anger. And remember, every good thing in life evolves from love.

(Mother gazes at Grandma for a moment and disappears. Outside Bokhi Lee is startled to see Jina run by her, crying. She gets up from the stool, walks to the door, and slowly pushes it open to peep in. She watches Grandma. A thought flashes in her mind. Bokhi Lee steps back, wondering. Grandma gets up, bends over picking up the flowers. Bokhi Lee enters. She takes off her shoes neatly in a proper place. She starts helping Grandma.)

BOKHI LEE: Your granddaughter ran away, crying. What happened?

(Grandma squats down, not answering.)

BOKHI LEE: You look —

GRANDMA: What?

(Soonja Park re-enters from the bathroom.)

GRANDMA: *(To Soonja Park.)* I am sorry. I did not mean to be rude to you.

SOONJA PARK: I understand. We all have demons inside us.

(Soonja Park picks up a few flowers and hands them to Grandma.)

SOONJA PARK: You don't look well now. Would you like to lie down?

GRANDMA: No.

(Grandma puts the flowers back in the basket and takes a pill box out of her pocket.)

SOONJA PARK: Shall I get you water?

(Grandma shakes her head and goes to the bathroom. Looking after her, Bokhi Lee stands with a thought. Soonja Park picks up the last flower.)

SOONJA PARK: Poor woman. She must be really sick.

BOKHI LEE: What shall we do?

SOONJA PARK: Well — we can't just leave her now. Let's wait and see.

BOKHI LEE: I suppose — we shouldn't leave without saying good-bye.

(Soonja Park sits on the chair. In a pensive mood, she gazes at the silk flower she holds and ruefully sings a sad Korean song. Bokhi Lee sits on the stool, preoccupied with her thought.)

SOONJA PARK: *(Singing in Korean.)* Ta hyang sari, myo tae dun ga—
son koba heyer boni—
ko hyang tternan, si byo—nyuneh—
chung choon maan, nu-hul ul ger—!
(Glancing at Bokhi Lee.)

So many years in a foreign land, my youth was wasted away — This song still tears my heart. *(Beat.)* What are you thinking?

BOKHI LEE: *(Pause.)* She looks really —

SOONJA PARK: What?

BOKHI LEE: She is like —

SOONJA PARK: She is like someone I know.

BOKHI LEE: Who?

SOONJA PARK: You.

BOKHI LEE: *(Sulks.)* I'm not a rude person.

SOONJA PARK: I'm teasing you. See how sensitive you are with no sense of humor?

(Amused by Bokhi Lee's reaction, Soonja Park laughs. Bokhi Lee makes a wry face.)

BOKHI LEE: I wonder where she's from. She doesn't have a North Korean dialect, so can't be from my hometown.

SOONJA PARK: She's from Choong Chung Province. Didn't say which city.

BOKHI LEE: She seems unhappy.

(Looking around the room.)

I would be happy to have a place like this, living with a family.

SOONJA PARK: But we don't have a family, so what's the use talking about it?

BOKHI LEE: I have a family.

SOONJA PARK: Yeah, in North Korea. You left them when? Fifty-five years ago? Think of your age. Your parents must have passed away long ago.

BOKHI LEE: I have two sisters — and a brother.

SOONJA PARK: *(Sarcastic.)* Your brother? Wouldn't he be surprised to see you! If he's still alive.

BOKHI LEE: I hope he is. When I was brought back to Pusan after the war, I should've gone to my family in Pyong Yang.

SOONJA PARK: *(Taunting.)* Yeah. Why didn't you?

BOKHI LEE: Well, better that they think I'm dead than find out what I was. I just wish I could visit my parents' tombs.

SOONJA PARK: Pray that the south and the north will be reunited in your life time. It's a damn shame — separating families and living as enemies!

BOKHI LEE: I need to go to the bathroom.

SOONJA PARK: *(Whispers, glancing at the bathroom.)* She's a strange sort, isn't she? A nasty old woman.

BOKHI LEE: You don't behave yourself sometimes. Talking too much —

SOONJA PARK: You know I try to make people understand about us.

BOKHI LEE: But you go too far. It's embarrassing.

SOONJA PARK: I'm sorry. I couldn't help myself. *(Beat.)* Well, you let the lid go off, too, sometimes. I've seen you —

BOKHI LEE: Not the way you go on and on — angry at a sick old woman like her. You push people pretty hard.

SOONJA PARK: Oh, I know. I can't control my anger when I'm provoked.

BOKHI LEE: You weren't even drunk. Thank Heavens, you weren't. I was afraid you might beat her up.

SOONJA PARK: Oh, no. Now you're making fun of me.

BOKHI LEE: I have no sense of humor, remember?

(They look at each other and laugh.)

BOKHI LEE: Why doesn't she come out?

SOONJA PARK: She'll come out.

(Soonja Park takes out a bottle from her purse, sits on the floor, and drinks.)

SOONJA PARK: Ah — I wish I had dried squid to go with ssoju. Want some?

BOKHI LEE: *(Shakes her head.)* No. You're some woman. You remind me of someone.

(Bokhi Lee sits next to Soonja Park.)

SOONJA PARK: Who?

BOKHI LEE: My landlord.

SOONJA PARK: That old drunkard?

(Bokhi Lee titters. Soonja Park playfully slaps her back. Bokhi Lee moans in pain.)

SOONJA PARK: Oh, I'm sorry. Did I hurt you? I forgot that you're more fragile than a dry leaf.

BOKHI LEE: You have the hand of a strong man. *(Beat.)* You should've been born a man. What a misfortune that you were born a woman. You could've made a general, if you were a man.

SOONJA PARK: You talk like a fortune-teller I met long time ago.

BOKHI LEE: I hate fortune-tellers.

SOONJA PARK: Why so?

BOKHI LEE: They all say the same things about me. "You have a miserable life. No fortune from your parents. No husband. No children. No money. I see that you are in great pain."
Damn them!

(Bokhi Lee involuntarily slaps her thigh and moans in pain. Soonja Park laughs, amused.)

SOONJA PARK: They're not fortune-tellers. They're "misfortune" tellers. I don't go to them anymore. They charge you good sum of money for making you miserable.

BOKHI LEE: I stopped, too. Too old for building hopes anyway. False hopes. You know something? *(Angrily.)* Hell with them. Hell with my life! That's what I say.

SOONJA PARK: Right. Let your sleeping volcano of "haan" erupt! *(Beating her chest.)* My volcano of "haan" settled in here — shoots out through my mouth. I can't control it sometimes, you know.

BOKHI LEE: Yes, I know.

SOONJA PARK: I have to let it all erupt in singing —

(Soonja Park sings a Korean song, "Han-o-baeng-nyun." Bokhi Lee hums along.)

SOONJA PARK: *(Sings.)* A-mu-ryum—gu-ruh-chi—, gu-ruh-ku-maal-ku—woo—han-o-bang-nyun— sa-ja-nun-deh—, wen-sung-hwa-a-yo—

(Re-entering, Grandma listens, deeply moved. Seeing Grandma, Soonja Park stops singing and smiles awkwardly.)

GRANDMA: You sing so well. Please sing.

(Bokhi Lee gets up, heads to the bathroom.)

SOONJA PARK: *(Sings.)* Gi-gu-han—woon-myung eui, jang-nani-ryun-ga—ah—wae-eedajidoh—ahm-nari—ahm-daaam—han-ga-ah—

(Stops singing, beat.)

Well — I sing when I burn inside. Damn Japs. If we spoke a word in Korean or sang a tune, they beat us up like dogs. But there were times we were beaten up if we didn't sing. When I was in Taiwan —

(Bokhi Lee stops. Behind Grandma's back, she discreetly gestures to Soonja Park not to talk much. Soonja Park smiles. Grandma turns around, and Bokhi Lee awkwardly smiles and exits to the bathroom.)

SOONJA PARK: *(In a whisper.)* When I was in Taiwan, bombing was heavy.

(Beat.)

We were all dragged into a cave — huge enough for the whole army. During the day we labored, digging ditches, or nursing the wounded soldiers. At nights — Jap officers wanted to be entertained. I was good at singing. That saved my life. You know what happened to those who couldn't sing or dance? *(Walks about the room with growing anger.)* The cave was huge, a hundred times bigger than this room. The officers were at the deepest end to be safe from the bombing. Then the soldiers, and the women — Those girls who were sick or couldn't sing and dance were placed near the entrance. They were the human shields! Got killed. Can you imagine that? *(Beat.)* We didn't know Japan was losing the war. They became more and more brutal. Most of us were massacred in the end. I survived by sheer luck! *(Plops down on the chair.)* When I returned home, my mother fainted. She thought the ghost of me returned.

GRANDMA: I used to faint a lot —

SOONJA PARK: Why so?

GRANDMA: Noises — I mean I hate violence — any kind, you know. Even the sound of gun shots from television used to scare me.

SOONJA PARK: That bad, uh? No wonder why you have no television in this room.

GRANDMA: I had bad experiences during the war. The Korean war.

SOONJA PARK: That was a tough time, too. What kind of bad experiences?

GRANDMA: My mother was always worried about me.

   (Beat.)

I still cry for my mother. She comes in my dreams.

SOONJA PARK: I have no tears to shed anymore. In a way, I'm glad my life is near the end.

GRANDMA: You are not that old.

SOONJA PARK: I'm seventy. How old are you?

GRANDMA: Old. *(Beat, sighs.)* I have aged badly —

SOONJA PARK: Something's eating you up inside, I can see.

GRANDMA: Shall we sit over there? It is more comfortable.

   (Grandma walks over to the bed. Soonja Park follows. Grandma watches her limping.)

SOONJA PARK: Where did your granddaughter go? She has to take us back to the protest rally.

GRANDMA: Oh — I am sure she will be back.

SOONJA PARK: She's a very sweet girl. I envy you for having a granddaughter like her. I wish I had a family.

GRANDMA: Having a family can be a burden, you know. I lost my husband when my daughter was only a few weeks old.

SOONJA PARK: So you became a widow at an early age? How old were you?

GRANDMA: I do not remember. *(Looking at her hands.)* I had to work hard — so hard.

SOONJA PARK: What happened to your finger tips?

GRANDMA: Nothing. Years of hard work and raising a family —

SOONJA PARK: What did you do?

GRANDMA: All kinds of work — using my fingers, you know. *(Beat.)* How do you cope with your pain?

SOONJA PARK: I smoke, drink, and sing.

GRANDMA: Do you dance?

SOONJA PARK: When I get drunk.
> *(Sings, shoulder dancing.)*
> Nil-liriya, nil-liriya, nil-lee-ri-ya-ah—
> *(Beat.)*
> I wanna tell you something. Last year, all the Jeong-shin-dae halmonies in Seoul, got together for the New Year's party. It was incredible. Crying, laughing, singing, and dancing — we were a bunch of wild drunkards. You know, it's been a great comfort for me to meet those survivors. We meet every Wednesday morning to protest in front of the Japanese Embassy in Seoul. Every Wednesday whether it's rainy or snowy — dragging our broken bodies there. Most of us live with incurable pain.

GRANDMA: I live on medicines.

SOONJA PARK: I suffered from syphilis for a long time and had to have my uterus taken out. There's not a single bone in my body that doesn't ache, you know.
> *(Bokhi Lee re-enters from the bathroom.)*

SOONJA PARK: It's a miracle I can walk after all the beatings and tortures —
> *(To Bokhi Lee.)* Come and sit with us. It's more comfortable here.
> *(Bokhi Lee walks over and sits at the edge of the bed.)*

SOONJA PARK: Lee halmoni is in worse pain than I. It's truly a miracle that she survived. Her story makes people cry. Even some Japanese cried when she testified in Tokyo last year. *(To Bokhi Lee.)* Tell her your story.

BOKHI LEE: Oh, you talk too much.

SOONJA PARK: You keep too much inside. That's not good.

BOKHI LEE: Don't worry. I know when to talk, when not to talk.
> *(Soonja Park takes out a cigarette, then she realizes that she shouldn't smoke here.)*

SOONJA PARK: I'm sorry. It's a habit.

GRANDMA: I will get you something for an ashtray. *(Beat, with a smirk.)* If I can find it — in my closet. *(Grandma goes into the closet.)*

SOONJA PARK: It's damn too hot — suffocating.

BOKHI LEE: *(Looks around.)* She doesn't even have a fan.
> *(Bokhi Lee wipes her face with her handkerchief. Soonja Park fans herself with her hand and sees the window. As she attempts to open the window, something falls from the windowsill. Bokhi Lee picks it up. It is a piece of driftwood. Bokhi Lee stares at it. Grandma re-enters from the closet with a small dish and three oranges.)*

GRANDMA: What are you doing there?

SOONJA PARK: It's hot in here. I was going to open the window a bit.

GRANDMA: No, please. I do not like the sun to come in my room.

(She pushes away Soonja Park.)

BOKHI LEE: This piece of driftwood reminds me of a girl I once met at Bai Chen comfort station. Yoshiko —

(Reminiscing.)

She would run naked or sit and cry quietly. One night I found her sitting in a puddle. Holding a piece of wood like this, she kept making rowing motions and chanted, "I'm going home — I'm going home — I'm going home — " *(Beat.)* Made me cry.

GRANDMA: That is just a piece of driftwood my granddaughter brought me from some beach. I use it as a spool for my knitting. *(Beat.)* Both of you — you can smoke, sing and dance, if you like. But stop telling me stories.

BOKHI LEE: You think I'm making up stories?

GRANDMA: People make up stories when they do not know the truth.

BOKHI LEE: Do you know the truth?

(Grandma takes the driftwood from Bokhi Lee. With her back to Bokhi Lee, Grandma stretches her arm to put it back in the windowsill. Bokhi Lee quickly lifts up Grandma's blouse. Surprised, Grandma turns around, grabbing her blouse tightly. In shock, Bokhi Lee stands speechless.)

SOONJA PARK: What is it?

GRANDMA: What?

BOKHI LEE: Hanako — !

(Grandma stands dumbfounded.)

BOKHI LEE: You're — Hanako?

SOONJA PARK: Hanako?

(Perplexed, Soonja Park looks at Grandma and Bokhi Lee.)

BOKHI LEE: The tattoo — I saw— *(To Grandma.)* Remember me? We met in Bai Chen — Bai Chen, Manchuria, remember?

GRANDMA: Manchuria? I have never been to Manchuria.

BOKHI LEE: Kyoko was my Japanese name. You probably don't remember me because we only met once. But I remember you — now.

GRANDMA: I do not know what you are talking about.

BOKHI LEE: You are Hanako, aren't you?

GRANDMA: I am not Hanako. I never had a Japanese name.

BOKHI LEE: Yes, you did. We all did.

(Bokhi Lee looks at Soonja Park for her approval.)

SOONJA PARK: We all had Japanese names — although most of us were called by the number, not by name.

BOKHI LEE: But Hanako was different.

GRANDMA: You do not know me!

> *(Grandma stumbles over the stool. Soonja Park tries to help her up. Grandma pushes her away.)*

BOKHI LEE: Honest to God, I never knew I was going to find you here!

GRANDMA: You are mistaken —

BOKHI LEE: I'm not mistaken. You were a comfort woman!

GRANDMA: *(To Soonja Park.)* Is she crazy?

BOKHI LEE: *(To Soonja Park.)* Look at her tattoo on her back. It says "Hanako" in Japanese.

> *(Soonja Park approaches Grandma, who backs with caution.)*

GRANDMA: What tattoo? My moxi burns?

> *(To Soonja Park.)*

She must be hallucinating. Maybe she sees me as that crazy young girl she was talking about —

BOKHI LEE: I just saw it on your back. Hanako was the only girl who had a tattoo on her back. She was a high-rank officer's exclusive girl. I saw you in a kimono going out in his jeep. You were the only one with privileges because you were beautiful and educated. Everyone knew Hanako.

GRANDMA: Hanako is Japanese.

SOONJA PARK: *(Gently.)* Please don't be afraid. I understand why you don't want to admit it, especially if your family still doesn't know about it. They'll understand, believe me.

GRANDMA: My family? Why are you trying to shame me?

SOONJA PARK: There's no reason to be ashamed. Times have changed. *(Beat.)* I know how painful it is to remember. Trust me, you'd feel so relieved if you told the truth.

GRANDMA: Truth? *(Pointing her finger at Lee and Park.)* You are accusing the wrong person!

BOKHI LEE: I'm not accusing you.

SOONJA PARK: We're trying to help you —

BOKHI LEE: Yes. Please —

SOONJA PARK: Believe me, it will set you free.

GRANDMA: I am free! *(Beat, to Park and Lee.)* Who the hell are you?

BOKHI LEE: Did you love that Jap, the officer, who sent you home?

SOONJA PARK: Love the Jap officer?

BOKHI LEE: Is that why you don't want to talk?

GRANDMA: You are a crazy woman! I have no memories of knowing you or anybody you are talking about.

BOKHI LEE: Memories never go away. Not those memories — !

(Bokhi Lee sobs, her hands wringing her white handkerchief. As her rage builds up, she speaks in her blood-dripping, quivering voice.)

BOKHI LEE: Confined in a cubicle as small as this bed, how we were forced to receive soldiers every day. Even when we lay in our own blood and puss rotting from injuries and syphilis, they kept coming — giving us no time to breathe. And only a fistful of rice was shoved down our throats. How can you not remember that? *(Beat.)* They beat us up, broke our limbs with kicks and sticks, cut our flesh with swords. All from a slight sign of resistance! Don't tell me you have no memories of those horrific, brutal, inhuman acts!

GRANDMA: How many times do I have to tell you that I was not a comfort woman?

(Watching Bokhi Lee and Grandma with growing anger, Soonja Park suddenly rises and speaks as a Japanese officer.)

SOONJA PARK: Chosenppi! You Korean whore. If you defy me, I'll cut your throat! Take off your clothes!

(Soonja Park stands like a Japanese officer and kicks as if kicking a woman. Grandma trembles. Bokhi Lee starts weeping, falling on her knees.)

SOONJA PARK: I said, take off your dress! It's an order! You disobey me, I'll kill you! You stupid Chosenppi! Bagayaro! Kitsama!

(Soonja Park brandishes her imaginary sword, motions to cut Bokhi Lee and stabs the floor, cursing in Japanese.)

BOKHI LEE: *(Screams.)* Murderers — !

GRANDMA: You are both mad!

SOONJA PARK: Let us all go mad! Why not, if only in madness you will see the truth!

GRANDMA: Both of you — get out of my room. Get out!

(Soonja Park helps Bokhi Lee rise.)

BOKHI LEE: Remember Fumiko? How she died? She was running away — got caught — Fumiko, your friend — Remember?

GRANDMA: No. I had no friend!

BOKHI LEE: Hung upside down, naked — in front of everyone, she was beaten with a rifle butt and stabbed to death with bayonets! And they wrapped her blood-dripping body in a straw mat and dumped her in a ditch! *(Beat.)* You were there — screaming —

GRANDMA: I was not!

BOKHI LEE: You were there!

BOKHI LEE: *(Pause, catches her breath.)* You were gone the next day. Where were you taken? Someone said — no, you tried to run away with Fumiko, but you were saved by your lover, the Jap officer —

GRANDMA: I curse you for all the lies your mouth spits out!

SOONJA PARK: Maybe, you weren't sent home, after all. Who gave you the scars on your fingertips? Were you tortured by the M.P.?

GRANDMA: I was never tortured. I have no scars —

(Hiding her hands behind her back, Grandma falls on her knees.)

SOONJA PARK: I recognize the torture scars. Bamboo needles pricking under the fingernails — until you bleed and scream — I know it well. Look at mine!

BOKHI LEE: So horrible — it would've been merciful if I could die!

GRANDMA: If it was so horrible, you — both of you — should have killed yourselves to be free from all these years of suffering!

SOONJA PARK: Oh, no. I'm glad I'm alive. I did everything to remain alive, so that I could be a witness. I had to survive.

(Bokhi Lee leans against the table, out of breath.)

BOKHI LEE: I — I tried — tried to kill myself — three times. But — failed. *(Beat.)* I still don't know the meaning of my life. The only thing I know now is that — I do not wish to die in vain.

(Bokhi Lee goes to Grandma, kneels by her.)

BOKHI LEE: Hanako. I am glad to see you alive.

(Grandma violently shakes her head, tears streaming down her cheeks. Jina appears outside the door. Jina wears a white headband and the white sleeveless smock with a banner across it.)

BOKHI LEE: We can't die in shame, can we? We're in our twilight years. Let's do something to redeem our lost youth. And our dignity!

SOONJA PARK: You can't remain a caterpillar any longer. If you come out of your cocoon, you'll be as free as a butterfly. Please join us. Let's fly together. *(Beat.)* We have a collection of testimonies from the survivors. We have gone to Japan to testify. We'll go everywhere until we can bring justice. Let's work together.

(Jina enters, takes off her shoes in the proper place. She catches the heavy mood in the room.)

JINA: What happened? Grandma, are you all right?

(Silence. Jina goes to Grandma. Grandma turns her head away, trying to regain her composure.)

JINA: *(To Soonja Park.)* What's going on?

SOONJA PARK: *(Beat.)* We've just found a long lost friend.

(Grandma defiantly stares at Soonja Park.)

JINA: Friend? *(Confused.)* My grandma — ? From where?

GRANDMA: I do not know them!

> *(Understanding Grandma's despair, Soonja Park remains quiet. Jina goes to Grandma.)*

BOKHI LEE: *(In deep sorrow.)* We were political hostages — sacrificed out of human greed and injustice. Yet, in our homeland, we were the outcasts hidden away. The faceless faces, the voiceless voices for over fifty years — *(Beat.)* Who can give us back our youth?

> *(Bokhi Lee slowly turns her tearful face to Jina.)*

SOONJA PARK: Your generation is our hope.

GRANDMA: *(To Jina.)* Take these crazy women away! I want to be alone now.

> *(Confused and embarrassed, Jina looks at Soonja Park and Bokhi Lee, then Grandma. Soonja Park picks up her bag. She leaves a copy of the petition on the table. Clutching onto her purse, Bokhi Lee sadly watches Grandma, who closes her eyes. Soonja Park points toward the main house to Jina, meaning "We'll wait." Bokhi Lee wants to say something but restrains herself. She follows Soonja Park to the door. They exit. Jina closes the door.)*

JINA: I'm sorry — I really am. I didn't mean to upset you.

> *(Without looking, Grandma waves her hand one more time for Jina to leave. Jina kneels by Grandma. Soonja Park and Bokhi Lee exit to the house.)*

JINA: What happened? What did they do to you? *(Beat.)* I should not have brought them here.

GRANDMA: Leave — Jina, please.

JINA: I can't leave you. Not like this. You don't look well. Shall I get you the medicine?

GRANDMA: *(Shakes her head.)* Just go with them. I will be all right.

> *(Grandma turns her face to Jina, tries to smile.)*

JINA: I love you, Grandma. I didn't mean to say I was ashamed of you.

> *(Jina sobs. Grandma pets Jina as if she were a baby in her arms.)*

GRANDMA: Hush — my baby, hush. I was — *(Beat.)* bad!

> *(Grandma separates herself from Jina, looks into her eyes with mixed emotion of love and unspeakable sorrow.)*

GRANDMA: You go on now.

JINA: Are you sure you're gonna be all right?

> *(Grandma nods and waves her hand for Jina to leave. She gets in bed.)*

JINA: All right. I'll come right back after the rally. I promise I won't do anything to make you worry. I want you to be proud of me, Grandma.

> *(Grandma waves her hand again. Jina takes out the telephone from the flower basket and leaves it next to Grandma.)*

JINA: I'll call you later. Grandma, please answer the phone.

(Grandma responds with a faint smile. Jina exits the room. Grandma drops the telephone into the basket and buries herself under the comforter. Outside the door, Jina gives one more look toward Grandma's door with great concern and exits to the house.)

(Lights change. "Pansori" music is followed by the sound of Mother's wailing. Grandma gets out of the bed.)

GRANDMA: Mother —

VOICE OF SOONJA PARK: Chosenppi, Korean whore! That's what the Japs called us.

VOICE OF BOKHI LEE: You were a comfort woman!

GRANDMA: No, no. I was not!

(Grandma sees the driftwood on the floor, picks it up. A memory comes to her.)

VOICE OF HUSBAND: How dare you lie to me! You, dirty Jap soldiers' whore!

(Sound of slapping.)

VOICE OF HUSBAND: Get the hell out of my sight! Take the damn baby and get out!

(Sound of a baby and a woman crying.)

GRANDMA: Oh, Mother — Help me!

(Behind the scrim, Mother appears, holding baby in her arms. Sound of ocean waves.)

MOTHER: I told you never tell anyone!

GRANDMA AS A YOUNG WOMAN: He said I talked in my sleep — I do not know, Mother. He got drunk, beat me up — *(Beat.)* Oh, Mother, why did you save me? I would rather die!

MOTHER: Damn your husband! He is despicable! I shouldn't have married you to him. It was my mistake. Damn him!

GRANDMA AS A YOUNG WOMAN: I want my body, my life washed away in that ocean —

MOTHER: Don't be foolish, Yuniya. Life is given as a gift to cherish. It is not for anyone to take away. Look at your baby. She was left alone in your room, starved and crying in a wispy voice.

(Holding up the driftwood.)

Look at this. Dead with no roots — abandoned on the beach or drifting to nowhere in the ocean. A child without a mother is like driftwood. Think of your baby. She is your hope, your life. You must give her the roots and nourish her with all your love. It will give you the strength to live.

GRANDMA AS A YOUNG WOMAN: But — my memories, Mother, the memories —

MOTHER: Your memories are only nightmares! You should never dwell on them. Promise me you'll never dwell on your nightmares as long as you live. Swear it to the spirits of our ancestors!

(Mother with baby disappears.)

GRANDMA: Mother, I have kept my promise. What now — ? Is this another nightmare? *(Sees the photo of her brother.)* Oh, Brother Insung. What am I to do? Were your war memories also nightmares?

(Grandma hears Soonja Park's singing of "Dokodai" song intermixed with a Japanese Army song, followed by "Kimikayo" sung by a multitude along with the sound of soldiers marching.)

VOICE OF A JAPANESE OFFICER: Let us all pledge our loyalty to our Emperor!

VOICES OF WOMEN/SOLDIERS: *(Reciting.)* We are subjects of Great Imperial Japan. We pledge to serve our Emperor and our country with loyalty!

VOICE OF A JAPANESE OFFICER: *(Shouting.)* Denno Heika Bansai! Long live the Emperor!

VOICES OF WOMEN/SOLDIERS: Long live the Emperor! Long live the Emperor!

VOICE OF A JAPANESE OFFICER: *(In contempt.)* Chosengin girls! Get up! *(Beat.)* Break them into the job. They need to be toughened right from the first day. Just like soldiers and horses. If they are not, they're no use at all on the battlefield. Understand?

VOICE OF HOUSE MANAGER: Yes, Sir! We do train them like the horses for the soldiers to ride on. And we shoot those who attempt to run away same as deserters, sir!

(Grandma squats down, covers her ears with both hands. Lights change. Grandma's memories continue. Isolated in light behind the scrim, Japanese Officer (played by Soonja Park) stands with a sword. Hanako (played by Jina) in a shabby Korean dress is pushed in and falls on her back. Towering over her with his legs apart, Japanese Officer holds his sword high and points it at her head.)

JAPANESE OFFICER: I name you — Hanako. A woman as beautiful as a flower. *(Amused, chuckles.)* Soon to be deflowered!

(He runs his sword over her body from head to toe.)

JAPANESE OFFICER: You are honored to serve Great Imperial Japan. Ha!

(In a swift motion, he cuts her skirt and stabs the floor. Hanako gasps, turns over, revealing her fresh tattoo, "Hanako," on her back.)

JAPANESE OFFICER: *(Pointing at the tattoo.)* HA-NA-KO. My good luck charm. My moan, my mark. This makes you mine!

(He laughs haughtily. A moment of Blackout. Grandma gasps and falls to the floor. She hears whispering voices.)

VOICE OF WOMAN #1: That is Hanako in kimono. Commanding Officer's exclusive girl.

VOICE OF WOMAN #2: The only girl with her name tattooed on her back.

VOICE OF WOMAN #1: She never starves as we do.

VOICE OF WOMAN #2: Watch out. She may be an informer.

GRANDMA: No!

VOICE OF BOKHI LEE: Fumiko, your friend. Remember?

(Lights come up on Fumiko (played by Bokhi Lee) in the washroom, washing condoms. Hanako enters with her cut dress and squats down to wash it. Both wear plain dresses.)

FUMIKO: You must be the new star. The Commanding Officer named you Hanako. Room seventeen. One blanket and a box of shatku, rubbers. Right? *(Beat.)* Look at these — thirty, forty a day. I hate washing these damn rubbers!

(Fumiko tosses around a few condoms.)

HANAKO: Do you have to?

FUMIKO: They make us do it. To reuse them. *(Beat.)* My name is Cho Young-Jin. The Jap name, Fumiko. Mostly called "number eleven, the troublemaker." You're very pretty. No wonder, officers go crazy over you. It will make your life easier. But watch out, sweet tongues are poisonous, Hanako.

HANAKO: Call me Yuni. Kim Yuni is my real name.

(Fumiko takes a rubber, turns its inside out and rubs it hard in the water basin. Hanako sees Fumiko's hand with two fingers missing and gives a questioning look. Fumiko lifts her hand to show.)

FUMIKO: It's only two fingers lost. Some crazy soldier — he could've cut my whole arm, but missed it.

HANAKO: How horrible — !

FUMIKO: These savages don't treat us as human beings because they're not! I'd rather die with dignity than be a collaborator. I won't be here too long!

HANAKO: Are they sending you home?

FUMIKO: They'll kill you before they send you home. If your body becomes useless, they starve you to death and dump your body in a ditch! But I will find a way —

(Sound of footsteps. Hanako and Fumiko hug in fear. Lights Down on them.)

VOICE OF BOKHI LEE: Fumiko, your friend. Remember how she died?

GRANDMA: Fumiko. Why did you —

(Grandma covers her face with both hands, crying. Behind the scrim, Lights Up on Japanese Officer and Hanako who is crying profusely.)

JAPANESE OFFICER: Hanako! This kimono is my special gift for you. Get up.

(Hanako gets up. He drapes the kimono around her shoulders. He then circles around her, enjoying her beauty.)

JAPANESE OFFICER: *(With a wide grin.)* Beautiful — Hanako, my beautiful flower! *(Beat.)* What is the matter with you — drunk and crying about nothing.

HANAKO: Fumiko is dead! My only friend — Your soldiers killed her! *(Feverish.)* They hung her upside down — naked! They beat her — and stabbed her to death with bayonets! How could they be so cruel! How could you let your soldiers kill her like that?

JAPANESE OFFICER: Enough! That girl was a deserter, deserved to die, understand?

HANAKO: You let them kill her. You killed Fumiko! You, Japanese soldiers are barbarians! Evil murderers! Worse than animals!

JAPANESE OFFICER: BAGAYARO!

(Enraged, he pulls his sword and raises it high as if to cut her head.)

JAPANESE OFFICER: You stupid Chosenppi!

(He trembles, throws the sword, and slaps her hard.)

JAPANESE OFFICER: How dare you accuse me of that killing! How dare you criticize any action of the Japanese Imperial Army! How dare you — !

(Japanese Officer kicks her repeatedly. Hanako crawls, picks up his sword. He glares at her. Hanako drops the sword, steps back. He picks up the sword and aims at her neck. Hanako closes her eyes, trembling.)

JAPANESE OFFICER: Ha!

(He stabs the floor. Looking at Hanako's frightened face. He lets out a roaring laugh, then abruptly stops, turning cold and vicious.)

JAPANESE OFFICER: For your treachery, you deserve to die. But — you are drunk — so am I. I tell you — this is my last favor for you, Hanako. I am going to hand you over to the Military Police.

(Hanako crawls and grabs his leg.)

HANAKO: No, please do not send me to the M.P. Just kill me. Kill me now! I would rather die than be tortured! Please — I will do anything for you. Do not send me to the M.P. Please — !

JAPANESE OFFICER: *(Calling.)* Guard — !

(Blackout. Lights on Grandma. She frantically searches her pocket for her medicine and can't find it. She manages to get up, feebly walks toward the table.)

VOICE OF BOKHI LEE: You were there!

    (Grandma stops, speaks defiantly.)

GRANDMA: Yes, I was there!

VOICE OF BOKHI LEE: You tried to run away with Fumiko, but you were saved by your lover —

GRANDMA: Saved by my lover? Ha! I was horribly tortured by the Military Police. And transferred to a Japanese military comfort station in Jangsa, China. None of you girls at Bai Chen knew that. I suffered as much. In Jangsa, I was one of "the dirty Chosenppies"!

    (Grandma kicks the footstool, throws away the flower basket. Flowers scattered around and the telephone is cast away into the far corner. She crushes the flowers with her feet in a rage.)

GRANDMA: Countless Jap soldiers crushing my body — ! Those bloodthirsty vultures, the royal hunters of Japan! I curse you all!

VOICE OF BOKHI LEE: Fumiko died, but you did not!

GRANDMA: *(Defiant.)* I wished to die! *(Beat.)* But — I was a coward. Afraid to die, afraid to live!

    (Grandma weeps. A wailing siren is heard from a distance. Grandma listens. Growing louder, it is accompanied with running footsteps and Voice from a loudspeaker.)

VOICE FROM A LOUDSPEAKER: Bombers approaching — Run to the shelter. Everybody! Hurry up!

    (Grandma looks all around in fear, clutches her chest. Behind the scrim, we see Hanako in kimono knelt down, crying.)

VOICE OF FUMIKO: *(Urgently.)* We must run away. The Japs are gonna kill us all! Hurry, hurry.

GRANDMA: Fumiko!

VOICE OF FUMIKO: There's no moon tonight. Everyone's running to the shelter. Come with me, Hanako!

    (Sound of bombing. Grandma ducks. Behind the scrim, Fumiko appears.)

FUMIKO: Hanako. How can you stand this shameful life? This is no life!

GRANDMA: *(In a whisper to herself.)* Fumiko — ! She has come to take me.

FUMIKO: Please come with me. There's no moon tonight. We'll be safe. I'll be waiting outside the gate. Remember, there's no moon tonight. Come with me, Yuniya — !

    (Hanako turns, revealing the tattoo on her back. Blackout on Hanako and Fumiko.)

GRANDMA: I wanted to come with you that night but could not get away — You must believe me—I did not betray you, Fumiko. Please forgive me!

(Grandma lets out a slow heartbreaking howl, falling on her knees. Her body half bent, she holds her chest as if to catch her broken heart.)

VOICE OF BOKHI LEE: Memories never go away. Not those memories!

GRANDMA: *(Violently shaking her head.)* NO — !

(Sound of whipping. Grandma doubles over, crawls. She lets out one blood-curdling scream and sinks to the floor.)

GRANDMA: M-O-T-H-E-R—!

(Like an echo of Grandma's scream, we hear a shrill Voice ruefully singing "chaang" (Korean Pansori music.). Mother appears in a dim light. She wears a black-and-white garment with a wide red sash, holding a large fan like a "moodang" (a Korean shaman). She moves in slow-motion dancing steps.)

GRANDMA: Oh Mother—help me.

(At drum beats, Mother dances furiously and ends it by snapping her fan.)

MOTHER: There! I've exorcised all the bad spirits lingering around you.

GRANDMA: The memories — all those horrifying memories are haunting me now.

(Sound of winds. A shaft of light is cast as a fog rolls in. Hanako with her hair cropped appears in a torn kimono, dragging the obi on the floor. Grandma shudders and curls up.)

GRANDMA: Hanako!

HANAKO: *(Rueful.)* A fog rolled in. The river was bloody red. Hundreds of heads and legs floating — There you saw soldiers collecting the legs, human legs — and piling them by the river bank. The soldiers burned those legs and gathered the powder. The powder of the bones — to cure syphilis.

GRANDMA: Syphilis — !

HANAKO: Oh, the stink from the heaps of flesh —

GRANDMA: Mother, help me.

MOTHER: Don't be frightened. I'm protecting you as I always have.

GRANDMA: Remembering the past is too painful. Like drinking poison.

MOTHER: Remember, nothing happened to you. You're having a nightmare.

HANAKO: That winter — you remember. On a cold snowy day in January 1945 —

GRANDMA/HANAKO: In ragged clothes and lice infested, I came home —

(Beat.)

In Jangsa comfort station, I was deadly sick with syphilis and bayonet wounds. My body became useless, and the Jap soldiers threw me out in the field. And one merciful Chinese saved my life.

MOTHER: What a miracle that was to see you alive! After three years, I thought you were dead.

GRANDMA: I should have died —

MOTHER: You DID die then. I gave you a new life. I cured your syphilis and found a man who would take care of you.

GRANDMA: I never wanted to marry any man.

MOTHER: The Jap M.P.s were like hound dogs taking women from everywhere. I was afraid to lose you again! You could not have survived.

HANAKO: For your own survival, you exchanged your human dignity with lies and hypocrisy.

GRANDMA: Look at my face, an old ugly face full of sorrow and hate! Do you think it was easy to live that way?

HANAKO: You must live with the truth now.

GRANDMA: How?

HANAKO: You know we cannot both live.

MOTHER: Hanako does not exist!

HANAKO: You can no longer deny me! Hanako is YOU no matter what!

MOTHER: Never!

GRANDMA: What should I do?

MOTHER: You were never Hanako! There is no proof.

HANAKO: Look at the tattoo on your back.

MOTHER: Those are moxi burns.

HANAKO: That is a lie!

MOTHER: I'll make them disappear.

HANAKO: You cannot!

MOTHER: I'll protect you, my daughter.

HANAKO: You cannot!

MOTHER: I will exorcise again!

HANAKO: No, you cannot!

GRANDMA: Stop it! Both of you — go away! *(Beat.)* Let me decide what to do with my life!

(Blackout on Mother and Hanako.)

GRANDMA: The memories — they were not just nightmares but real! I remember them. *(Beat.)* The two old women from Korea — One of them remembers me. Saw my tattoo. See it, Mother?

(Grandma lifts her blouse, showing the tattoo on her back.)

GRANDMA: Oh I remember the pain! Hundreds of needles piercing into my skin—!

(Grandma's body writhes in pain.)

GRANDMA: With HA-NA-KO in Japanese branded on my body, how can I deny those horrific memories! *(Beat.)* Oh, Brother Insung. The night I was abducted in the street, you went out looking for me and got yourself in trouble — All because of me! I am so sorry, Brother. I am sorry I could not even tell you —

VOICE OF BOKHI LEE: You were a comfort woman!

GRANDMA: Death would have been more honorable!

(Mother appears in her white Korean dress, performing "salpuri" dance.)

GRANDMA: Mother. You have protected me all these years, and I am thankful that I could raise my family. But now — how can I face my daughter, my son-in-law? And Jina! I will only bring shame to them! My life has come to this end, I am more afraid to live than to die! *(Beat.)* I need the courage — to be truthful. Please understand, Mother. I want you to know — I was Hanako!

(Mother stops dancing. As Grandma weeps herself into exhaustion and falls to the floor, Mother lets out one long wail. Hanako in her Korean dress appears behind the scrim. Mother faces Hanako and opens her arms. A moment of Blackout.)

(Outside, Jina appears, her face puffed up from crying. She runs to the door, stops for a moment and enters. The sunlight shoots into the room. Jina kicks off her shoes, sees Grandma on the floor. She runs to her.)

JINA: Grandma — Grandma — !

(As Jina tries to lift her, Grandma squints at the bright light. Afraid and dazed, she shrinks her body.)

JINA: Grandma. It's me. Jina!

GRANDMA: Jina?

JINA: Yes, it's me. Shall I call the doctor?

(Grandma waves her hand meaning no.)

JINA: I'll call Mom.

GRANDMA: *(Shakes her head.)* No — no!

JINA: *(Cries.)* Grandma, I'm sorry. I didn't know you suffered so much!

(Jina embraces her. Grandma breaks down as if she is in her mother's arms. Together held, they weep for a while, no words necessary to explain.)

GRANDMA: I am so sorry — ! *(Beat.)* What am I going to do?

JINA: Please don't worry about anything now. I'll take care of you. You know I will. *(Jina straightens Grandma's disheveled hair.)*

GRANDMA: *(Beat.)* I had long braided hair, you know — beautiful black silky hair — *(Beat.)* Fifteen I was — The Japs — they first cropped my hair ruthlessly and stripped my Korean dress off of me. I wanted to die then. But I was so young and afraid — *(Beat.)* Perhaps, I should have died then.

JINA: I am so glad you didn't. I love you, Grandma.

GRANDMA: Your mother and father — will never understand —

JINA: Everything will be all right. I'll help you. *(Beat.)* You'll help me with your stories — the truth.

GRANDMA: My stories — ?

JINA: Yes. Please —

(Grandma looks at the scattered flowers on the floor and then toward the door where the sunlight is bright. Jina seats Grandma on the stool.)

GRANDMA: *(Nods, beat.)* Where are those halmonies? Upstairs?

JINA: No. They're at the protest rally. I'm to pick them up later.

GRANDMA: Oh. *(Beat.)* If you want — you may bring them back here.

JINA: Are you sure?

GRANDMA: *(Slowly nods.)* Yes.

(Jina gives Grandma a hug. She picks up a flower from the floor and gives it to Grandma. Grandma looks around the room.)

GRANDMA: Will you open the window?

JINA: Yes.

(Jina opens the window. Bright sunlight shoots in.)

VOICE OF BOKHI LEE: We can't die in shame, can we? We're in our twilight years. Let's do something to redeem our lost youth. And our dignity!

VOICE OF SOONJA PARK: You can't remain a caterpillar any longer. If you come out of your cocoon, you'll be as free as a butterfly! Please join us. Let's fly together.

(As Grandma holds the flower to her heart and contemplates, tears roll down on her face in a mixed emotion of relief, fear, sorrow, and hope. Lights fade.)

END OF PLAY

TEXAS HOMOS

Jan Buttram

PLAYWRIGHT'S BIOGRAPHY

Most recently tapped by American Movie Channel to create a pilot for a new television series, Jan Buttram began her professional theater career as an actress with the New Orleans Repertory Theatre under the direction of June Havoc. She has since acted Off Broadway, Off-Off Broadway, and in regional theaters. While touring nationally with *The Best Little Whorehouse in Texas*, she began writing plays. Her works have been produced in New York by the York Theatre, One World Arts Foundation, Pulse Ensemble Theatre, Circle Rep Lab, the Samuel French Short Play Festival, La Mama, ETC., the New Rude Mechanicals, Lightning Strikes Theatre Co., and Abingdon Theatre Company, which introduced her "comedy with hymns," *Glory Girls*. Other plays include *Zona, the Ghost of Greenbrier, Private Battles,* and *The Parker Family Circus*. Her plays *Private Battles* and *The Parker Family Circus* received options by commercial producers for Off Broadway. *Captive* and *The Parker Family Circus* are published by Samuel French (*The Parker Family Circus* was selected by Smith and Kraus for *The Best Scenes for Actors of 2001–02.*). Her play *Texas Homos* (directed by Tony–award winner Melvin Bernhardt) played to sold-out houses in Abingdon's June Havoc Theatre and has been optioned for a feature film by Sterling Zinsmeyer and Eric Morris. She received commissions to create original scripts for Capital Rep and Greenbrier Valley Theatre. Her plays have also been performed mainstage at the University of Memphis, the American Folk Theatre, and Greenbrier Valley Theatre. Her play *Backwoods* won the 1995 Roger L. Stevens Award from the Kennedy Center's Fund for New American Plays. Her short plays are published in several anthologies by Heinemann Books. A founding member and Artistic Director of Abingdon Theatre Company, a not-for-profit company located in Manhattan dedicated to developing and producing new plays by American playwrights, she has produced seventeen mainstage productions, seventeen workshop productions and hundreds of play readings. She leads Abingdon's playwrights' unit. Ms. Buttram graduated from the University of North Texas with a Bachelor of Arts (1968.) and a Masters of Fine Arts (1969.) in drama.

ORIGINAL PRODUCTION

The world premiere of *Texas Homos* was January 28 to February 27, 2005, at June Havoc Theatre in the Abingdon Theatre Arts Complex in New York, N.Y. Directed by Melvin Bernhardt; Jan Buttram and Pamela Paul, Artistic Directors and Samuel J. Bellinger, Managing Director. Kim T. Sharp, Associate Artistic Director. Mary E. Leach, Production Stage Manager. James F.

Wolk, scenic design. Susan Scherer, costume design. Matthew McCarthy, lighting design. Julie Hegner, Dramaturg. Rick Sordelet, fight direction. Cindi Rush, casting. Press Representative, Shirley Herz Associates. Cast, in order of appearance:

CECIL RAY BONNER ....Reed Birney
JIM BOB MASON .... Richard Bekins
HAROLD D. CARNEY ....David Van Pelt
JUDY KAY MURPHY ....Karen Culp
DELBERT SIMMONS ....Michael Busillo

TIME

Saturday, 8:00 AM, early November. The present.

PLACE

The supply office, Carney & Sons, Tyler, Texas; population 80,000.

CHARACTERS

In order of appearance:

CECIL RAY BONNER: forty, a general practitioner with surgical skills. A good person under many layers of bullshit.

JIM BOB MASON: forty, a full-time Methodist minister and part-time accountant. A truly good person.

HAROLD D. CARNEY: forty, a dapper, precise lawyer. A so-so person.

JUDY KAY MURPHY: thirty-five, a legal secretary, single mother and ex-mistress of Cecil Ray Bonner.

Delbert Simmons: twenty-five, very cute boy, two years too old to audition for *American Idol.* He's gay and a very good person.

Texas Homos

Jim Bob Mason and Cecil Bonner enter. Both are in rumpled clothing and have had a bad night.

CECIL: What the hell? Harold D. put us way back in the back room. What is this, the broom closet?

JIM BOB: My ears are still ringing from the clanging of cell doors.

CECIL: Somebody in that cell was suffering from acute gastric distress.

JIM BOB: How could you get any sleep in there?

CECIL: If you make it through medical school, you can sleep in a pigpen.

JIM BOB: My head itches.

CECIL: It's probably mites.

JIM BOB: Awe, no!

CECIL: Don't get your freak on! We just need to be dipped in a vat of disinfectant. Ten hours of pure dee hell. I'm filing a class action suit against the State of Texas for secondhand smoke contamination. I'll never get the nicotine out of my nose hairs.

JIM BOB: Cecil?

CECIL: What, babe?

JIM BOB: Are you mad at me?

CECIL: Naw. You are always in the right lane with me.

JIM BOB: You wouldn't talk to me.

CECIL: You were busy talking to everyone else. You were a Chatty Cathy.

JIM BOB: I was trying to help the other men.

CECIL: Talk about your captive audience.

JIM BOB: All night I was spreading the gospel in slow motion.

CECIL: You had that black kid on his knees, praying for an hour.

JIM BOB: He was a troubled man.

CECIL: Nice butt.

JIM BOB: I've seen him before.

CECIL: That ass was familiar.

JIM BOB: I never should have gone in that restroom without you. I thought I'd missed you.

CECIL: I was running late. I was trying to get to you.

JIM BOB: I'm sitting in the patrol car handcuffed and I see you drive up and walk inside. Why didn't I call out to you?

CECIL: Surreal. This good-looking Mexican walks up and offers to suck my dick. I did not see it coming.

JIM BOB: Mexican?

CECIL: Very. I unzip my fly and quicker than you can say "tortilla" he had handcuffs on me.

JIM BOB: This Mexican, was he short, stocky . . . with an innocent mouth?

CECIL: Yep.

JIM BOB: Same one that took me.

CECIL: I saw him standing by the urinal and, I thought, hmmmm, Jim Bob is going to love this.

JIM BOB: If Tulie finds out . . .

CECIL: Oh, hell, if Kay Nell finds out, she'll divorce me for the third time.

JIM BOB: Cecil, you can tell them you were looking for me . . .

CECIL: I'm not telling them a damn thing.

JIM BOB: We have to tell them something. We were arrested for sexual misconduct in public.

CECIL: Do not worry. I'm going to fix this. Nothing bad is going to happen to us, not with me working my magic. It's going to be over real quick . . . bim, bam, boom . . . record expunged . . . history. That Mexican was gay. I'll bet money on it.

JIM BOB: Sitting in the patrol car watching my life slip through my hands into God's hands . . .

CECIL: Heh, I treated most of the politicians in this two-horse town for crabs. They won't touch us. I won't renew their Viagra prescriptions. Besides, Tyler, Texas, is the only town where you don't need five doctors to treat you . . . I cover your piehole to your toenail. I studied medicine every damn day of my life to take care of these yokels.

JIM BOB: The Lord giveth and the Lord taketh away.

CECIL: Kay Nell will be the one doing the taking . . . she'd skin and filet my ass.

(Harold D. Carney enters. He wears a white shirt and suit pants. His collar is unbuttoned.)

CECIL: What took you so damn long, Harold D.?

HAROLD D.: I told you I was going fishing.

CECIL: Jesus H. Christ! They bailed out the Channel 5 weatherman in less than an hour.

HAROLD D.: I've been telling you this was coming. You never listen to me and I'm your lawyer.

CECIL: Yeah, well, I've been telling my patients to stop overeating and quit smoking for thirty years, and they don't listen to me either.

HAROLD D.: How many times have I warned you?

JIM BOB: Lord help me, every time you warned us, I thought, "Harold D. is right."

CECIL: We shoulda gone fishing.

HAROLD D.: I hope this won't turn into a total disaster. The Texas Penal System and get costly.

JIM BOB: How much do I owe you for bailing me out?

HAROLD D.: You owe Cecil.

JIM BOB: Cecil, God love you.

CECIL: I got you covered.

HAROLD D.: Ten grand. So don't leave town.

CECIL: We're not going anywhere.

JIM BOB: I signed a paper swearing I wouldn't.

HAROLD D.: Mexico might start looking awful nice. As I remember "yo hablo espanol" pretty good.

JIM BOB: We built a church in Brownsville; I got fairly proficient in Spanish. I can say, "Hand me the hammer" and "Bring me some nails."

CECIL: We did have a couple of insane nights in Nuevo Laredo.

JIM BOB: Cecil, I'll make it up to you.

HAROLD D.: It's his fault you're in this mess.

JIM BOB: It's not Cecil's fault. It's mine.

CECIL: It's nobody's fault.

HAROLD D.: C'mon, Jim Bob, I've been in the end zone with you boys. Cecil's the quarterback. He calls the plays.

CECIL: That's right. OK, huddle up. We fumbled the ball but it's back in our possession. Let's score quick and get out of here. Harold D., run it straight down the middle.

HAROLD D.: Now, Cecil, I arranged your release but that's it for me. I have limited experience with criminal law.

CECIL: Time to expand your portfolio. My buddy Marty Richards took our fingerprints at the station. I put in his mother's pacemaker. He told me to make a lot of noise about suing the city for false arrest and demand the charges be dismissed . . . so set that up.

HAROLD D.: Judge Peters won't be in court until early Monday.

CECIL: I've got a stomach stapling Monday morning.

HAROLD D.: Until he sets the arraignment, you're under my custody.

CECIL: The Longhorns play at 2:00. "Hook 'em Horns."

HAROLD D.: I'll try to get Judge Peters on the phone. You can't leave this office until he sets the time.

CECIL: Not good enough.

HAROLD D.: Well, the Longhorns may be kicking off without you.

CECIL: Harold D., listen carefully. I don't want an arraignment. I want the charges dismissed. I want a clean slate and I want it now. I'm hungry. Jim Bob, you feel like catfish?

JIM BOB: Maybe later . . .

CECIL: Are you all right?

JIM BOB: I think so.

CECIL: You haven't eaten all night, babe. You sound like you could use something to eat.

JIM BOB: I'm fine.

CECIL: Let's hit Murray's for lunch.

JIM BOB: I've got the missionary committee at 2:00.

HAROLD D.: Cecil, look, I'll assist in your defense but I'm advising you to find another lawyer . . .

CECIL: I've got a lawyer, you.

HAROLD D.: I'm your cousin.

CECIL: Second cousin by marriage.

HAROLD D.: I go to Jim Bob's church. He prepares my taxes.

CECIL: He prepares half the town's taxes because he never gets audited.

JIM BOB: I've had several clients who were audited.

CECIL: Baptists. If anyone asks, this was a DWI. Right, Jim Bob? I had a couple of dead soldiers in the floorboard of the car and I was getting out and two beer cans fell out smack dab in front of a patrol car . . .

JIM BOB: When did that happened?

HAROLD D.: It didn't. The Sheriff told me they had those bathrooms under surveillance for a month. There's been way too much traffic in and out. Just why in hell you like to risk everything in public bathrooms . . .

CECIL: Harold D. Just because the only time you touch your dick is to take a piss, doesn't mean the rest of us have to live like the flying nun.

HAROLD D.: I don't know why not. She was cute and she had a clean arrest record.

CECIL: Damn Kay Nell to hell and back. This is all her fault. If I ever got any pussy worth a goddamn, I wouldn't be in this mess. Where's Delbert, anyway? I bailed him out, didn't I?

HAROLD D.: At the station.

JIM BOB: They've *still* got Delbert Simmons?

HAROLD D.: He was caught flagrante delicto.

CECIL: Yeah, well, they got the Channel 5 weatherman too and he was out before midnight. I'm starving.

HAROLD D.: Call Judy Kay if you want to bring in some take out.

CECIL: Judy Kay?

HAROLD D.: Judy Kay Murphy. My secretary.

CECIL: I thought I told you to fire her last week.

JIM BOB: Cecil . . .

HAROLD D.: And replace her with what? She has a family and she's not hurting you.

CECIL: She's got conflict of interest written all over her . . .

HAROLD D.: I can't replace her. She's an excellent legal secretary.

CECIL: Jim Bob and I will replace her. He has a whole slew of qualified folks at the church looking for jobs.

JIM BOB: Not at someone else's expense. Leave Judy Kay alone.

CECIL: The hell I will. She tried to wreck my marriage! And there's a thing called loyalty, Harold D. Judy Kay doesn't help pay for these fancy offices or bankroll your political career.

HAROLD D.: She was in here at 7:00 AM to spring you from jail.

CECIL: Well, I sure as hell don't want Judy Kay Murphy coming in here.

HAROLD D.: Don't ask for anything.

JIM BOB: Can I use the phone?

HAROLD D.: Dial 8.

(Jim Bob dials the phone.)

CECIL: I wouldn't ask that bitch to wipe my butt.

HAROLD D.: Could you just can the complaining, Cecil?

CECIL: Sure, Harold D., after you can your condescending crap. I'm your richest client and I expect to be treated accordingly.

HAROLD D.: Dammit to hell, Cecil, I'm trying to contain this circus to a one-ring extravaganza.

CECIL: Well, tell Judy Kay to stay the hell away from me.

(Harold D. exits, muttering.)

HAROLD D.: God forbid anyone says, "thank you."

CECIL: I bet Harold D. squats to take a piss. Harold D.'s wife makes him shave his armpits. I know that for a fact. She made him jerk off in a test tube so she could get her dainty cooch artificially inseminated — twice!

(Jim Bob gets an answering machine.)

JIM BOB: Tulie . . . it's me. Are you there? *(Beat.)* Tulie . . . are you sleeping?

CECIL: She's probably at Carol Ann's.

JIM BOB: Maybe you're at Carol Ann's. I'll call over there. I'm at Harold D.'s office . . . when you get this . . . I hope you get this . . . I'm sorry I didn't get home last night. Hope I didn't worry you. I had an emergency . . . please, call me?

(Jim Bob hangs up.)

CECIL: Babe . . . you don't sound so good. Let me look at you . . . *(Looking into Jim Bob's pupils.)* You're shaking.

JIM BOB: Nerves got me a little.

CECIL: Symptoms of aftershock . . . some serious pupil dilation.

JIM BOB: I haven't been this scared since you made me play football in high school.

CECIL: You were the fastest running back in the region. No one could catch you.

JIM BOB: I was running for my life.

CECIL: He's at the 40, he's at the 30, he's at the 20 . . .

JIM BOB: I have a congregation that loves me, a wife who drug three kids half way around the world twice doing missionary work, a home with everything I ever dreamed of owning, friends . . . grandkids . . . a relationship with God and I risked it all because I wanted to lay hands on another man's cock.

CECIL: You need a couple of Valium. My pharmacia is in the Corvette.

JIM BOB: Cecil? Aren't you scared?

CECIL: Naw. Glad to be alive, babe. It just reminds me of elementary school, stealing that shitload of Double Bubble off the candy truck . . .

JIM BOB: We flushed it down the toilet. The plumbing system was backed up for months.

CECIL: But we got away with it and we'll get away with this. Watch my fingers fly . . . *(Cecil picks up the phone, dials.)* Hi, honey . . . did I wake you? Still tucked in? You must have downed a couple of serious martinis last night . . . I called you about midnight. Jim Bob and I spent the night in jail . . . picked up for a damn DWI . . . No, it's all right. Harold D. sprang us from the can. Awe, jail wasn't too bad. The room service sucked. Jim Bob converted a bunch of heathens. Pretty funny stuff. I'll be home later. Yes, I am out of shirts. Thank you, baby, you're the only one who can do my collars so they don't scratch. No, don't wait for me . . . we're going for catfish and catch the game. "Hook 'em Horns . . ." Take the girls mall hopping or something, I'll find you later.

I don't have my cell phone . . . call me at Harold D.'s if you need me. Love you.

(Harold D. re-enters.)

HAROLD D.: I told Judy Kay to stay out but if you need her, just dial "6".

CECIL: More like "666." Now Harold D., I need to make my hospital rounds before the game.

(Jim Bob redials . . . waits.)

HAROLD D.: I'm working as fast as I can. The office is going to start filling up.

CECIL: It's Saturday.

HAROLD D: I do pro bono work on Saturday.

CECIL: Yeah, well, you see what I get for my pro bono work. I donated $50,000 to that park. I built the goddamn toilet they arrested me in.

HAROLD D.: Cecil, Merle Watson is right down the hall here . . . he is an excellent criminal lawyer.

CECIL: Merle doesn't play on my team.

HAROLD D.: My schedule is tight . . . the runoff is next week.

CECIL: You've got my vote and Jim Bob's.

HAROLD D.: I'm only three points ahead in the polls.

CECIL: Jim Bob, you're looking at the next Texas State Representative from Smith County, Harold D. Carney.

HAROLD D.: If the Democrats get wind of this, I'll be sunk. All that campaigning for nothing.

CECIL: Hell, relax, you'll be the champion of wronged citizens.

HAROLD D.: Not the cause I was hoping for.

CECIL: Harold D., find your balls, they're tucked up under your dick.

(Harold D. exits.)

JIM BOB: *(On the phone.)* Carol Ann, it's Daddy. Are you there? I'm looking for your mother. Tulie, are you there? I left you a message at home. I just thought . . . OK. Carol Ann? I'm at Harold D.'s office . . . and, well, I hope you're OK. Did the baby keep you up all night? Well, call me? Or ask your mother to call me.

CECIL: They probably went out for breakfast.

(Judy Kay Murphy enters, a sassy looking thirty-five-year-old. She carries a newspaper.)

JUDY KAY: What's new, Jim Bob?

CECIL: No one asked you to come in here.

JUDY KAY: *(Tossing down the paper.)* I thought you boys might want to read this old newspaper.

CECIL: For what?

JUDY KAY: It's got both your names in it. I'm hoping it's a typo in your case, Reverend.

JIM BOB: *(Reading the paper.)* It's on the front page? My God, have mercy.

JUDY KAY: I just want to know one little thing, Cecil.

CECIL: Get the hell out of here, Judy Kay.

JUDY KAY: Were you doing men all the time you were doing me?

CECIL: I was doing my wife when I was doing you.

JUDY KAY: Now if I had just had me a girlfriend, we could have had some real fun.

CECIL: I could never get you to have any real fun.

JUDY KAY: No you couldn't. Not as hard and long as you tried . . . and now we all know why. Well, should I go get tested?

CECIL: For mental instability?

JUDY KAY: For AIDS?

CECIL: I'm clean. But I'm not your doctor. Do any thing you want.

JUDY KAY: You're my doctor on this test and it's on the house. I am so disappointed in you, Jim Bob.

JIM BOB: A lot of people will be.

CECIL: I don't know why the hell they would be, it was a false arrest.

JUDY KAY: Is that true, Jim Bob?

CECIL: Yes, it's true. We can explain everything.

JUDY KAY: How do you intend to explain indiscriminate sodomy?

JIM BOB: I'm going to pray for tolerance and forgiveness.

CECIL: Two subjects beyond your comprehension, Judy Kay.

JIM BOB: *(Reading the paper.)* I'll resign immediately.

CECIL: Why would you? We are not guilty.

JUDY KAY: I hope he's telling the truth, Jim Bob, for your wife's sake. For my sake, too. If you two get sent to prison, who'll do my taxes?

CECIL: Who said anything about prison?

(Jim Bob goes to the phone. Dials.)

JUDY KAY: You think you're going to weasel your way out of this?

CECIL: Hell, I got away from you, I can get out of anything.

JUDY KAY: Jim Bob, I hope you learn your lesson, it's dangerous to have assholes as friends.

CECIL: Jim Bob is the only person in this town who understands the meaning of friendship.

JUDY KAY: I hear your kind has lots of buddies.

CECIL: Jim Bob doesn't lie to me.

JUDY KAY: I never lied to you.

CECIL: You said you were looking for a good time and that was bullshit. I trust Jim Bob.

JUDY KAY: Jim Bob? Do you trust Cecil?

JIM BOB: No one's at the church office.

(Jim Bob hangs up the phone.)

JUDY KAY: You know? If I were a man, I'd just beat the living shit out of both of you. I mean, get a motel for Christ sake. You're a fucking millionaire, Cecil.

CECIL: That's what you want to believe.

JUDY KAY: Honey, I've seen your bank account. I work for Harold D., your lawyer. I know you inside out . . . and now me and the entire State of Texas knows you for a queer faggot . . .

CECIL: Get the fuck out of here, Judy Kay, or pay me back the shitload of money I gave you for your goddamn mortgage. I'll also send you a bill for setting your boy's broken leg.

JUDY KAY: *(Indicates the newspaper.)* Yesterday was Kid's Day in the park. How would you like it if one of your kids waltzed in there to witness that perversity?

CECIL: I've had you in some pretty perverse positions myself . . . so just get the hell out of here.

JUDY KAY: Sure thing, hon'. Happy reading you little shit!

(She exits. Cecil picks up the newspaper.)

CECIL: Damn it, the arrest sheet!

JIM BOB: We're right between blowing up Iraq and tryouts for the Apache Bells.

CECIL: It gives our ages. I keep forgetting that you're a year younger than me . . .

JIM BOB: *(Moving to the phone.)* Nobody home. Nobody at the church office. They probably firebombed the parsonage.

CECIL: Hell, sensationalism is good for business . . . might even juice up your congregation.

JIM BOB: If we lived in Houston.

CECIL: Harold D. is the best damn lawyer in the State of Texas. He'll get us off . . . Jesus, God almighty, where's the Channel 5 weatherman? They must have pulled out the big checkbook.

JIM BOB: Delbert Simmons, twenty-five, public lewdness, indecent exposure, and solicitation.

CECIL: They caught him with his pants down.

JIM BOB: I tried to help him in the lock up. Delbert's eyes were so big he looked like a hoot owl. He wouldn't even talk to me, he just kept staring off into space.

CECIL: Hell, I warned him to cool hanging in the park every damn night. The first time I decide to play close to town and we get busted and we get busted with Delbert.

JIM BOB: His mother will read that.

CECIL: Yep, she's going to have trouble. She's had two triple bypasses. I bailed him out because of his daddy.

JIM BOB: Perry Simmons was so beautiful. And tough.

CECIL: He had webbed toes. Fascinating.

JIM BOB: Straight as a straightedge ruler.

CECIL: And snaggle-toothed. He could spit through his two front teeth . . . ten feet in the sand. The combination was very erotic.

JIM BOB: I didn't know you had such a thing for him.

CECIL: I had a huge crush on him. He was unique.

JIM BOB: Call him up if you're so intrigued.

CECIL: I don't even know where to find him.

JIM BOB: Is it hot in here to you?

CECIL: A lot of dust . . . no air . . .

JIM BOB: I'm sweating. I've got a fever.

(Cecil feels Jim Bob's forehead.)

CECIL: You're fine.

JIM BOB: I'm having a panic attack. I think I'm dying!

(Drops to his knees.)

My God, why have I forsaken you? Yea, though I walk through the valley of the shadow of death . . .

CECIL: Get up off the dern floor, Jim Bob. *(Cecil pulls Jim Bob up from the floor.)* Listen to me. Are you listening to me? *(Cecil massages Jim Bob's shoulders.)* Jim Bob. It's going to be OK. Just breathe. Whoa . . . goose egg . . . no, two . . . two goose eggs. Breathe!

JIM BOB: I've got to talk to Tulie.

CECIL: You haven't had any sleep in twenty-six hours. You're not in any condition to talk to anyone.

JIM BOB: I've got to get it together.

CECIL: You will. You will. It's a good thing I bailed out little Delbert. We need him. One is suspect, two is a couple . . . but three, my good buddy, is an alibi.

(Judy Kay enters. Cecil doesn't move away from Jim Bob.)

What?

JUDY KAY: Kay Nell on line one.

CECIL: Tell her I left for breakfast.

JUDY KAY: I told her you were here.

CECIL: Haven't you got an intercom or something so you don't have to sashay your cynical ass in here?

JUDY KAY: I wouldn't want to miss the chance of rubbing you the wrong way.

CECIL: Fuck you, Judy Kay.

JUDY KAY: Not after the places your dick has been.

(She exits. A pause as the phone light blinks and beeps.)

CECIL: Christ. Kay Nell saw the paper! I don't want to talk to her. How are you doing, Jim Bob?

JIM BOB: Better.

CECIL: Will you talk to her?

JIM BOB: What should I tell her?

CECIL: Just tell her . . . hell, I don't know . . . tell her I'm doing my nails . . . I'm doing Judy Kay . . . I'm doing myself . . .

JIM BOB: I'll try. *(Picks up the phone.)* Hi, Kay Nell, this is Jim Bob. *(Beat.)* He's not doing real well. I understand. I hear you. I know. Well, I know it looks bad. He'll talk to the kids. I'll talk to my kids. We're all going to have to talk a lot. *(Beat.)* I'll let him answer you on that. Well, he can't talk right now. He's asking for some time, Kay Nell. We've been through a lot in the last twelve hours and I guess we're just asking for some time to sort this out . . . have you heard anything from Tulie? Well, of course we're sorry.

CECIL: Don't say "sorry" . . .

JIM BOB: We'll pay for it . . . I know, we'll pay . . .

CECIL: Don't say "pay"!

JIM BOB: Pray for us . . .

(Cecil grabs the phone, speaks.)

CECIL: Honey, honey . . . I just walked in the room . . . no, of course I want to talk to you . . . I was in the other room. I was talking to Harold D. Baby, baby . . . It's a mix-up. It's . . .

(Kay Nell hangs up.)

Dammit to hell! Never ever use words like "sorry" or "pay" to Kay Nell . . .

JIM BOB: *(Dialing the phone.)* She's got to be home.

CECIL: Before you start calling everyone in east Texas . . . we need to get our stories straight.

JIM BOB: Thank God for Alzheimer's . . . Mother won't know it's me she's reading about.

CECIL: Thank God my folks died at fifty otherwise I'd still be loaning them money.

JIM BOB: On your mother's deathbed, she told me you had no moral compass and she asked me to take care of you and I promised I would. She'd be so disappointed.

CECIL: My mother was psychotic.

JIM BOB: Your mother was a saint. *(On the phone.)* Tulie? Pick up the phone . . . Tulie? It's twenty past eight. You're usually up by this time . . . Tulie? I've got to stay at Harold D.'s until he gets some things settled . . . I hope I'll be home soon . . . all right. Good-bye.

(He hangs up.)

CECIL: We'll sue the damn paper.

JIM BOB: What good will that do? Guilt by association. We're listed — eleven altogether.

CECIL: There were twelve. The Channel 5 weatherman got off! We'll get off because we're innocent.

JIM BOB: We get the paper delivered . . . so does Carol Ann.

CECIL: Jim Bob, if you want an aneurysm keep it up.

(Delbert enters with Harold D. Delbert is a nice-looking man (twenty-five) and very upset.)

DELBERT: They said it was a dangerous weapon. My grandfather gave it to me.

HAROLD D.: You've got bigger problems than getting your pocketknife confiscated.

DELBERT: And I want to talk to Mother.

HAROLD D.: Didn't you talk to her last night?

DELBERT: She hung up.

HAROLD D.: I don't want you talking to anyone right now.

DELBERT: I want to thank her for putting up the bail.

CECIL: I put up your bail. Your mother would have left you in there.

DELBERT: It's OK. I kinda liked being in jail.

CECIL: Delbert, trust me. You don't want to be in jail.

(An intercom buzzer sounds.)

JUDY KAY: *(Offstage.)* Harold D.?

CECIL: Don't worry, Delbert. I'm going to help you.

HAROLD D.: I'm coming!

DELBERT: Mr. Carney?

HAROLD D.: Yes, Delbert?

DELBERT: I'm very hungry.

HAROLD D.: All right, Delbert. We'll see about getting some food.

(Cecil picks up the newspaper, shows it to Harold D.)

CECIL: And how the hell did this happen?

HAROLD D.: *(Reading.)* Good God, you made the arrest sheet.

CECIL: Add a retraction in the paper on your "to do" list.

HAROLD D.: This is way over the top for me.

DELBERT: Our names are in the paper?

CECIL: What did they do? Stop the presses so they could print this shit? And the Channel 5 weatherman isn't here.

HAROLD D.: Who?

CECIL: The weatherman who works for Channel 5 . . . I don't know his damn name . . . I told you about him, he was arrested and he was bailed out within an hour and his name isn't in the paper.

HAROLD D.: If you don't know his name, how do you know it's not in the paper?

CECIL: Because when we started there were twelve of us and then they came and got one . . . the Channel 5 weatherman, somebody recognized him.

DELBERT: His name is Bobby Titus.

HAROLD D.: I can't touch this, Cecil.

DELBERT: I've never had my name in the paper . . .

HAROLD D.: Mother of God . . .

JIM BOB: Shit! Tomorrow is communion Sunday.

(Jim Bob grabs the phone. Dials.)

HAROLD D.: The press will make it impossible to get an out-and-out dismissal. Once the State of Texas announces an execution, they'll put Little Bo Peep to death before they'll admit to a mistake.

JIM BOB: There's no dismissal?

CECIL: Settle down, Jim Bob! What did Judge Peters say?

HAROLD D.: He's still asleep.

CECIL: Wake him up!

HAROLD D.: *(Reading.)* Public lewdness, indecent exposure. It's a felony.

DELBERT: I'm a felony?

CECIL: I can personally guarantee y'all that Judge Peters will throw these charges out, without a doubt.

(The intercom buzzes again.)

JUDY KAY: *(Offstage.)* Harold D.?

HAROLD D.: I'm coming . . . Write me three cohesive and credible statements to give to the judge.

JIM BOB: To swear we're not three Texas homos?

CECIL: He's using the Latin, Harold D! We're Texas "homos . . ." Texas men, not Goddamn queer homosexuals . . .

JIM BOB: *(Hanging up the phone.)* Not one person in the entire congregation is home on a Saturday morning?

(The intercom buzzes.)

JUDY KAY: *(On the intercom.)* The Gay and Lesbian Defense League on two . . .

CECIL: Don't talk to those people.

DELBERT: I'd like to talk to them.

JUDY KAY: *(Offstage.)* Harold D.!

CECIL: Judy Kay! Shut it!

HAROLD D.: They've got some top notch lawyers and they've had excellent results with entrapment.

CECIL: To hell with entrapment. Entrapment says we're guilty. They entrap hookers and dope dealers. We're innocent!

HAROLD D.: The Gay Defense League could get you an expert attorney.

CECIL: I don't want to be affiliated with a bunch of gay crusaders.

HAROLD D.: The police arrested a lot of men so it could stand to reason that three of them were innocent bystanders.

DELBERT: Well, I told Officer Leviticus that I was guilty.

CECIL: *(To Harold D.)* You didn't tell me that?

HAROLD D.: I didn't know it. Delbert, did you confess?

DELBERT: Uh huh. In the interrogation room.

HAROLD D.: How many officers were in the room with you?

DELBERT: Two . . .

HAROLD D.: And did they scare you?

DELBERT: No.

HAROLD D.: I bet they did.

DELBERT: No.

HAROLD D.: OK. Did they ask you who you were at the park with?

DELBERT: Yes.

HAROLD D.: And what did you say?

DELBERT: Well . . .

CECIL: What did you say, Delbert?

DELBERT: I said I wasn't there with anyone in particular . . .

HAROLD D.: So you didn't name names?

DELBERT: Well, they did ask me for the names and addresses of all my friends.

CECIL: Christ almighty.

JIM BOB: We're his friends.

HAROLD D.: And what did you tell them?

DELBERT: Well, I told them that my momma doesn't like people coming to the house. And then they asked about my restroom buddies.

HAROLD D.: Delbert, did they ask you to name any of your friends who were at the public bathroom last night?

(A beat.)

DELBERT: Well, yes . . .

HAROLD D.: Because I know the two officers in the room with you . . . one of them was very big . . . right, Delbert?

DELBERT: Right. Leviticus.

HAROLD D.: Leviticus has a record of scaring prisoners . . . so he might have scared you, right?

DELBERT: I'm not into being around big men . . . but he was very nice. Leviticus is massive. He has to get his uniforms specially tailored.

CECIL: Delbert, if you say you were there to meet Jim Bob and me, we'll swear you were lying through your teeth. Right, Jim Bob?

JIM BOB: What?

CECIL: You're too damn quiet. Say something.

JIM BOB: What do you want me to say?

CECIL: If he names us as faggot queers, you and I will swear Delbert is lying, right?

JIM BOB: I can't call Delbert a liar. I'm an ordained minister of the cloth.

HAROLD D.: I repeat. Engaging in sexual acts in public bathrooms is a felony.

CECIL: Then just tell the truth, Jim Bob, you were just taking a piss.

JIM BOB: There were nine other men arrested. Somebody's going to tell the truth.

CECIL: I'll spread a little cash around and the hardened queers will be glad to take the heat off us.

HAROLD D.: Don't say that in front of me!

CECIL: Bullshit!

HAROLD D.: I'm serious, Cecil. Bribery has a nasty habit of coming back up as blackmail.

CECIL: We're respected citizens. We were football heroes in high school!

JIM BOB: We won one game our senior year.

CECIL: Doesn't matter. We played.

JIM BOB: I don't know.

CECIL: Don't know what?

JIM BOB: This is what God wants us to do? Lie?

CECIL: What about going home to your wife every night? What do you say you've been doing?

JIM BOB: Driving around, working on my sermon.

CECIL: What about getting up in the pulpit every Sunday?

JIM BOB: Cecil, I know I've fallen short.

CECIL: A few thousand times by my count. Look. You can work it out with God when you meet up with Him. But while you're down here on earth, let me take care of it. *(To Harold D.)* Jim Bob is having trouble so I'll lie for both of us.

(Judy Kay enters.)

JUDY KAY: Harold D.! Judge Peters is on the phone!!!

(Judy Kay exits. Harold D. begins to exit.)

CECIL: Take it here!

HAROLD D.: You let me handle this, agreed?

CECIL: Just do it.

HAROLD D.: *(Picks up the phone.)* Judge Peters? Good morning . . . how you doing? Sorry to be calling so early. It's an emergency, your honor. No, the race is going well, real well . . . now, I'm just slightly ahead in the polls . . . yes sir. I understand why you had to endorse him . . . he's your nephew . . . Yes, your honor. Sure. Right. The reason I'm calling . . . is . . . the police had this sting in City Park last night . . . so you know . . . Well, yes, I agree . . . but, your honor, they botched it . . . they got a couple of the good guys. Well, Dr. Cecil Bonner, that's one . . . and the Methodist minister, Jim Bob Mason . . . *(A beat.)* Your honor, they're innocent. If you could just read their statements . . .

CECIL: *(Hissing at Harold D.)* You want a dismissal!

HAROLD D.: I was hoping for a dismissal . . .

CECIL: And a retraction in the paper! For slander . . .

HAROLD D.: I'm not trying to circumvent justice . . . Well, what about an early arraignment . . . *(A beat.)* Thank you your honor. Yessir. It won't happen . . .

(Judge Peters hangs up. Harold D. does the same.)

OK, according to Judge Peters, he's going to put away as many queers as he can for as long as he can.

CECIL: And what about us?

HAROLD D.: I quote, "Felons automatically lose their medical license."

CECIL: That piece of petrified shit.

HAROLD D.: He left Jim Bob's church because his sermons were too liberal.

JIM BOB: I'll tie myself to the bumper of the church van and let Tulie drag me down Main Street.

HAROLD D.: He began ranting about how aggravating factors can increase sentences. I misjudged what an evangelical asshole he is.

CECIL: Call him back. Remind that evangelical asshole that I cured his girlfriend of a huge case of crabs that he gave her.

HAROLD D.: His girlfriend?

CECIL: His girlfriend! Candy Jones . . . I dated her myself.

HAROLD D.: You can't blackmail a judge.

CECIL: The hell I can't. If I could have gotten a hold of you, I wouldn't be in this mess. Hell, the Channel 5 weatherman is probably tracking storm patterns right now.

HAROLD D.: I can't have anything to do with extortion. I could get disbarred.

CECIL: Now listen here you coward pansy motherfucker. I've got some beautiful snapshots of you in your sister's prom dress.

HAROLD D.: If Delbert sticks to his story you haven't got a case.

CECIL: Delbert is changing his story.

DELBERT: No, I won't. This will make me a star. I'm finally going to be the professional dancer I've always dreamed of being.

CECIL: You don't know how to dance. You're a Southern Baptist.

DELBERT: But I've been practicing in my room. I'm going to be a dancer. Or an actor . . .

CECIL: People study to dance. They study how to act . . . they go to schools for this shit.

DELBERT: So, I'll study.

CECIL: Good God almighty, Delbert. I've known you since you were in Little League with Doodie. Christ, when I think that both you and Doodie are twenty-five damn years old. I had accomplished a shitload by twenty-five . . . finished medical school, Jim Bob and I both had kids . . . Harold D. had passed his bar exam...

JIM BOB: Times are different.

CECIL: Neither you nor Doodie has held down a job for more than six weeks.

JIM BOB: Youth struggle . . .

CECIL: With what? Ways to hang onto Momma's titty. That's what. Bullshit. Kay Nell keeps giving Doodie money. That's why he can't find a direction. I shoulda cut that supply line years ago and I shoulda left you sitting in that lockup.

DELBERT: I didn't ask you to bail me out.

CECIL: You were whining about your goddamn cat so I bailed your butt out. Well, I'm not going to let you ruin my life because you can't control your self-destructive personality.

HAROLD D.: Look. By law the judge has forty-eight hours to set the arraignment.

CECIL: I'm not waiting forty-eight hours!

HAROLD D.: Under the circumstances, I suggest you plead guilty to a misdemeanor . . .

CECIL: We're not admitting anything.

HAROLD D.: . . . take a plea bargain, pay a fine as first-time offenders.

CECIL: Hell, no!

HAROLD D.: Then get another lawyer!

(Judy Kay saunters in.)

CECIL: Get the fuck out of here, Judy Kay.

JIM BOB: Cecil, that's enough! Stop it!

JUDY KAY: I just think you are the least bit touchy today, Cecil. Your bedside manner has gone all to hell. Harold D., you've got five people waiting to talk with you. So, at your convenience . . .

(She exits.)

CECIL: Get back on the phone, get that son of a bitch out of bed and tell him that three upright tax-paying citizens have been framed. Framed by the liberal media. Framed by the foreign doctors who steal all my patients. Framed by the corrupt cops. These cops have secrets. Heh, heh, heh! Let's see if this one will fly. Find out about that Mexican that came onTo audience. Where the hell did he come from, anyway?

HAROLD D.: They brought him in from Houston.

CECIL: Score!

HAROLD D.: He's a top-rate officer.

CECIL: Every Mexican is on the take. It's a part of their culture.

DELBERT: That's racist and you should be ashamed.

CECIL: *(To Harold D.)* I'll take you down with me, boy. Just remember, I hold a lien on this goddamn office . . . I'll jog Judge Peters' memory bank. You settle this before the damn Longhorns kickoff!

HAROLD D.: Jim Bob?

JIM BOB: I just want this all to be over with.

CECIL: Jim Bob is with me. So, let me see some dust fly!

(Harold D. exits. Cecil dials the phone.)

Loretta. I need you to get over to the office, pronto! Pull up the file on Candy Jones. I saw her a couple of years back . . . xerox it and fax it over to Judge Gerald Peters . . . I know it's confidential information, that's the point . . . no message . . . just the medical record, and get me last year's total contributions I made to the Democrats and the Republicans . . .

(A beat.) What? When did that come in? God almighty! No, I didn't get the message. Because I don't have my goddamn cell phone . . . I know my language has gone all to hell . . . E-mail her chart over to Dr. Brewer. Reschedule all my appointments. Loretta, stop questioning me or find a new job, and good luck on finding one that pays as much as you're making now. *(Cecil disconnects the phone. Dials a number.)* Bobby? How's it going, pal? Listen, I need you to cover my rounds today. I was arrested. I was driving home last night and I had to take a dump, so I stopped in the park because I was about to poop my pants, and I walked into this homosexual ring and the police had some sting happening, and those idiots handcuffed me and threw me in the lock up. Hell, yes, I told them who I am. I didn't do a damn thing except look at this Mexican kid kinda funny when he asked me if he could suck my dick. You know I always have to protect my hands so I couldn't just sock the shit out of him, and I guess he took that as a "yes." Harold D. is getting the charges dismissed. Now, Mrs. Adele Potts has got a tumor the size of a golf ball in her abdomen that's causing some bowel blockage. It's benign but painful as hell. I had scheduled some surgery Monday afternoon . . . sounds like it may be more pressing. Yeah, the shit is backing up. Well, just see her and don't let her take any of that homeopathic crap. Sweet-talk her. I know you don't like to do that but she's my girl, so sugarcoat it. Yeah, thanks. Loretta will e-mail you the other patients. Well, just read the paper . . . and, do you believe, Jim Bob is here with me and he's innocent, too. *(Gives thumbs up to Jim Bob.)* And they got that poor little Delbert Simmons kid. Hell, yes, he's innocent. *(Gives thumbs up to Delbert.)* We just walked in and they slapped cuffs on us. That Supreme Court has turned them hysterical. Hell, I don't blame 'em either, if you can't get rid of the queers one way, get 'em another way. But these yokels took civilian casualties. It's going to be one hellavu lawsuit before I'm finished.

So, if you talk to anyone, we were framed. Out and out framed. You got it. I'll be there for you next time . . . *(Hangs up. Dials another number.)* See, Jim Bob? Everything is going to be fine.

DELBERT: I need to use the men's room.

JIM BOB: Down the hall . . . men's room is on your left.

CECIL: No messing around in the restroom, Delbert. Be careful who you talk to . . . and I don't want to hear anymore about that dancing shit.

DELBERT: I might travel to Europe.

CECIL: They don't allow felons into the nice countries.

DELBERT: I could be an interior decorator. I have talent.

CECIL: You have a fantasy life.

(Delbert exits. Cecil talks on the phone.)

Good morning, beautiful . . . yeah, it's your favorite doctor. No apology needed. Mrs. Potts, a woman as good-looking as you can call me anytime, day or night. I know you're ninety-two . . . I like my women old. Now, I've got a little family crisis brewing so I'm sending Doctor Bobby Brewer to check on that little discomfort . . . no, he's not going to operate. I'll be in this afternoon to collect on my bet. It's good to hear you laugh . . . The Longhorns will take it, depend on it. Now, no more racing down the hallway with your IV pole . . . that thing is fragile. Well . . . thank you, I always feel better after talking to you, too. Bye, bye, sugar.

(Hangs up. Jim Bob picks up the phone immediately, dials.)

Judge Peters will give us a dismissal, a thunderbird, and blow me before I'm finished with him.

JIM BOB: "For when I am weakest, then I am strong."

CECIL: Damn straight.

JIM BOB: The disciple Paul taught that only when you are most vulnerable are you open to true love.

CECIL: Well, then, I love everyone in the whole world.

JIM BOB: Even the poor little black crack babies?

CECIL: Even them.

JIM BOB: Even Judge Peters?

CECIL: If he acts right.

(Jim Bob hangs up the phone.)

JIM BOB: Nobody's anywhere. It's just me. Oh, my . . . *(Beat.)* I walked out of that bathroom last night in handcuffs, and I was giddy. My legs were trembling. The policeman placed his hand on my head, guiding me into the back seat of the police car, and it was like he was blessing me . . . I felt the steel handcuffs dig into my wrists. I thought, I have finally done it . . . I forced God's hand to reach down from heaven and say, "This is it, Jim Bob . . . you're mine."

CECIL: I hate it when you get that ethereal look on your face.

JIM BOB: I've had a wonderful life so far, and I'm grateful for it . . . but it's all been preparation for this moment. Because the truth is, I've always been afraid of people knowing the real me. Cecil, God's truth, you're the only person who knows who I am. And last night, praying with Wally . . . *(Looking at the newspaper.)* Where is he . . . there's his name, Wally Byrd . . . solicitation and indecent exposure . . . his name was Wally Byrd . . . when I was helping Wally find the Lord . . . it was like I was talking to you, Cecil. Even though I'd just met him, Wally knew me, he knew me like the Lord has always known me . . . because Wally and I were in the same jail for the same reason. And we prayed long and hard, and in the prayer, I was walking along a road in Jerusalem and I met Jesus, face-to-face. And Jesus held up his hand and stopped me. He spoke to me, and when he spoke to me, I spoke to Wally Byrd. I said, "Wally Byrd, here's your chance to leave uncertainty behind. There's a greater picture, a larger version of you and me and the Lord wants the world to know the truth of who we are."

CECIL: You know, Jim Bob, if you keep talking like this we're all fucked.

JIM BOB: Cecil, last night I found myself. I found me, the man I would like to be. I was out in the open for everyone to see. I felt a relief, a weight lifted from me . . .

CECIL: Whoa, whoa, babe, you shared some secrets . . . you played some "I'll show you mine if you show me yours." You were doing what you do best, little diversionary tactic . . . helping a scared man get through a bad night. I do it all the time with my patients.

JIM BOB: A diversionary tactic?

CECIL: That's all. A little quarterback sneak.

JIM BOB: You're not hearing what I'm telling you.

CECIL: I do. I hear you. You got to saving souls and you fell for your own bullshit. You're very good at what you do.

JIM BOB: Cecil. We're ruined.

CECIL: I'm not ruined.

JIM BOB: Well, I'm ruined. They run preachers out of town for mispronouncing a baby's name. There's a population of 80,000 people and they are all talking about us right this second. The deacons will not let me walk through the door of my church.

CECIL: They will if I say they will.

JIM BOB: How can you do that? Delbert, this kid . . . walks in here and says he's going to be honest and tell the truth . . .

CECIL: Delbert is not a kid. He's twenty-five years old. We will change his mind. Just be careful what you say in front of him. Confusion is contagious.

JIM BOB: I'm not confused.

CECIL: Jim Bob, you're getting all tangled up in the replay. Look at the end of the game. In less than an hour, we'll be eating breakfast. You can grab a catnap, I'll make my rounds, you go to your missionary thing and meet me to watch the Longhorns score the final touchdown.

(Delbert enters.)

DELBERT: The most awesome thing just happened.

JIM BOB: What was it?

DELBERT: I walked through a room and every single person in it turned and looked at me.

CECIL: Good God.

DELBERT: That has never happened to me before.

CECIL: And it will never happen again.

DELBERT: But it could. If I capitalize on the moment, I could even write a book.

CECIL: It would be a short one about the same size as your dick . . .

DELBERT: I could write a book and you would be in it.

CECIL: You put me in any book and I'll sue your ass for slander.

DELBERT: It's only slander if it's a lie.

CECIL: It's a lie.

DELBERT: We were there, Cecil.

CECIL: It was not sex.

DELBERT: A blow job is not sex?

CECIL: If the president of the United States swears it's not sex, it's not sex.

DELBERT: But the president got caught no matter what he called it.

CECIL: Delbert, I'm telling Harold D. that you've gone loco. You hooked up with an ecstasy smuggling ring and you're a runner for drug lords.

DELBERT: One day, I'm going to try ecstasy.

CECIL: I'll get you some ecstasy if that's all you want . . .

DELBERT: I could be as big as Ricky Martin.

CECIL: Who the hell is that?

DELBERT: He's like a major rock star.

CECIL: You're never going to be a rock star.

DELBERT: If we all plead guilty, we'd be heroes.

CECIL: We'll be pariahs. And if you keep talking like this, I'll drown your sorry ass in Lake Palestine.

JIM BOB: Cecil, that's enough! Delbert, Cecil and I have a lot to lose here.

DELBERT: He can drown me if he wants to. I don't care.

JIM BOB: Don't say that.

DELBERT: Why not? Nothing matters if Momma won't talk to me. I'm going to have to find a new home and find my cat a new home. If I can't keep my cat, I might as well go to jail.

JIM BOB: Don't worry, Delbert, your mother will forgive you.

DELBERT: I don't know. She's so mad at me.

CECIL: I hope she's taking her Prozac.

DELBERT: The one time I didn't come home at night, Soupy stopped eating. She didn't eat a bite for two days.

CECIL: You tell the truth about last night and she'll kill your cat.

JIM BOB: It's all right. She won't kill your cat.

DELBERT: She might. When I turned sixteen and told her I thought I was gay, she gave away my cat and my dog to people who were leaving town. And I asked her why she did it, she said it was to shock me into not being gay. And after a couple of years, she let me have Soupy, but when she sees that it didn't work, she'll probably just kill Soupy. Last night, Momma said I was the devil and she probably thinks my cat is the devil, too.

JIM BOB: She's upset.

DELBERT: She's going to get back at me by hurting my cat. Do you think I could call the ASPCA and tell them Momma is a religious fanatic and she's going to kill my cat because her worse fears have been confirmed. Her son is gay and he is the devil.

JIM BOB: She'll calm down, Delbert.

DELBERT: She may calm down but by then it will be too late because Soupy will be dead. I've sacrificed my cat for my sexual identity.

CECIL: I hate cats.

DELBERT: That's because you're an insensitive person like Doodie says.

CECIL: My son is an asshole and I'm a discerning individual. The only good cat is a dead cat.

DELBERT: You are the straightest gay man there ever was.

CECIL: I'm not gay. I just have a very strong libido.

DELBERT: Leviticus said the police had known about me for a long time.

CECIL: I knew it! You were the one that got us nailed! I told you to stop hanging out at the showers at the college.

DELBERT: The showers at the college were safe.

CECIL: C'mon, Delbert. The word was out — you showered for two hours at a pop.

DELBERT: It's OK. I'm glad it happened. My time has arrived. I'm going to be a star!

(Cecil goes after Delbert, who retreats.)

CECIL: I'm going to bust you up . . .

(Delbert heads for the door.)

DELBERT: Harold D. . . . help!

(Cecil blocks the door.)

CECIL: I'm going to end your dancing career early!

JIM BOB: Cecil, stop it! Leave him alone!

CECIL: I am going to hurt him!

(*Harold D. enters.*)

HAROLD D.: Cecil, cut it out!

CECIL: This little pissant wants to ruin us.

JIM BOB: He's not out to ruin us, he's just telling the truth.

CECIL: Fuck the truth.

HAROLD D.: I'm fielding phone calls from half the State of Texas and you two are in here fussing? I want you to quit it!

CECIL: And I want you to explain hard labor to this kid.

DELBERT: YOU CAN'T JUST SNAP YOUR FINGERS AND GET YOUR WAY!

CECIL: (*Reaching for Delbert.*) You little shit!

JIM BOB: Cecil!

HAROLD D.: Heh! This is my party! I've got good news.

JIM BOB/CECIL/DELBERT: (*Speaking together.*) Can we go home?/What the hell is it?/Did Mama call?

HAROLD D.: Chill! I'm not going to tell anything until we get some control. This is a time-out. Sit down and nobody says a word for one minute . . .

(*Jim Bob sits.*)

DELBERT: One minute?

HAROLD D.: One minute . . .

HAROLD D.: And after the one minute, I will tell you what I've got.

CECIL: That's bullshit.

Harold D.

All right, thirty seconds.

(*Cecil sits.*)

DELBERT: Can I dance . . .

CECIL: Nitwit!

HAROLD D.: You can do what you want to as long as you don't talk. I'm timing starting now . . .

(*Jim Bob prays. Harold D. scribbles on a Palm Pilot, Delbert break-dances, Cecil glares at Delbert, and thirty seconds pass.*)

Do we all feel better?

JIM BOB: I do. Thank you, Harold D.

DELBERT: That was really interesting. I could feel the difference between like noise and no noise.

HAROLD D.: OK, now . . . I talked to my buddy in Houston, the officer that arrested you has a past.

CECIL: The Mexican kid?

HAROLD D.: Yes.

CECIL: Hot damn, I knew it.

HAROLD D.: He was on probation for six weeks for use of excessive force.

CECIL: Thank you, Harold D. Gentlemen, we've got him.

JIM BOB: That has nothing to do with us.

HAROLD D.: We'll say he overstepped his authority. He tried to bring in a huge bust to redeem his reputation.

CECIL: Hell, if he's a bad cop, let's just bribe the son of a bitch to say it was a false arrest.

HAROLD D.: I keep telling you, bribery is real dangerous, Cecil.

CECIL: So are Texas jails. We'll say he took a bribe from us.

JIM BOB: I didn't bribe him. Did you bribe him, Delbert?

DELBERT: No.

JIM BOB: Nobody bribed him.

CECIL: I bribed him.

HAROLD D.: How did you do that?

CECIL: I paid him $500 cash to get himself hired on for this particular sting operation so Jim Bob and I could scare the hell out of Delbert.

HAROLD D.: Cecil, are you serious?

CECIL: Damn right, I'm serious. *(To Delbert.)* You want "out?" We'll "out" you. *(To Harold D.)* Doodie told me Delbert was a sex addict and Jim Bob has been counseling him on his homosexuality for years. Kay Nell's brother in Houston owes me severe pay back. We'll say he put me in touch with the Mexican officer, but the muchacho took it too far.

DELBERT: But what about you? You were there.

CECIL: Well, Jim Bob and I were trying to experience the world as you saw it, Delbert.

JIM BOB: This is beneath us, Cecil.

HAROLD D.: Bribery is like sinking a dead body in the river, eventually it rises up.

CECIL: Bribery is a hallowed Texas institution. And it's a damn site better than being pegged a fairy in Tyler, Texas.

HAROLD D.: Cecil, are you up to this?

CECIL: Harold D., I drug myself out of the white trash landfill by cheating my way through elementary and high school. I wore one coat from the age of six to fifteen. Bagged groceries 'til my hands bled, bluffed my way into the University of Texas and pimped my way through medical school. I married one of the richest girls in this town. I have patients running out my ears because I am the best damn doctor they know, and at this moment in time, my medical practice is worth just over fifteen million. I helped put you through law school so you could keep me out of trouble. Now, as Billie Holiday wrote, "Them that's got shall get."

JIM BOB: She quoted the Bible.

CECIL: For once, the Holy Scripture was right. My work is done.

DELBERT: But we were in there at the same time. I saw you come onto the officer.

CECIL: You lied. He lied.

DELBERT: The officer lied?

CECIL: The Mexican tried to shake me down for more money. When I wouldn't agree, he got pissed and ran me in with Delbert.

HAROLD D.: Because?

CECIL: Because he thinks I'm a pompous, rich white man and that I own this town but he's wrong, the Channel 5 weatherman owns the town.

JIM BOB: We're going to blackmail Judge Peters, discount Delbert, get Harold D. disbarred, and now . . . we're lying about a man we don't even know . . .

CECIL: But God will forgive me, Jim Bob. And He'll forgive you, too.

JIM BOB: I have made so many allowances for you because you struggled mightily as a child.

CECIL: Kiss my ass.

JIM BOB: Your mother and father were wonderful people.

CECIL: Right. My parents were mild-mannered, downtrodden assholes. They were the meek and they inherited shit.

(Judy Kay enters with a huge laundry crate filled with dirty clothes, mostly white shirts. She dumps it in front of Cecil.)

What the . . .?

JUDY KAY: Your prissy little wife delivered your laundry not seconds ago with the following message. "I am not Cecil's slave. He can do his shirts himself, the fucking worthless piece of queer shit."

(She exits.)

DELBERT: You have some really nice shirts, Cecil.

END OF ACT I

ACT II

Moments later. The same location. Cecil is on the phone.

CECIL: What in the hell is the matter with you, woman? Don't you ever embarrass me like that again! Kay Nell, you want your constant supply of money and drugs to vanish? You better "stand by your man" or you'll be standing by your house trailer instead of a two-million-dollar mansion. Now, go get my cell phone. It was in the front seat of the Corvette. How the hell do I know where they took it?
(To Harold D.)
Harold D. where's my Corvette?

HAROLD D.: The police impounded it.

CECIL: That car better not have a scratch on it. I just had it washed yesterday.

HAROLD D.: That's not my immediate concern.

CECIL: God dammit to hell. *(On the phone.)* Stop screaming! That's all I need right now is a hysterical woman.

HAROLD D.: Keep it down!
(Harold D. exits.)

CECIL: *(Changing tactics.)* Now, honey, pull over . . . just pull the damn car over before you wreck it! *(A beat.)* Now, you never even asked me if this was a setup which it is. Now, honey, you know I have enemies in this town, enemies who are jealous of my success. *(Softening even more.)* Jim Bob and I were trying to help little Delbert Simmons. He played with Doodie. I hate to tell you, but he is. Doodie's not gay . . . he was always bringing girls over to the house and he doesn't live in Houston . . . Now, I know we've had some rough times but just think about it, I'm not a Goddamn faggot. You know that. I love you. I have strayed in the past but it was only because you wouldn't have a damn thing to do with me because of postpartum depression and we talked all through that . . . hell, you divorced me twice . . . you do it again and that's it! Stop crying. Just stop crying. It'll be all right.
(Jim Bob moves to Delbert.)

JIM BOB: I'm sorry, Delbert. Cecil is under a lot of pressure.

DELBERT: It's OK.

JIM BOB: It's nothing against you. I'm proud of you for wanting to stick to the truth.

DELBERT: Well, they caught me pretty good.

CECIL: *(On the phone.)* Kay Nell, you do not want to do that . . .

JIM BOB: Poor Cecil . . . chasing his own tail.

DELBERT: Do you think they'll believe him?

JIM BOB: He has a lot of power in this town.

DELBERT: Well, I don't have any.

JIM BOB: You'd be surprised.

DELBERT: No, I don't think I would be.

CECIL: *(Managing a few sniffles.)* Now you've got me crying, honey. Hell, I'm crying because I'm scared. I love you. Now, Kay Nell Bonner, I don't want to lose you. You got to believe I wouldn't ever do anything to lose you.

JIM BOB: The Lord Jesus was tested for forty days and forty nights.

DELBERT: Tested for what?

JIM BOB: His faith. And he was without sin.

DELBERT: I don't know if I have any faith.

CECIL: *(On the phone.)* The kids will believe what I tell them.

JIM BOB: You got to have faith, boy, if you don't have faith you don't have anything.

DELBERT: I'm not very religious. Momma just scares you to death . . . with all her screaming.

CECIL: *(On the phone.)* You're going to make yourself sick . . .

DELBERT: She used to handle snakes. She almost died from getting bit so she doesn't do that anymore. But she speaks in tongues. I hate going to church with her because I have to sit next to her and she holds onto my arm and shakes and drools.

JIM BOB: It's just people talking to the Lord, Delbert. She's been tried . . . your daddy leaving her to raise a child all by herself.

DELBERT: Because she screamed all the time. My friend Sara thinks she's crazy.

JIM BOB: It could be that she was crazy before she found religion.

CECIL: *(On the phone.)* Honey, don't beat that dead horse again.

JIM BOB: I could talk to her. Maybe I could help her.

DELBERT: If she won't have anything to do with me, she won't have anything to do with you.

CECIL: *(On the phone.)* Honey, honey!

DELBERT: Daddy told me he left because she kept screaming that he was going to hell. Now she screams at me.

JIM BOB: It's never too late to find faith in a "good" God. One that doesn't judge or punish, one that loves you, no matter what.

DELBERT: Well, I'd like to believe in that kind of God.

JIM BOB: Delbert, do you trust me?

DELBERT: No.

JIM BOB: Why?

DELBERT: You say that Cecil's acting like this because he's under so much pressure but I think you're under just as much pressure as he is. You're going to do anything he says. That's how you are.

JIM BOB: I wish you could trust me.

DELBERT: I don't know why you think I would. Cecil's your best friend. You'll always put him first.

JIM BOB: I put our Lord Jesus Christ first.

DELBERT: Really?

CECIL: *(On the phone.)* Kay Nell, I swear on the lives of our children, "no."

JIM BOB: If I could just spare my wife the pain . . .

DELBERT: It won't matter. If your wife is anything like my momma, she'll never trust you again.

JIM BOB: You're probably right.

CECIL: *(On the phone.)* When you get home, take two tablets of that new drug — there's some samples on my nightstand — depathon . . . drink a lot of water. And, remember to eat something. No. Forget the damn cell phone. Don't worry about the Corvette. I'm going to buy you a new car . . . how would you like a Porsche? *(Pause.)* I'm going to beat it because it's a lie. The whole thing is a lie. I love you. Kay Nell? Did you hear me? I love you. *(He hangs up. Cecil sizes up Delbert.)* Now, Delbert, I'm not out to ruin you. Hell. You want to go to Europe for the summer? I'll send you there, all expenses paid. You want a new car? You got it. You want to go off to school. I'll pay your Goddamn tuition for the next year at any school that will accept your sorry ass, and that's just for starters.

JIM BOB: I've never seen you so scared.

CECIL: I'm not scared.

JIM BOB: You are about to wet your pants, Cecil. Did Kay Nell finally realize she can take you for everything you have?

CECIL: Kay Nell has a hangover. She'll be fine after a medicated nap and her 5:00 martini.

JIM BOB: Would it be such a terrible thing to face up to the reality of our lives?

CECIL: No, Jim Bob. Let's just chuck it all. Forget Tulie, forget Kay Nell, forget our kids . . .

JIM BOB: "Everyone that is of the truth hears my voice." Cecil, my wife is a very intuitive woman.

CECIL: Meaning?

JIM BOB: I wonder if Tulie has known about me all this time.

CECIL: Tulie doesn't know a thing.

JIM BOB: She's never asked, never pried. But sometimes she'll smile at me with a kind of benevolence . . . I hope she does know . . . maybe then it won't be such a shock when I lose my church.

CECIL: Babe. Take a sabbatical. Schedule another missionary trip . . . Ghana. You were all worried about Ghana.

JIM BOB: Another quarterback sneak?

CECIL: Hell, yes. I'll buy them a new bell for the steeple. We'll get them a new organ. That'll change their tune . . .

JIM BOB: Cecil. I can't be part of all this wrangling and lying.

CECIL: Well, we're in a little bit of a mess.

JIM BOB: I just wish, for once, we could do the right thing.

CECIL: We are doing the right thing. And, Delbert, this is where friends hang tough and strong . . . they don't rat on each other.

DELBERT: But you just outed me to your wife.

CECIL: No, I did not.

DELBERT: I just heard you.

CECIL: No, you didn't.

DELBERT: Yes, I did.

CECIL: Well, I was talking fast . . . sorry . . . all I hear from you is how you're going to tell the truth . . .

JIM BOB: I think it would have been kinder to let Delbert tell the truth himself.

CECIL: Oh, hell, Kay Nell won't say anything.

DELBERT: And you were the one told me about going to the restroom in the park.

CECIL: Oh, c'mon, Delbert. You knew. Everyone knew.

JIM BOB: But you went because you heard Cecil raving on about what fun it would be.

DELBERT: Right.

JIM BOB: Cecil likes to have a decoy. We're bait.

CECIL: You think what we do is wrong?

JIM BOB: Anonymous sex? For me, yes.

CECIL: But you go without me.

JIM BOB: I went because you wanted me to go, you tempted me. My whole life.

CECIL: Well, you tempt me, buddy. That's the excitement of it.

JIM BOB: You tempted Delbert.

DELBERT: You did. You tempted me, Cecil.

CECIL: I may have loaned you money. I never tempted you.

JIM BOB: Every time I think I have the taste for it licked, here you come. Let's take a ride to the Red Dragon. Let's find some strange at the truck stop. Let's risk it all at the Motel 6. At least you always insisted on safe sex.

CECIL: Hell, that's a good one. He was having fun all those years just to keep me company. How safe. How nice. How about a steaming plate of horseshit!

JIM BOB: I'm realizing, right this moment, all these years, I've been following Satan.

CECIL: Satan! That's good! Heh! If I am the devil, then I am evil. And there is evil in us all. And that includes you, preacher.

JIM BOB: I'll take responsibility for my actions. Just say you had a hand in it. Just say you were caught last night. Why can't you just say that?

CECIL: You know. Eat me. I'll see you both in court. I'll sue your ass.

JIM BOB: So now you're suing me?

CECIL: Yes. For solicitation, for enticing me into the bathroom.

JIM BOB: I watch you dancing around, finding ways, improvising, trying to put people off balance.

CECIL: What the hell do you think? You've got a family. I've got a family.

JIM BOB: Cecil, you know what I preach every Sunday?

CECIL: How the hell should I know.

JIM BOB: That's right. You stopped coming to the Methodists. You go to the Episcopalians.

CECIL: Is that what this is about?

JIM BOB: No. That's not what it's about. But if you did hear me you'd know that I preach about self-control. And we don't practice self-control. We practice sin.

CECIL: Don't do this to me.

JIM BOB: The sex isn't the sin. I don't believe the sex is the sin. The sin is the lie.

CECIL: We've been friends a long time.

JIM BOB: The sin is not telling the people who love you, "This is who I am."

CECIL: You know who I am.

JIM BOB: The sin is when you ignore the truth.

CECIL: If you don't back me I swear to God!

JIM BOB: Let's tell the truth. Let's announce who we are!

CECIL: Think about your wife.

JIM BOB: I'm thinking about Tulie.

CECIL: Jim Bob. She's my patient. She has a major weight problem complicated by a pre-diabetic condition exacerbated by a dependency on Mounds bars.

JIM BOB: I've been so unfair to Tulie, all these years. Bless her heart, she'll be better off without me.

CECIL: And your daughters?

JIM BOB: I'll pray that they can forgive me.

CECIL: *(To Delbert.)* I should have never bailed you out. You've infected Jim Bob.

DELBERT: I did not!

JIM BOB: The grace of God infected me. The grace of God led me to that bathroom.

CECIL: You are shitting me!

JIM BOB: I'm as serious as I've ever been in my life, Cecil.

CECIL: I'm your best friend. And there's one thing that's wrong with your thinking. I'm not announcing anything.

JIM BOB: Hiding from the truth is just making it worse. We could make a difference in the world, in people's lives.

CECIL: Look. I had to go over to the Episcopalians. Half of my patients belong to that congregation.

DELBERT: I hate church.

JIM BOB: You think I care if you don't come to my church?

CECIL: Yes.

DELBERT: I'll never go to boring old church again. Hallelujah.

JIM BOB: I'm sorry you feel that way, Delbert.

CECIL: Look. I'll be in the front pew tomorrow morning.

JIM BOB: Tomorrow?

CECIL: You'll preach and I'll be there. We will face them together.

JIM BOB: If you come with me I'll preach! If you come out with me before my congregation and Jesus Christ . . .

CECIL: Next you'll be wanting me to marry you! Stop equating Jesus and recreational sex. It's a fuck club, for Christsake.

DELBERT: Really? Am I in it?

CECIL: No. It's only Jim Bob and me. And Harold D. if we're across the county line.

JIM BOB: Cecil, I've never gone against you. But it's time for me to get right here, to be strong. I want us to tell the truth. I want you to go to sleep at night thinking that you didn't lie to anyone. You're always saying that you're a powerful person. Well, have some compassion for yourself, for me . . .

CECIL: That's the way we keep sane, Jim Bob, by telling little lies. We don't lie, we stretch the truth.

JIM BOB: I just wish for once in your dadgum life, you'd take responsibility for one thing but you never do. If someone dies while they're on the operating table, it's always their own damn fault.

CECIL: Neither doctors nor preachers can help it when people are set on dying.

JIM BOB: I've never once heard you say you made a mistake or you could have done better.

DELBERT: You're very egotistical, Cecil.

JIM BOB: You paid that pretty little Tomkins boy to show us his dick in the second grade.

CECIL: You gave him your allowance.

JIM BOB: But it was your idea! Cecil, even if we do get the charges dismissed, it won't matter to this town. It's a done deal. Now I don't have to be afraid of Tulie, of my family, of my congregation, and . . . I don't have to be afraid of myself . . . praise the Lord, I'm having an epiphany.

CECIL: We don't have time for any epiphany.

JIM BOB: Cecil?

CECIL: What?

JIM BOB: We're gay.

CECIL: The hell we are.

JIM BOB: And now . . . everyone knows.

CECIL: They haven't got a shred of evidence. There wasn't a Goddamn videotape.

JIM BOB: We were arrested for buggery, Cecil.

CECIL: Listen up. You are my best friend. Now, you are not gay!

JIM BOB: Yes, I am.

CECIL: Well, that's news to me.

JIM BOB: Cecil, c'mon . . . look . . . I'll give you living proof . . . Delbert?

DELBERT: What?

JIM BOB: Did Cecil hit on you?

DELBERT: Actually, we kind of hit on each other. The first time we were together was in the restroom at The Catfish King. That was two years ago. I didn't even know he was gay.

CECIL: I'M NOT FUCKING GAY!

JIM BOB: Yes, you are!

CECIL: I AM FUCKING NOT GAY!!

JIM BOB: Yes, you are. You're gay, I'm gay and he's gay. Just admit it.

DELBERT: It's good to be gay!

CECIL: The hell it is!

JIM BOB: Either you admit it . . .

CECIL: Or what?

JIM BOB: Or I'm siding with Delbert. Heck, I may side with Delbert anyway.
(Harold D. enters.)

HAROLD D.: Why the hell are you yelling? You want people to hear this shit?

CECIL: Go get me my gun and change the plea, Harold D. Change it to double homicide.

HAROLD D.: Just keep it down, damn it! I've got clients out there.
(Harold D. exits.)

CECIL: Harold D. is my man, Jim Bob. He's going to save me and he's going to save you, despite yourself.

JIM BOB: I'm gonna to tell the truth and Delbert is gonna to tell the truth. I'm delivering you.

CECIL: Deliver me? Hell, I'm committing you! You want to walk into some lion's den but I don't. I repeat. I do not want to slay dragons, I do not want to change my life, to become some gay fucking political icon . . . And if you want to have . . . what did you call it . . .

JIM BOB: An epiphany.

CECIL: That's right, an epiphany. So be it. I'll play it without you. It's you and me, Delbert. You and me. Anything you want, Delbert. You want to be a star? I will bankroll your career . . .

JIM BOB: It's Lucifer . . . see him changing into Lucifer?

DELBERT: Jim Bob, you're sounding more and more like my momma. I don't know which is more frightening — you or Cecil.

CECIL: I couldn't agree more, Delbert. So, what will it be? New York City . . . want to go to New York? Or Hollywood? Nice apartment . . . new wardrobe . . . you could take your damn cat with you.

DELBERT: You'd really give me a lot of money?

CECIL: I'll get Harold D. to transfer the money right now. Damn right! Name the price.

DELBERT: To move to New York . . . with an apartment and furniture and new clothes . . . hmmmm . . . fifty thousand dollars.

CECIL: Deal.

JIM BOB: Poor Cecil . . .

CECIL: Poor my ass. You mean rich Cecil, "smart" Cecil. Which is why you'll never take me alive.

JIM BOB: Delbert?

DELBERT: I don't like it when you start calling people the devil.

JIM BOB: C'mon, Delbert. You helped me see it. You helped me see the truth and now I'm asking you to stand with me. Will you do that, Delbert? Will you be independent and strong and stand up for who you are and what you believe?

(Harold D. breaks into the room.)

HAROLD D.: Nice work, Cecil. Judge Peters will be at the courthouse at noon to set the arraignment but there's a chance he'll go for a complete dismissal.

CECIL: And why aren't you smiling?

HAROLD D.: I checked in at the Sheriff's office. You can't play the bribery angle. The Mexican covered his butt . . . he was wearing a wire.

CECIL: Shit!

HAROLD D.: Now, is there anything incriminating on those tapes?

(Judy Kay's voice over the intercom.)

JUDY KAY: Someone is dying on line one . . . Cecil, get your dick outta Delbert's mouth and answer the phone!

CECIL: I am going to hurt that woman if she keeps this shit up.

HAROLD D.: I promised Judge Peters three statements by ten . . . it's just after nine o'clock. That gives us about thirty minutes. Let's stick to the plan. But if that tape is real, we're toast.

(Harold D. exits.)

(Cecil picks up the phone.)

CECIL: Hello? . . . Heh, Ken . . . buddy . . . how are you feeling? Malpractice! I didn't give you a heart attack! You were bragging about combining Viagra and poppers to hump some mommacita! I warned you, poppers are amyl nitrate. That's why you're in the hospital with a mild cardio infarction. Hell, you're lucky you're alive. Wait! The park bust doesn't change a thing. The police are in more trouble than I am. You watch! I'm coming over . . . just calm down and let me speak to the nurse. *(Pause.)* Heh, Betty. What's his blood pressure? Good God! And what's the heart rate? OK, give him 5 milligrams of morphine and don't let him make anymore phone calls. You don't need my signature . . . get Bobby to sign it. Jesus H., what if I was sick and in the damn bed? Now just get Bobby . . . why has everyone there has gotten so dern dense? *(Hangs up phone.)* Jesus, it's impossible to get anything done sitting in this room. I am not missing this game. I have not missed a Longhorn game in twenty years . . .

JIM BOB: Remind me. What happens if you miss watching the Longhorns play?

CECIL: Big explosions, Jim Bob. Thunder, lightening . . . monumental locusts. Delbert, did you say anything in the restroom?

DELBERT: Like what?

CECIL: I don't know. Like "Mister, come look at this . . . come home with me, or just come here?"

DELBERT: I think I just talked about my poison ivy . . . I wish someone would call me.

CECIL: Delbert, you'll get phone calls in New York. You can tell your story to all those pansy activists and you'll get a ton of calls, because you can be queer in New York and you can be queer in Houston but you can't be queer here. Besides which, no one in Texas gives a rat's ass what kind of perversity happens in New York.

DELBERT: Really?

CECIL: In New York, last night turns into titillating dinner conversation. *(A beat.)* I think I said something to Pancho Gonzales about his smile. Jim Bob?

JIM BOB: Oh, I talked on and on.

CECIL: Will you quit it?

JIM BOB: Cecil, don't you see? We're going to die one day.

CECIL: Jesus, Jim Bob, lighten up.

JIM BOB: I thought I was going to die last night in the cell. I thought I was dying in this office. I didn't die. I was reborn.

CECIL: Jim Bob, just tell me if you said anything incriminating on the tape.

JIM BOB: I did. I prayed for a divine intervention and my prayer has been answered. We're on the tape.

CECIL: You know, Jim Bob, it's not going to be too long before I look out my rear view mirror and I'll be thinking, what ever happened to my good buddy, Jim Bob Mason? Where did he go? He hasn't got his church anymore. He hasn't got me. He hasn't got his wife or his family. Well, maybe you'll move to San Francisco and start a new religion. The religion of fanatic faggots who tell all to anyone who is interested.

JIM BOB: I like that idea, Cecil.

CECIL: Didn't you hear what I just told Delbert, Jim Bob? Nobody is interested in your story. Nobody cares. These good folks want to hear about the rose festival or whether Medicare is going to pay their doctor bills, they don't want to hear your version of how a couple of fellows like to beat off in public.

DELBERT: Then why do I have to leave town?

CECIL: It's for your own good, Delbert. And Jim Bob can pack up and go with you.

JIM BOB: No, Cecil, I'm staying here.

CECIL: We weren't doing anything wrong. We were doing what you always preached. Celebrating life. Celebrating the glory of God. *(A mild roar is heard.)* What the hell was that?

DELBERT: My stomach. Do you think we could order out?

CECIL: Sure, Delbert, let's have breakfast. I've got to eat something before the game starts.

DELBERT: I'm really hungry . . . like some pancakes and eggs . . .

CECIL: Hungry, Jim Bob?

JIM BOB: I'm straining to make a connection between the glory of God and me disappearing in your rear view mirror.

CECIL: Stay with me. Back me up. There wasn't any coercion. We didn't force anything on anyone. We weren't hitting on pre-teens, we weren't screwing the babysitter, we weren't watching pornography or we weren't involved in pedophilia. We have some fun. That's all, we offer. A friendly hand job, an anonymous blow . . . no invasive procedures. Now in your heart, is a friendly offer worth tearing your soul out?

DELBERT: Should I go outside and ask Harold D.?

CECIL: Ask him what?

DELBERT: About getting some food.

(Cecil presses the intercom.)

CECIL: Judy Kay, order us some food . . . pancakes, eggs . . . how do you like them, Delbert?

DELBERT: Over easy. And bacon?

CECIL: You got it.

(On the intercom.)

Bacon, over easy eggs . . .

DELBERT: And the bacon, well done . . . I'll have pancakes and eggs . . . keep the eggs separate from the pancakes . . . not on top.

CECIL: Keep the eggs separate.

(She hangs up on Cecil.)

Bitch!

DELBERT: And some orange juice.

CECIL: Just give me a damn second here . . .

(Judy Kay enters. Slams down a menu.)

JUDY KAY: Order your own damn food, faggot!

CECIL: Judy Kay! Will you order pancakes with eggs on the side separate for

Delbert and I will pay you 500 dollars. OK? You can go dancing and drinking in a new dress on me.

JUDY KAY: Do you even remember, Cecil, when I called you last month, in absolute hysteria because my baby had swallowed a quarter, and you were too damn busy to come over.

CECIL: I told you to turn him upside down and shake him.

JUDY KAY: He was traumatized.

CECIL: Did it work?

JUDY KAY: Yes.

CECIL: That was the same thing I would have done.

JUDY KAY: It's better if a doctor does it.

CECIL: No, it's not.

JUDY KAY: And you stood me up on my birthday.

CECIL: I had an emergency!

JUDY KAY: You always had an emergency. And now we know what the damn emergency was! You had to get to the park bathroom to suck some dick.

CECIL: I did not suck!

DELBERT: There was one time . . .

CECIL: Delbert, shut the fuck up! Face it, Judy Kay, this is about the sex . . .

JUDY KAY: You know, you do suck, Cecil. I know you suck and Delbert knows you suck and Jim Bob knows you suck. And now the whole town knows you suck. I mean I feel sorry for Delbert because he has never tried to make anyone believe anything different. I mean, child, you are gay. You have always been gay.

DELBERT: I know.

JUDY KAY: God help me. Cecil, Cecil, Cecil . . . I cannot believe you. I have held you in my arms and listen to you talk about your poor parents and how much you loved them and hated them at the same time. You even cried . . . growing up wanting so much and having so little.

CECIL: I was just trying to get laid.

JUDY KAY: You lying little prick! I believe you deserve any hardship that comes down on you because even though you've helped a lot of people, you've hurt a lot, too. Every time poor Harold D. leaves this room, his face gets paler . . . he's trying, God love him. We're all trying.

JIM BOB: Thank you.

CECIL: You need professional help.

JUDY KAY: You know, I'm almost relieved. I thought it was me. I thought I had failed you in some way. I kept thinking, if the sex is this good, how could he just lose interest?

CECIL: Hell, Judy Kay, I lost interest because you were too needy, hysterical, and demanding.

JUDY KAY: That is so wrong.

JIM BOB: Cecil asked Harold D. to fire you.

CECIL: Nice going, Jim Bob.

JIM BOB: I'm just telling the truth.

JUDY KAY: Why would you ask Harold D. to fire me?

CECIL: I don't think hysterical people should be working in law offices.

DELBERT: Doodie told me that he never invited any girls over to his house because Cecil would hit on them.

CECIL: Doodie's paranoid.

JUDY KAY: I was so crazy over you . . . I woke up crying for a solid two weeks. I thought you were different. Finally, I had found a man who didn't have cow shit under his fingernails, who talked to me, even if it was mostly about sick people . . . who didn't fall asleep on top of me. I worked so hard to treat you really good. Well, you know, Cecil, $500 is not enough money for ordering breakfast. Nope. Not nearly enough. Ordering breakfast is going to cost you $10,000 a month for six months of heartbreak . . . let's see that's $60,000 . . . yep. And either you pay or I'll tell Kay Nell where you were parking your shoes two times a week for two damn years.

CECIL: Kay Nell knows about you because you nearly ran me off the road twice with her in the car. So, whatever you have in mind won't make any difference . . .

JUDY KAY: Oh, I'll make a difference. I've got some tapes myself. I taped a few of our phone sex conversations . . . to get me through those lonely, lonely nights.

JIM BOB: Are you sure you want to do this, Judy Kay?

JUDY KAY: Jim Bob, you've lost your moral authority over me. I don't know if you're guilty or not, but if you are guilty, that you would lay down beside this mongrel dog just depresses me beyond belief. But, I'm wising up. So, I guess I'll pray you don't go to jail so you can still do my taxes.

CECIL: You greedy bitch!

JUDY KAY: You know where to send the check.

(She exits.)

DELBERT: Does this mean she'll order us breakfast?

CECIL: God, she is a mess!

JIM BOB: She's got some resentments.

CECIL: So here I stand. Lucifer.

DELBERT: If Cecil gives me money, will I have to pay taxes on it?

CECIL: No.

JIM BOB: But your soul will pay, Delbert.

CECIL: More bullshit propaganda, Delbert.

(Harold D. enters.)

HAROLD D.: The Channel 5 weatherman bought the tape.

CECIL: I have got to date this man.

HAROLD D.: I don't want to know one iota more than I found out. Must have cost him a bundle.

CECIL: Look for the clouds to part with mild temperatures and sunny skies all around.

JIM BOB: Just like you predicted.

HAROLD D.: We are squeaking by . . . squeaking by . . . but not a word leaves this office . . . ever!

JIM BOB: No divine intervention. He's leaving it up to me.

CECIL: I told you this would be an easy one.

HAROLD D.: You did. You were right. So, we're all agreed here?

JIM BOB: I'm telling the truth.

HAROLD D.: Exactly what are you saying?

JIM BOB: I was caught offering to perform oral sex on an undercover police officer.

HAROLD D.: Jim Bob, I thought we were trying to stay out of jail.

CECIL: It's exhaustion. I'll write his statement.

HAROLD D.: Look. Cecil, I can't be a party to out-and-out perjury.

CECIL: Relax. Look. Jim Bob is my best friend. He's a little confused.

JIM BOB: You keep saying that. I am not confused.

HAROLD D.: I can't risk my practice. I've got a family. I can't coerce someone to lie.

JIM BOB: Harold D., bless you.

CECIL: So, you can forget your runoff . . . I'll pull everything, everything . . . I'll smear you across the radio, the television, the newspapers. You want me to tell your in-laws the truth about your fishing trips to Houston?

HAROLD D.: Her daddy is sick, Cecil. He's an old man . . .

CECIL: Your stuck-up wife will kick your ass out and you'll never see your kids again.

HAROLD D.: We've got the new baby.

CECIL: That's why I would hate to do it, of course . . .

HAROLD D.: Cecil . . . be realistic. Obstruction of justice? Jim Bob could out all of us. I can't afford that. None of us can afford that.

CECIL: Let's jump-start your imminent ruin right now. Judy Kay is up for an eye-opener. Let's call her back in here. *(Hits the intercom.)* Judy Kay!

JUDY KAY: *(On the intercom.)* WHAT DO YOU WANT NOW, FRUIT FLY!

CECIL: Come in here!

HAROLD D.: ALL RIGHT!

CECIL: *(Hits the intercom.)* Judy Kay?

JUDY KAY: WHAT??

CECIL: Never mind. *(A beat.)* See, Jim Bob? Nobody wants to "come out."

HAROLD D.: Jim Bob . . . I was trying to spare you until you could leave. Your daughter called a few minutes ago. She took Tulie to the emergency room with chest pains.

JIM BOB: Is she all right?

HAROLD D.: She's stabilized. She's at Trinity.

DELBERT: I wish something would happen to Momma . . .

CECIL: I'll transfer Tulie out of Trinity first thing.

JIM BOB: Lord, help me.

HAROLD D.: And you've had four heart attacks in your congregation . . .

CECIL: Now you know why you couldn't get anyone on the phone.

JIM BOB: My Lord, forgive me.

HAROLD D.: Jim Bob, now is not a good time to be sent to a Texas prison. You're looking at a year behind bars. Prison has never been an easy ride but I expect it's gotten worse since they've legalized sodomy. If you survive the prison gangs, vendettas, strip searches, and boredom, you'll come home HIV positive. Delbert will be a career criminal.

CECIL: His butthole will be stretched from here to Kansas.

HAROLD D.: At best, you'll spend a year building a highway in 100 degree weather. It will ruin you physically and spiritually. I would think long and hard about letting yourself and your family in for a ride like that.

DELBERT: I wouldn't want to build a highway.

HAROLD D.: That's smart thinking, son. Now, let's get this in front of Judge Peters and then you can go see Tulie.

(Harold D. exits.)

JIM BOB: My Lord, what have I done?

CECIL: Got your priorities tangled up a bit.

JIM BOB: If I had one iota of courage as a human being, I would not have wrought this shame and misery.

CECIL: Courage? You're human. You are a hot number, Jesus H. Christ! You're a sexy minister who occasionally likes sex with men.

JIM BOB: That's not me.

CECIL: Look, when I cross the highway and see a semi coming I might freeze for a split second, mesmerized by the oncoming power . . . but when I come to and see that I'm in danger, I run like hell so I won't get squashed. How about not getting squashed? Jim Bob, I can't say this about myself. Well, hell, I'm a half decent doctor but I'm not much of a person. You — you are a good man. You make lives better. You've made me better. I'd be a moral catastrophe without you watching over me. Everybody you touch, and I'm not being facetious, they are all better for knowing you. Now cut yourself some slack, stop being so goldarn hard on yourself. Let's go home and forget this happened.

DELBERT: I don't think Momma will let me come home.

CECIL: We've got your problems under control, Delbert, let's not pick that wound anymore.

(Harold D. enters, calling out.)

HAROLD D.: Judy Kay, come in here. Bring your book.

CECIL: I don't want that cunt in here.

HAROLD D.: Don't start, Cecil. I don't want it on tape. I want it on paper so I can burn it when we edit the hell out of whatever bullshit you're going to tell me. And all these stories, ALL THREE, are going to match up . . .

(Judy Kay flounces back with a steno pad. Sits.)

CECIL: Can she be trusted?

JUDY KAY: As long as the check arrives by tonight.

CECIL: It will arrive.

HAROLD D.: Who wants to start?

CECIL: Hell, I will. I was just coming in for a friendly piss. I no sooner walked into the bathroom, unzipped and stood at the urinal when I see this Mexican kid looking at me with this grin and all I said was "You've got a nice smile." But I said it with a spin. A real irony attached to it. It was like I was saying, "What are you looking at motherfucker . . ." but I didn't because he was a Mexican and could have been a drug lord for all I knew besides which I can't get in a fight. I have to protect my hands. I never touched the son of a bitch. I never stood two inches close to him. *(Pause.)* That's it. He cuffed me and read me my rights.

HAROLD D.: You didn't show him the size of your dick?

CECIL: If he looked, it was his problem. I did not display the merchandise.

HAROLD D.: A simple yes or no . . .

CECIL: No.

HAROLD D.: You got that?

JUDY KAY: I got it.

HAROLD D.: Who's next?

CECIL: Jim Bob? *(Pause.)* OK, play hard to get . . . Delbert?

DELBERT: OK, Cecil?

CECIL: What?

DELBERT: After you pay Judy Kay . . . will you still have enough money to send me to New York?

CECIL: Yes.

DELBERT: Sweet.

HAROLD D.: Someone is paying off Judy Kay?

JUDY KAY: It's a personal debt.

HAROLD D.: I don't want to know!

DELBERT: OK, I was having this problem with some poison ivy that I got working in Momma's backyard last summer. It flares up something awful, it's like I never quite got rid of it. So, I stopped in the bathroom to put down my pants in the stall . . . and I was looking at it and kind of rubbing it and I heard someone come in . . . and without any help on my part . . . the door to the stall . . . the latch must not have caught . . . so the door to the stall just crept open and suddenly I'm looking at this Mexican guy looking at me and I kinda smiled because I was embarrassed and I think I sorta said this was the only way I could get it to stop itching . . . and he said he had the same problem and I said I might help him out.

(Judy Kay stops taking notes.)

JUDY KAY: Harold D., you want me to keep writing?

HAROLD D.: No. OK, Delbert . . . you didn't proposition him?

DELBERT: Not really.

HAROLD D.: I'm sorry. That was a statement. You did not proposition the undercover officer.

DELBERT: No.

HAROLD D.: You were making conversation about your poison ivy. That was it.

DELBERT: That was it.

HAROLD D.: And what next?

DELBERT: His hands went down to his trousers and I thought he was going to show me his poison ivy so I went down on my knees . . .

JUDY KAY: Looking for salvation?

DELBERT: Looking to help him . . .

HAROLD D.: And?

DELBERT: He slapped my hands away, pulled me up real rough, turned me against the wall and I thought I was really in for something great when he said, "You're under arrest" and read me my rights.

HAROLD D.: OK. You know the first part of the story? The part about the poison ivy?

DELBERT: Yes.

HAROLD D.: That part is good. Where does it begin going bad, Judy Kay?

JUDY KAY: I think about the part where he was jerking off with the door open.

HAROLD D.: Right. So keep the door coming open but then cut the rest of the story. He pulled you out of the stall, turned you around and cuffed you. Got it?

DELBERT: Uh huh.

HAROLD D.: OK, Jim Bob?

JIM BOB: Right.

HAROLD D.: Let's hear it.

JIM BOB: I saw this Mexican outside. I'd been waiting for Cecil . . . we stop in some place like this twice, sometimes three times a week looking for rough trade . . .

CECIL: Damn you . . .

JIM BOB: I went inside. Cecil wasn't there. I was standing at the urinal when the Mexican walked in just when the night-light over the door lit up and it formed a halo, shining onto that thick black head of hair and I almost came from excitement and anticipation of the glory . . . I said, "I can give you a blow job that will part the clouds and let you see a glimpse of heaven."

JUDY KAY: Preacher, how you talk.

JIM BOB: And he smiled and I had this vision of Jesus smiling at me and I walked into his light and praised his goodness.

(A pause.)

CECIL: You're fucking delusional.

HAROLD D.: Right. They have you on record for being there for a while. So, you were sick. You got food poisoning . . . it gave you a bad stomach . . . a real bad stomach.

JIM BOB: I was caught.

HAROLD D.: You felt like you were going to puke . . . it made you hallucinate and when the undercover policeman came in, you were delirious . . .

JIM BOB: I was caught.

HAROLD D.: You didn't say "blow job," you said blessing . . .

JIM BOB: I said . . .

HAROLD D.: Judy Kay, use the second story for Jim Bob. I want the appeal on my desk in ten minutes.

JUDY KAY: You got it.

HAROLD D.: It will take us ten minutes to process this, Jim Bob. You have that long to change your story.

JIM BOB: My story is staying the way it is.

HAROLD D.: Will you incriminate Cecil?

JIM BOB: Won't I have to?

HAROLD D.: *(To Cecil.)* There's your problem.

(Harold D. and Judy Kay exit. A pause.)

CECIL: You know I won't be able to see you anymore.

JIM BOB: I knew that was coming.

CECIL: Just answer me one question, Jim Bob, why is it so easy for you to give me up?

JIM BOB: It's not.

CECIL: There's nothing here that can't be undone. That we can't chalk up to a sleepless night. I'm just finding it hard to believe you'd end our friendship over this.

JIM BOB: You're the one ending it.

CECIL: Well, you're the one betraying me. Let's see . . . if I'm Peter and you're Jesus, I'm saying I don't know you. And if you're Peter and I'm Jesus, you're saying you don't know me. But either way, you're playing Jesus because you're setting yourself up to be crucified . . .

JIM BOB: Not to my death.

CECIL: But why you would sacrifice me . . . after all the years and successes and failures and all the nights and days . . .

JIM BOB: I've done you harm by staying silent, by not speaking up sooner.

CECIL: We weren't hurting anyone.

JIM BOB: We've hurt a lot of people, Cecil. A lot of people.

CECIL: What if I said you were hurting me? What about me?

JIM BOB: Well, Cecil, now that I think about that . . .

CECIL: What?

JIM BOB: I'm suspect.

CECIL: Of what?

JIM BOB: That you can be hurt. Well, you cried for Judy Kay. I find that interesting. I've tried to get you to talk about your family for thirty years and you wouldn't ever confide in me.

CECIL: So this is jealousy? Because I was trying to get Judy Kay to loosen up?

JIM BOB: Actually, you cried when you were six years old and my daddy took your family a Christmas turkey because your mother and father were so poor.

CECIL: I don't remember that.

JIM BOB: Daddy always felt bad about it because you were so upset.

CECIL: We never took any damn charity.

JIM BOB: Yes, you did. You stood next to your mother crying and begging her not to take it but she did and you ran off into the woods, yelling back that you hated her and wished she was dead.

DELBERT: That's so sad.

CECIL: Your father had me mixed up with someone else.

JIM BOB: I was sitting in the back seat of my father's car, Cecil.

CECIL: I saw you in the back seat. For Christ sake. My parents couldn't afford to buy a damn turkey for Christmas. I always appreciated it that you had the courtesy not to mention it to me or anyone else. That's why I wanted you for my friend.

(A beat. Cecil goes to Delbert.)

How many friends have you got, Delbert?

DELBERT: Let's see. I mean, like to talk to?

CECIL: Yeah. You've got Doodie.

DELBERT: Doodie moved to Austin and we don't talk anymore.

CECIL: Well, who else?

DELBERT: Like to talk to a lot?

CECIL: God, yes. To talk to, to tell your troubles to . . .

DELBERT: I talk to my friend Sara.

CECIL: I don't count women.

DELBERT: Then I don't have any friends. But, it's OK. I'm used to being alone. I try to blend in because I got beat up a lot in high school. I make a better impression in the short term.

CECIL: Well, see, now, it's the same with most men. They don't have friends. They do if they're forced to have them, like in the Army or fighting someone. But I've always counted myself lucky that there was one person who was loyal — knowing me for the asshole that I am — one friend that I could count on. I had Jim Bob.

JIM BOB: We were never friends.

CECIL: Well, what the hell were we?

JIM BOB: Lovers.

CECIL: What?

JIM BOB: We were lovers.

CECIL: The hell you say. We were friends who had occasional sex.

JIM BOB: For thirty-two years?

CECIL: What the hell are you trying to do to me?

JIM BOB: I'm trying to tell you the truth. I fell in love with you the day you ran away from your mother. You broke my heart. You were beautiful and tragic. You wrote in my senior yearbook, "We exist in a place where souls meet."

CECIL: I was in my poet phase.

JIM BOB: "Let him deny himself and follow me."

CECIL: I don't get it.

JIM BOB: I didn't follow Jesus, I followed you . . . Cecil, you have ruined my life, you've ruined my family's lives, you've ruined your life and your family's lives because you could never admit that you loved me.

CECIL: Good God. You are so confused.

JIM BOB: No. I never saw clearer than I see at this moment and I thank God for my clarity.

CECIL: If I could get my hands on 200 milligrams of Thorazine, I'd force-feed you.

JIM BOB: I thought it was a Christian thing, never thinking of myself. But now I see my self-denial was my self-contempt. If you don't love me, I can't love myself, no matter how worthy I am.

CECIL: I will surely miss you.

DELBERT: *(To Jim Bob.)* You and Cecil are lovers?

JIM BOB: That's right.

CECIL: Jim Bob, now . . .

JIM BOB: Just admit three things to me. One, that you're gay.

CECIL: No.

JIM BOB: Two, that you're scared.

CECIL: I'm not scared, buddy.

JIM BOB: Three, that I'm not your buddy, that you love me.

(A pause.)

CECIL: Like a brother.

JIM BOB: Well, and that's that.

CECIL: Oh, hell, what's the big deal here Jim Bob?

JIM BOB: The truth, God help us!

CECIL: Well, here's the truth, friend. You know, it's like Delbert says, it's good to be gay. He's got it right. Hell, these days everyone is gay. And that's fine by me except for one stinking point. I don't give a fuck if someone is gay or not. I don't care if they fuck a pig. It's not anybody's goddamn business what I do and I don't want sex interfering with my damn life, understand?

JIM BOB: Then you shouldn't entice people to have sex with you in public places.

CECIL: I did not entice. I make use of a public facility.

JIM BOB: And me, you don't want me to interfere with your life.

CECIL: Not if you can't act right.

JIM BOB: Good. We'll just break up.

CECIL: You keep on talking like we've been together and I don't know where the hell you ever got that harebrained idea.

JIM BOB: You can honestly look at me and say that?

CECIL: I'm looking at you and I'm saying it.

JIM BOB: I love you.

CECIL: That's your problem.

JIM BOB: I've loved you my entire life.

CECIL: Like I say . . .

JIM BOB: Like you say what?

CECIL: You were wrong about that. I'm sorry. Look, now. I'm your best friend.

JIM BOB: Tulie is my best friend.

CECIL: All right, then I'm your next best friend. Jim Bob, I have given you everything you ever wanted. When did you ever want anything? When?

JIM BOB: I never needed your money.

CECIL: You needed it when I bailed your butt out of jail.

JIM BOB: Cecil, you can't buy me. You can buy Harold D. and Judy and Delbert but you can't buy me. I'll get you your bail money back.

CECIL: You're just tired. You always get cranky when you don't eat.

JIM BOB: It doesn't work for me anymore. If you learn anything from this, Delbert, learn this.

DELBERT: What?

JIM BOB: Don't take anything for granted. Especially when it comes to love. Find out exactly where you stand.

(Jim Bob begins giggling, hysterical. Cecil motions Delbert out of the room. Delbert exits. Cecil moves to Jim Bob.)

CECIL: Are you laughing or crying?

(No answer.)

Good God, Jim Bob. I wish I could help you out, buddy. I wish I could snap my fingers and feel a different way. You just never talked to me about any of this. You just presumed that I was taking this seriously. I never did. I'm sorry. I'm just like overwhelmed with this serious turn you've taken here and . . . damn, I'm grateful that somebody loves me, I am. I mean, thank you . . . *(A beat.)* Jim Bob, you're just worried about Tulie and all this shit. Look, I'm going to find us a way out. We'll wind up this thing pretty quick. Grab a shower, get some clean clothes. Find our cars. I'll get Tulie transferred to a private room on my ward. She'll be all right. We can order in a couple of pizzas, watch the game at the hospital . . .

(Another spasm of laughter.)

You're just in a mood. Moody since the first damn grade. A preacher can't afford to be moody. It's lucky you're a part-time accountant. I'm prescribing a complete physical for you once we get through this.

(No response.)

Look. You want me to say I was scared? I was scared. Last night I was scared. Those other men in the cell scared the shit out of me. I mean, I like sex but I like it on my terms, not somebody else's. So, I was scared.

(A moment.)

Just settle down, now. You don't want Delbert to see you like this. And Harold D. Christ, if Judy Kay comes in, she'll have a field day.

JIM BOB: Just tell me you love me.

CECIL: All right. Christ in Heaven, I love you.

(Jim Bob embraces Cecil.)

JIM BOB: I know it.

CECIL: But not like you want me to, not like I love Kay Nell.

JIM BOB: You don't love Kay Nell.

CECIL: She's the mother of my children. Now . . . I kid around but I do. I love my wife and my kids . . . let go of me . . . Jim Bob?

JIM BOB: You LOVE ME!

(Jim Bob kisses Cecil. Cecil reacts badly trying to pry Jim Bob's arms from around his body. Jim Bob has a firm grip on him.)

CECIL: Let go of me, GOD DAMN YOU! YOU TWISTED Mother-FUCKER!

(With one final wrench Cecil flings Jim Bob across the room.)

JIM BOB: OK! I'm sorry. I'm sorry. I get it!

(Cecil upends furniture, furious.)

CECIL: You don't have to do this. I can make it up to you. I'll make it up to you. I need you.

JIM BOB: No, you don't.

CECIL: I do.

JIM BOB: For what?

CECIL: To be there.

JIM BOB: For what?

CECIL: To just know me . . . you said before that I was the only one who knows you . . . well, that goes both ways . . .

JIM BOB: Somehow, I thought it did.

CECIL: Not like you want it to be. I'm not brave enough. Maybe if we had come at it from a different place.

JIM BOB: It's OK. I'm not asking . . .

CECIL: You are. YOU ARE! YOU ARE ASKING ME TO GIVE UP MY LIFE!!!

JIM BOB: No. Not anymore.

CECIL: OK. Then . . .

JIM BOB: I'm still telling the truth.

CECIL: Jim Bob.

JIM BOB: I won't bring you into it.

CECIL: They'll put you in jail.

JIM BOB: Well. I'll throw my net into the deep waters and take a plea bargain. I'm not making any more excuses.

CECIL: I'm not asking for excuses.

JIM BOB: My gosh, Cecil, not for you. I can't make excuses for myself.

CECIL: You say you love me.

JIM BOB: I do.

CECIL: Well I'm stumped. You don't betray the people you love.

JIM BOB: I give you my word. I won't incriminate you.

CECIL: They'll never believe I wasn't a part of it.

JIM BOB: People need you, you can save their lives.

CECIL: What about you? Don't you need me?

JIM BOB: You've given me so much — I'm truly grateful. I'll pray one day you'll understand why I'm doing this, Cecil. I'll pray to forgive you and I'll pray that you forgive me. I'll pray for you . . .

CECIL: Do not pray for me! I don't want you praying for me.

JIM BOB: I love you, Cecil.

CECIL: Then act like it.

(Jim Bob exits.)

CECIL: If you love me stay with me for Christ's sake!

(Jim Bob is gone.)

Jim Bob! Jim Bob?

(Cecil slumps in His chair.

Jesus H. Christ . . . Jim Bob?

END OF PLAY

LEARNING CURVE

Rogelio Martinez

PLAYWRIGHT'S BIOGRAPHY

Rogelio Martinez's new play *My First Radical* was workshopped this past summer at the Ojai Playwrights Conference. *Displaced* will have its world premiere in March 2006 at the Marin Theater Company. *Arrivals and Departures* was produced as part of the First Annual Summer Play Festival. In the fall of 2002, Mr. Martinez appeared on the cover of *American Theater* magazine where he was profiled as a playwright to watch. His play, *I Regret She's Made of Sugar,* is the recipient of a Princess Grace Award. *Sugar* was originally commissioned by South Cost Repertory. His one act, *Union City, NJ, Where Are You?,* was produced by Ensemble Studio Theater as part of the 25th Annual Marathon of One Act Plays and starred Rosie Perez. Mr. Martinez recently won a prestigious NEA/ TCG Residency Grant. He has worked extensively with younger writers through the Lincoln Center Open Stages program. Mr. Martinez is a graduate of Syracuse University and the Columbia University School of the Arts. He has taught at Columbia University and the City College of New York. Mr. Martinez is also a recipient of a grant from the New York Foundation for the Arts, and he is an alumnus of New Dramatists.

ORIGINAL PRODUCTION

Learning Curve, written by Rogelio Martinez, directed by Michael Sexton was presented by Besch Solinger Productions Inc. February 10 to 27, 2005, at The Beckett Theatre at Theatre Row Studios. The cast, in order of appearance:

JEFF/MARK/PAT/PHIL/STEVE	Daniel Talbott
JACKSON	Mike Hodge
DAVID	Demond Robertson
SALLY/STUDENT	Natalia Payne
LENDING LIBRARIAN/SUPERVISOR	John McAdams
STRAND	Graeme Malcolm
HENRY/PRICE/HOWIE	Chadwick Boseman
Set Design	Narelle Sissons
Costume Design	Suttirat Anne Larlarb
Original Music and Sound Design	Shane Rettig
Lighting Design	Justin Townsend
General Manager	Joseph Rosswog
Casting Director	Stephanie Holbrook
Production Manager	Craig SaNogueira
Stage Manager	Yvonne Perez
Public Relations & Publicity	Publicity Outfitters, Timothy Haskell
Portrait of David	by photographer Charlotte Nations

CHARACTERS

DAVID, eighteen in 1968
JACKSON, his older self in the present
SALLY/STUDENT
PROFESSOR HOLGER STRAND
HENRY/ PROFESSOR PRYCE/HOWIE
PROFESSOR LENDING
LIBRARIAN
JEFF/MARK/PAT/PHIL/STEVE

PLACE

A leading university in the Northeast.

TIME

The play takes place in 1968/69 and in the present.

ACKNOWLEDGEMENTS

I want to thank Rashaad Green, Matt Rauch, Royce Johnson, Greg Bratman, Airrion Doss, Laura Breckenridge, Leigh Silverman, and Mandy Hackett. Their talent and wisdom were invaluable. New Dramatists has always been there for me, and much of this play grew inside its walls. I would also like to thank Arielle Tepper and Rachel Neuberger for all their help. In addition, I'd like to thank the actors who gave so much of themselves. The director, Michael Sexton, collaborator and friend, created a theatrical world that flowed elegantly from past to present and vice versa. Lastly, I'd like to thank Betty Ann Besch Solinger for commissioning the play and then producing it. This play holds a special place in my heart. In writing it, I found myself outside a certain comfort zone. It made for an exhilarating experience — an experience I would not have had if it weren't for Ms. Solinger's perseverance and dedication.

LEARNING CURVE

ACT I
SCENE ONE

The present. Afternoon. A university classroom. Jackson, early fifties, is on stage. He looks around, slightly bewildered. After a moment, Jeff, twenty, enters.

JEFF: Hi.

JACKSON: Oh.

JEFF: I didn't mean to startle you.

JACKSON: It's OK. I should get —

JEFF: I can come back closer to the time.

JACKSON: What time is it?

JEFF: 2:40.

JACKSON: I must have been standing here . . . a very long time.

JEFF: Are you OK, man?

JACKSON: Yeah.

JEFF: First day of classes. No one knows where they're going. I used to think it was just a student problem. It isn't. Professors get lost too.

JACKSON: You're right.

JEFF: Room 319. This is —

JACKSON: It is.

JEFF: Good. Then this is where I belong. Look, the reason I'm here early is that I'm not registered. I messed up. Computer thing. Registration. Can't figure it out. Anyway, I was hoping to get in. I know the class is probably full, but well . . . Africana Studies . . . what can I say. What can I say? All right. It's important. It means a lot to me. OK. You're saying why does a white boy care but I do. I need this class. And I know because other people have told me that . . . well you don't make exceptions, but can I please get in to your class?

JACKSON: OK.

JEFF: Wow! Really? OK. That was easy.

JACKSON: If I were teaching the class, but I'm afraid . . . I'm afraid I'm just a student here.

JEFF: Uh-huh.

JACKSON: My first semester back in a long time. In a very long time.

JEFF: Oh. Well. OK. I'm sorry. I just thought — how old are you? Forget it. Don't answer that. Sometimes I can't stop myself. Would you like to be my study partner? Share notes. If I skip class — which I often do — you tell me what happened. That kind of stuff.

JACKSON: You're not in the class.

JEFF: I will be.

(Lights shift. At that moment, David enters. He is dressed conservatively — maybe a dark gray single-breasted polyester/wool blend suit. He looks around but does not see Jackson. After a moment, we start to hear sounds from a gymnasium. Soon we understand the sounds to be those of hundreds of teenagers running around introducing themselves to one another. A loud sound. A shift of light. The past has been set in motion.)

(1968. Sally enters, nineteen, and approaches David. She has a small camera around her neck.)

SALLY: Why aren't you playing?

DAVID: I'm OK.

SALLY: Not into the whole getting-to-know-you thing?

DAVID: No.

SALLY: You don't want to run around and try to meet as many young women as possible.

DAVID: I thought this was freshman orientation.

SALLY: It is. Kind of — what it really is . . . They guaranteed you'd meet fifty new people today. Kind of cool, isn't it?

DAVID: It all depends on who the people are.

SALLY: A young man with standards — that's rare in the middle of the sexual revolution.

DAVID: Is that what's going on?

SALLY: It's been going on. You're getting here kind of late.

DAVID: I'm sorry I missed it.

SALLY: You haven't — not completely. Stick with me.

DAVID: I'll just stand right here.

SALLY: You just like to watch?

DAVID: I didn't say that. Sometimes I watch; sometimes I join in.

SALLY: Oh, really. But tonight —

DAVID: I watch.

SALLY: What this is — want to know what tonight is about since you obviously haven't a clue?

DAVID: What are you talking about?

SALLY: First of all the way you're dressed. It's so sixties.

DAVID: It *is* the sixties.

SALLY: You got to be forward thinking — already I'm thinking about 1980. What will it all be like? Us for one.

DAVID: Us?

SALLY: Everything's changing. Everyone's throwing out old labels, trying out new things. Hey, do you shoplift?

DAVID: No! Why would you suggest —

SALLY: I do. Kind of. You go to the store. You switch sticker prices on items. You confuse the person at the register. That's what's happening. Everyone breaking out of what they were but into what . . . . I don't know. I guess even if you do switch sticker prices, you still have to pay for something, even if it is the wrong price.

DAVID: You've totally lost me.

SALLY: What's your major, mysterious black man?

DAVID: What did you say?

SALLY: Your major?

DAVID: No. Not that.

(Steve enters.)

STEVE: Hi. Steve. From Kalamazoo. Physics.

SALLY: Hi. Sally. From Hell. Get lost.

(Steve exits.)

SALLY: You're a fashionable man. The carnation on the lapel is a nice touch. Do you always do that?

DAVID: As long as I can remember.

SALLY: Why?

DAVID: Just something my father did.

SALLY: You're different, aren't you. All my life it's been Steve from Kalamazoo or Larry Lawrence from Lawrence, Kansas. Frightening. Who would do that to their kid, huh? Anyway, what matters is not where you come from, who your family is — what matters is this. Attraction.

DAVID: You're attracted to me?

SALLY: I wouldn't be talking to you if I weren't.

(She extends her hand.)

SALLY: Write on me.

DAVID: What?

SALLY: Your room number.

DAVID: People are looking.

SALLY: So?

DAVID: So? People are looking!

SALLY: Oh, just do it. Nothing is going to happen to you.

DAVID: How do you know?

SALLY: No one cares. Really.

(He writes it out for her.)

SALLY: I promise never to wash this hand as long as I live.

DAVID: I've got to go outside and get some air.

(He starts to exit. Sally runs after him almost bumping into Jackson. At the last minute, he moves out of the way.)

SALLY: What's your name?

DAVID: David.

SALLY: Hi, David. I'm Sally.

(She takes the flower and goes.)

(Blackout.)

SCENE TWO

1968. The university library. A stack of books. David is looking for a book. On the other side of the stack, Phil, a student, is doing the same. They find the book they're looking for at the same time. It turns out it's the same book. They pull, politely, for the book. Librarian stands nearby.

DAVID: I was —

PHIL: It's mine.

DAVID: What are you talking about?

PHIL: Let go.

DAVID: No.

PHIL: Let go, man.

DAVID: I need this book.

PHIL: And I don't?

DAVID: Find another one.

PHIL: I was here first.

DAVID: Who says?

PHIL: LET GO!

DAVID: NO!!

LIBRARIAN: Shhhhh!

DAVID: I'm not letting go.

PHIL: I'll flip you for it.

DAVID: No.

PHIL: Just be reasonable.

DAVID: Forget it.

PHIL: What is your problem? Take the fucking book. I hope you fucking flunk — forget hoping, you're going to flunk. YOU HEAR ME. FLUNK. FAILURE.

LIBRARIAN: Gentleman!!!

(David walks over to the desk with a large stack of books. As soon as he sees him, the Librarian starts talking.)

LIBRARIAN: Oh, no. No. No. No. No. No good.

DAVID: Huh?

(Librarian points to a sign.)

LIBRARIAN: Five-book maximum.

DAVID: Oh. Sorry.

LIBRARIAN: Some of those have to go back now. Let the brilliant Melvil Dewey help you. Now which five?

(David looks through the books.)

Where is your ID?

DAVID: I don't have one yet. I'm a freshman. They told us we'd get ours —

LIBRARIAN: Oh, no. No. No. No. No. No good.

DAVID: What?

LIBRARIAN: You have to wait. I can't do anything without — how do I know you didn't just walk off the street?

DAVID: I'm just trying to get ahead —

LIBRARIAN: Do you have a driver's license?

DAVID: No. But I can't afford —

LIBRARIAN: Next!

DAVID: What can I do?

LIBRARIAN: Not my department.

DAVID: Can you hold these for me while I go try to get this —

LIBRARIAN: I'm responsible for everything on this desk. This is the nerve center of the university. What if you don't return and those books don't make it back on the shelves? Do you know what happens then? The university has a nervous breakdown. You wouldn't want this school to shut down, would you?

DAVID: Five books?

LIBRARIAN: Next! I can't deal with someone without an ID. I have BIG responsibilities. Ordering books — private collections — authors leave us their letters — where are you going?

(David exits. He leaves the books behind.)

Hey. These have to go back. Young man. Hey!
(*Blackout.*)

SCENE THREE

*Night. David enters his room. His roommate, Pat, is there wearing pajamas
and conducting Janacek. David watches. After a moment, the roommate
spots David.*

DAVID: Would you turn that down a little. I just need to get some rest.
   (*Pat does. David lies down to get some rest. After a moment, the music swells.
   David bolts up.*)
DAVID: Come on, man. I need to get some sleep.
PAT: There's a half hour left.
DAVID: A half hour?
PAT: It's about a woman who possesses the secret of eternal youth. This knowl-
   edge destroys her. I want you to listen to this moment.
   (*He gets up on the bed and continues to conduct his private orchestra. David
   looks on. After a moment, Pat falls back exhausted.*
PAT: So, what do you think?
DAVID: I think you're nuts, man.
PAT: No, really, what do you think?
DAVID: No, really, I think you're nuts. You're going to be playing that all se-
   mester?
PAT: I don't say anything about the kind of music you like.
DAVID: You don't know the kind of music I like.
   (*David walks over and shuts off the record player.*)
PAT: Don't touch that. This record player, it's a gift — graduation. What I'm
   trying to say — not that I don't think you know how to . . . or that you
   wouldn't — what I'm trying to say — . I have a great idea! I'm going to
   draw a line on the floor. That way we can separate the room, two spaces,
   you understand? (*Pat draws a line.*) That over there is your side. I'm a
   total mess, and I wouldn't want it to spill over to your side. That make
   sense? Now I'm going to go spend the night with someone who appreci-
   ates Janacek. (*Pat takes his record and leaves.*)
   (*David lies back in bed. A moment of peace. Then there is a soft knock on
   the door. He walks over and opens it. Sally walks in.*)
DAVID: What are you doing here?

SALLY: You gave me your room number.

DAVID: I know. I know. But you're not supposed to be here. It's after hours.

SALLY: Then why did you give me your room number?

DAVID: I guess . . . to get you to go away.

SALLY: Now does that make much sense to you?

DAVID: People were starting to look over. I was nervous. Anyway, it's after hours. You really can't be here. They have rules, Sally.

SALLY: For people who choose to follow them.

DAVID: I'm a dead man. If someone found you here in my room . . . . What if my roommate comes back?

SALLY: David, you're in college. People walk in on one another all the time. As soon as he walks in I'll talk to him.

(Pause.)

DAVID: He's not coming.

SALLY: What?

DAVID: He said he was going to spend the night over at a friend's. He drew that line there. I'm not supposed to cross over to his side.

(She crosses over.)

SALLY: There. There aren't any barriers I'm not willing to cross.

(David smiles.)

DAVID: God, Sally, what are you doing here!

SALLY: I'm here because I like you.

DAVID: You don't even know me.

SALLY: And you don't know me. So what?

DAVID: I'm here on scholarship — to get an education.

SALLY: That's what I intend to give you.

DAVID: Very funny.

(They kiss.)

SALLY: Why are you so nervous? *(She laughs.)* An education, huh? Have you seen what's happening? What educated people are doing to the world. If you want an education, go over to Vietnam. Get a job cleaning toilets. Get out of the university, for God's sake. This is not the place — this is not where you come to get an education. This is where you come to get laid — if you're lucky, which you are — this is where you experiment with drugs, disappoint your folks, and drink a lot. Make love to me.

DAVID: I've never —

SALLY: Sure you have.

DAVID: No, I mean with someone like you.

SALLY: What do you mean someone like me?

DAVID: Like you . . . like . . . well like you.

SALLY: Oh, with a photography major — it's understandable. Not a big department. Well, I can tell you that it's not that different — other than the nude photos I'll have to shoot for the student newspaper.

DAVID: You know what I mean.

(Pause.)

SALLY: I know what you mean, but college is a whole different world.

DAVID: Is it?

SALLY: I promise it is. OK?

(Sally is almost undressed. She goes into her large purse and takes out two wigs, a blond and a red.)

Now who do you want me to be?

DAVID: You carry those around.

SALLY: Variation. In case you get bored with who I am.

DAVID: I don't even know who you are.

SALLY: Do you like me this way?

DAVID: Yes.

SALLY: You won't always.

DAVID: That's not —

SALLY: Everyone gets bored, David.

(They kiss. It's more passionate than before. Intense.)

Groovy.

(Lights off on Sally and David.)

(Lights shift.)

(The present.)

(Jackson. The library. The Librarian is there.)

JACKSON: I was hoping to find some information on Professor Strand.

LIBRARIAN: Oh, no. No. No. No. No. It's not my job to look things up.

JACKSON: You're a librarian.

LIBRARIAN: You think that's all we do. We have BIG responsibilities. Ordering books — private collections — authors leave us their letters — everything from an outline for a novel they didn't write to a Con Edison bill they didn't pay. Why a Con Edison bill is of any scholarly interest is beyond my imagination. Regardless, we catalog it. The past is well documented here.

JACKSON: I just thought I would ask you —

LIBRARIAN: There are two computers over there.

(Jackson starts to walk toward the computers.)

You need an ID to use them.

(Jackson returns and takes out an ID. The Librarian examines it.)

JACKSON: How long have you worked here?

LIBRARIAN: Why?

JACKSON: Not everything changes.

LIBRARIAN: Thank God!

(Jackson goes.)
(Lights shift.)
(Sally and David. Morning.)
(A light is turned on over a bed. Sally and David lie naked there. She reaches over for her camera and gets ready to take a picture. Then she puts her bra over his eyes and takes a picture. He wakes.)

DAVID: What the heck is this?

SALLY: Don't take it off. Leave it.

DAVID: What is it?

SALLY: What does it smell like?

DAVID: Baby powder.

SALLY: And?

(He takes it off and opens his eyes.)

DAVID: Your bra. You put your bra on my face. You're a weird bird, Sally.

(She takes another picture.)

Hey! What are you doing?

SALLY: I'm taking a picture of you.

DAVID: Why?

SALLY: You're interesting.

DAVID: Should I expect it in tomorrow's paper?

SALLY: No one will see it. Now do you want to keep the bra? I think you should have something of mine.

DAVID: Your bra?

SALLY: A souvenir. Aren't you sentimental?

DAVID: I'm surprised you even have one. The first day I was here I saw a bon-fire — girls just like you just burning their bras.

(She pulls on it.)

SALLY: Oh, no, see here. This is an expensive one. For demonstrations I use cheap bras — the kind that almost always combust as soon as I light them.

(She tosses him the bra.)

SALLY: Let me take another photo.

DAVID: I'm feeling kind of naked right now.

SALLY: That's because you are kind of naked, Sweets.

(She throws him his jeans then jumps into bed with him. They kiss.)
Thank you.

DAVID: I want to ask you a question.

SALLY: What?

DAVID: Did you come up to me last night . . . .

SALLY: Say it.

DAVID: Was it because . . . I just need to know. Was it because I'm —

SALLY: Variation on a theme. *(Short pause.)* Of course, it wasn't just because —

DAVID: But that means —

SALLY: That I like you. That's all it means. Did you sleep with me because I was —

DAVID: No.

SALLY: You didn't let me finish. Was it because I was the only one who came up to you last night?

DAVID: What do you mean?

SALLY: No one was talking to you.

DAVID: I didn't think we'd end up doing it — fooling around, yeah, but how did we end up —

SALLY: You were on top.

DAVID: Am I making this up or were there wigs involved?

SALLY: There were a lot of things involved.

DAVID: I think it was . . . good.

SALLY: It was GREAT!

DAVID: OK. It was. I wanted to make sure you had a good time.

SALLY: A sensitive man. How lucky.

(She takes another picture of him.)

DAVID: Hey!

SALLY: You're in good company. You know who was in my first picture? Ike. Dad was shaking hands with him. A little Canon P, basic camera, but I was hooked. Later Dad gave me his old Ensign Commando which he got during the Korean War and I was off and running, exploring classic cameras, that kind of thing. But this Leica M4, it's the best. Silent, you know.

DAVID: What did you just take a picture of?

(She starts laughing.)

Did you just take a picture of my underwear?

(It's on the floor. She picks it up.)

I want to know everything about you. Size—

DAVID: Give me that.

SALLY: Mmmm. Let me be the first one to say it, David, you've outgrown this size. You need new underwear.

DAVID: Give it to me now.

(She plays with his underwear. He tries to grab it from her. He chases her. Finally he catches her but not before she takes a second picture of his underwear.)

SALLY: I like you holding me like this.

DAVID: I like it too.

SALLY: It's so convenient having the room to yourself.

DAVID: This kind of thing would never happen at home.

SALLY: Why?

DAVID: If you saw me you'd probably cross the street.

SALLY: You don't know me. Sex doesn't give you the right to assume things about me, David.

DAVID: It's just that most people —

SALLY: I'm not most people. Haven't you figured that out by now? And anyway this isn't the real world. This is a university. As far from reality as you can possibly get. You know last year's freshman orientation wasn't as exciting.

DAVID: You're a sophomore?

SALLY: I'm a junior.

DAVID: A junior?!

SALLY: You can learn a lot from an older woman. You're here for an education, aren't you?

DAVID: Yeah. OK. What would you call last night?

SALLY: I'd call it S321. Variations in Human Sexuality.

DAVID: Is there a second part to this class?

SALLY: Why? Do you intend on taking it?

DAVID: Of course.

SALLY: S322. Deviant Behavior and Social Control. Still interested?

DAVID: As long as I'm teaching it.

SALLY: OK, Professor. I'm there. Shit. What time is it? I'm going to be late. What about you?

DAVID: What?

SALLY : Any classes today?

DAVID: In the afternoon. This guy who I think — no I know — hates me. Just has this awful way of looking at me.

SALLY: Why don't you just drop the class?

DAVID: I'm not about to give him the satisfaction.

SALLY: What class?

DAVID: Nineteenth Century European History.

SALLY: The Utopian Socialists?

DAVID: How did you know?

SALLY: Oh, dear. I think I know the professor.

DAVID: He's full of himself. Loves to hear himself talk.

SALLY: I think it's he.

DAVID: The man doesn't even bother learning the students' names. It's as if we didn't exist.

SALLY: It's definitely he.

DAVID: You know who I'm talking about?

SALLY: Professor Strand. He's my father.

DAVID: That's your father?!

SALLY: Yes.

DAVID: Your last name is Strand?

SALLY: What's yours?

DAVID: I can't believe this.

SALLY: Tell him you're screwing his daughter — you might get some extra credit.

DAVID: It's not funny.

SALLY: Hey, I'm the one who has had to live with him these last twenty years.

DAVID: I can't see you again. What if he finds out?

SALLY: I'm not going to tell him. Are you? Look, people like my father — their world is coming apart because of people like us . . . because of what we're doing here.

DAVID: We've had sex once and we can't be seen in public.

SALLY: Why not?

DAVID: You know what would happen to me if they caught us? I'd lose my scholarship.

SALLY: That's not true.

DAVID: Or worse.

SALLY: I get it. OK? But I really like you, and if you want to keep it a secret that's all right with me.

DAVID: Sally?

SALLY: And we did it more than once.

DAVID: You're overwhelming. This whole thing is overwhelming. They told me I'd have to adjust. I wasn't sure what they were talking about. Then I come here. I start to walk around and no one looks like me. I can't let the people back home down.

SALLY: *(Smiling.)* So last night was kind of like a letdown — is that what you're saying?

DAVID: No. I was —

SALLY: I know what you're saying. But now you have someone who's on your side. We're in this together. You're not going to let anyone down. I promise, Professor. See you next class.

(Sally goes.)

(Blackout.)

SCENE FOUR

Holger Strand is on stage lecturing.

STRAND: "At this moment nothing but the Army preserves us from that most dreadful of all calamities, an insurrection of the poor against the rich, and how long the Army may be depended on is a question which I scarcely dare ask myself . . . the country is mined beneath our feet." Sir Walter Scott.

It's during this time that history — with a wicked smile I might add — watches the Utopian Socialists fumble their way through life. Inspired. Contradictory. Mystifying. You could say they were pretty much down right nuts. That's what makes them so much fun.

Robert Owen born in 1771, died 1858. Mr. Owen spends the first half of his life profiting off his fellow man, his second half making up for it through a series of wild schemes that fail time and again. At the foundation of each of these schemes was the belief that education was the key to reform — how naïve. Though praised for his unusual pedagogy — he was fond of having children spend time with watercolors and music — he was nevertheless a failure in his most ambitious project: to reform those he had taken such pleasure in exploiting.

Mr. Owen tried to do the impossible, create villages of cooperation in which no less than a thousand men and women worked together in hopes of what? Forming a self-sustaining unit. Owen was convinced that mankind was as good as his environment and that if the environment was a positive one a real paradise on earth might be achieved. He was sure that the wretched of the earth — or some other more fashionable term — that these men and women would become the producers of wealth and that their social habits — their deviant ways — would change if the environment around them were a more pleasing one.

Owen was laughed out of England along with his merry paupers who by then knew how to take tea and smile politely, play the piano and paint. They found a new home in New Harmony, Indiana. Yes. America. I'm often surprised they didn't end up here at this university. Regardless, after a few years, several members of the community got caught with their hands in the cookie jar; and that along with bad planning, lack of realistic goals, sent Mr. Owen home. No environment could do for these men what Owen wanted done.

Please read Engels' essay on Robert Owen. You will be tested.

Next week I'll discuss Count Henri de Rouvroy de Saint-Simon, who argued that the beaver would one day replace man as the most intelligent animal. And looking at you now, I'm afraid that day has arrived. Class dismissed.

(Blackout.)

SCENE FIVE

Jeff and Jackson studying in the cafeteria.

JEFF: Hey. David. What were you thinking about?

JACKSON: Years ago. I used to work here.

JEFF: Was the food always this bad?

JACKSON: Believe it or not, it was worse. Now at least they put something green on the plate.

JEFF: You worked here every day.

JACKSON: We have a test tomorrow. That's the reason we're here.

JEFF: Oh, come on. You were a ladies' man, weren't you?

JACKSON: What?

JEFF: I bet they lined up just to get your number.

JACKSON: First question.

JEFF: What's it like to be back?

JACKSON: He's not going to ask that.

JEFF: Obviously something brought you back.

JACKSON: The test.

JEFF: Huh? Oh. Pryce is definitely going to ask about Tuskegee. Founder?

JACKSON: Booker T. Washington. Criticism?

JEFF: The Great Accommodator.

JACKSON: Go on.

JEFF: He didn't push for civil/political rights with whites. More? His emphasis on vocational training. Not interested in a university education for African Americans. Well?

JACKSON: A little more complicated than that. He was interested in African Americans taking responsibility for themselves. He pushed for a vocational education because it would improve our economic situation.

JEFF: I don't need that much information to get it right.

JACKSON: You're trying to learn something.

JEFF: I'm trying to pass a test. The learning is what I do hanging out with you.

JACKSON: What do you mean?

JEFF: You can teach me more than that book. I mean, how does it feel to be discriminated against? How does it feel to be singled out?

JACKSON: Not my job, Jeff. Sorry. Wrong guy. Not your instructor.

JEFF: Not your job but . . . I don't know. Have I just — did I just offend you? OK. Let me . . . I'm wondering why I don't have one single black friend.

JACKSON: You're going to have to ask yourself that question.

JEFF: I hear about everything that happened in the sixties . . . wonderful things, right? But nothing has changed, has it?

JACKSON: Some things have.

JEFF: Really?

JACKSON: Back then there were only two black students in my residence hall. Fewer than three hundred in the entire campus.

JEFF: Did you have any white friends?

JACKSON: I knew some white people. Some of them wanted to save me. Some of them wanted to hit me. I'm not sure any of them were my friends.

JEFF: The instructor thing before . . . I was just . . .

(During the following conversation, an African American student is walking around collecting dirty dishes. This same student will play Henry in the next scene.)

JACKSON: I walk around and it's odd, but I start to catch glimpses of myself — lying on the Arts Quad before classes, drinking coffee near McGraw Tower; but back then I always felt like I was being watched. Like someone was waiting for me to do the wrong thing. That's different now. People for the most part leave me alone.

JEFF: Do you have a picture?

JACKSON: A picture?

JEFF: I would love to see what you looked like back then.

JACKSON: You don't need to see. I can tell you. Scared. I was scared out of my mind.

JEFF: Why?

JACKSON: First time away from home.

JEFF: I've been waiting all my life to get away from home.

JACKSON: When I was young I never thought I would leave Florida. Ever. It never crossed my mind.

JEFF: So what happened?

JACKSON: Someone talked to me about possibility and snow and I bought into it all.

(Lights shift.)

(The past.)

(David is doing the dishes in the cafeteria. Next to him is Henry, a black student of David's age. For a moment they do their work. Then Henry whispers.)

HENRY: Revolution.

DAVID: What?

HENRY: Nothing.

(They work some more.)

Revolution.

(David works.)

Revolution.

DAVID: All right, man. I heard it.

HENRY: You heard it but did you understand it. Revolution, David.

DAVID: How do you know my name?

HENRY: Keep your voice down.

DAVID: Who are you? What do you want?

(Henry hands David a newspaper.)

HENRY: Take a look at page 23.

DAVID: We got work to do.

HENRY: That there is *The New York Times.* The newspaper of record. Go on. Page 23.

(David looks at the newspaper. He opens it.)

DAVID: This is just an ad for Quaker Oats.

HENRY: Huh?

DAVID: Quaker Oats. Look. Whoever you are.

HENRY: Let me see that.

DAVID: Leave me alone.

(Henry looks through the newspaper.)

HENRY: Page 32. Look. Come on. Just look at it.

(David does.)

DAVID: So?

HENRY: My brother at Columbia.

DAVID: This really your brother?

HENRY: They took his picture at a sit-in. He's got the Denton family profile. Huh? Good looking.

DAVID: Yeah, well. What's your point?

HENRY: That's just a sit-in and look at the coverage it got. What we have in mind, what we want is bigger than that.

DAVID: What are you talking about?

HENRY: I've been keeping fit all semester 'cause I know I'm going to be in *The New York Times.*

DAVID: OK. Now I got some real work to do.

HENRY: Work? You call this work? Word is you a bit of a fool? Is that true?

DAVID: Who are you?

HENRY: I'm your brother, man. One of the only brothers you got.

(Suddenly, a Supervisor walks by. The two young men return to working.)

SUPERVISOR: You got to really scrub these. Hey, you hear. You're the new kid, right?

DAVID: Yeah.

SUPERVISOR: A couple have been sent back. That's not the first complaint. You got to use real force. No one said it was going to be easy. I got my eye on you.

(Supervisor exits.)

HENRY: That guy is nuts. He takes his job a little too seriously — thinks this some kind of prison. And you know what, he's right — he don't know it but he's right. I let them go dirty.

DAVID: You?

HENRY: They let us in this school just so we could do their dishes, David. They got no intention of doing anything for us. I mean, look around, most people working here are black. They give us some money to get here and they expect us to serve their food, wash their dishes, a new kind of servitude. That's higher education in this country. Oh, name's Henry.

DAVID: Look, Henry, I need this job. Just leave me alone.

HENRY: They killing our people and you just playing with your dick. This is war, David.

DAVID: I just want to finish this and go home. I got to read the last fifty pages of a novel by noon.

HENRY: What novel?

DAVID: *Hard Times.*

HENRY: Oh, brother, I'll tell you something about hard times — you want to hear about my life?

DAVID: Look, man, just leave me alone.

HENRY: You learning?

DAVID: Yeah.

HENRY: I don't have time to learn — too busy teaching brothers like you who think you can stay outside of it all. This is about you as much as it is about me.

DAVID: Thanks, but I'm not interested.

HENRY: Hard times. Hard times, my ass. You're living in the most historically important moment in the history of the country, and all you want to do is look back.

DAVID: Are you serious? You actually believe that?

HENRY: I'm alive, ain't I? I'm living in it. And I happen to think I'm very important.

DAVID: If things are so bad here, why don't you just drop out?

HENRY: I have a purpose. Watch out when a black man discovers his purpose!

DAVID: And what's your purpose?

HENRY: I'm here to change the monolithic system that is Western Thought. In fact, today we pulling some books out from the library shelves. Why don't you come?

DAVID: I got to study — probably from the same books you pulling.

HENRY: We ain't pulling Dickens yet. The guy wrote too many books. He'd be more of a long term project.

DAVID: Just do your thing and I'll do mine.

HENRY: You're in the middle of a revolution. You're either in or out. You join the Afro American Society or you lose. What's it going to be?

DAVID: Look what you're doing with those dishes.

(He grabs a dish from Henry and starts to clean it.)

HENRY: David?

(David turns his back to Henry. He continues to clean the dishes.)
(Lights shift.)

SCENE SIX

David is in Strand's office.

STRAND: Mr. Jackson.

DAVID: Yes.

STRAND: I am professor Holger Strand.

DAVID: I know that. I'm in your class.

STRAND: We haven't met. Officially. Have a seat. Now do you have an itch, Mr. Jackson?

DAVID: What?

STRAND: You fidget — in class. Often. Do you need me to scratch your back? I'm not a touchy-feely professor but if that's what this university asks of me . . .

DAVID: No.

STRAND: You must be absolutely still. Even now. You're fidgeting.

DAVID: When?

STRAND: I saw you.

DAVID: You serious?

STRAND: There.

DAVID: But —

STRAND: You just did it again. I have things to say but the moment someone moves — you just did it again, and I know this time you did it on purpose.

DAVID: All right. All right.

STRAND: You've declared an interest in a history degree; therefore, I have somewhat ironically been given the job of academic advisor. How wonderful for the both of us. I see that in your transcript —

DAVID: Is that it?

STRAND: Yes. I was looking over it and it states you're Negro.

DAVID: What?

STRAND: Surprised, Mr. Jackson? You are Negro according to your transcript.

DAVID: Uh-huh.

STRAND: Do you disagree — some color variation I'm not aware of?

DAVID: No. If it's written down it must be correct.

STRAND: You're here courtesy of the Committee on Special Educational Projects. In other words, you don't have to do well, you just have to do your best. That's unfortunate.

DAVID: Look, I'm just here for some advice. I want to know about this language requirement. I'm not sure what to take —

STRAND: Mr. Jackson.

DAVID: What?

STRAND: Did you hear me? How unfortunate.

DAVID: How unfortunate what?

STRAND: That this university has put us all in a terrible position. I'm not sure what to do with you — not even sure what to do with my class. In fact, I am sure. I'll continue to teach it the same way. I will expect no less from them, from you. But. And this is important, so please listen —

(Students are heard outside protesting the war. "Hey, hey, LBJ, how many kids did you kill today?" "Ho, ho, Ho Chi Minh!" At that moment, a smoke bomb comes flying through the window landing right on the desk. It fails to go off.)

DAVID: What's that?

STRAND: That's democracy in action. Things are done differently nowadays. Forget old-fashioned values, hard work, merit — now anyone with a magic marker and a loud enough vocal instrument feels they have the right to tell you how the world should be run.

DAVID: Is that a bomb?

STRAND: This? It's the sixties, Mr. Jackson. What do you expect?

DAVID: What are you going to do?

STRAND: They can't even get a smoke bomb to go off. Throw it back out at them.

DAVID: You want me to pick that up?

STRAND: Would you rather it stay there?

DAVID: It's a bomb, man.

STRAND: It's a smoke bomb. What are you afraid of?

(Strand goes over to the window.)

Let's see who it is now. Oh, of course. Students for a Democratic Society. Half of them don't even know what the word *democracy* means because supposedly they've spent all their college years fighting for it.

(Strand handles the bomb.)

There. It should go off now. Would you like to do the honors?

DAVID: I'm not touching it.

(Strand throws the bomb back out. We hear students run for cover.)

STRAND: COWARDS! You want advice, Mr. Jackson? Don't pull that kind of stunt — don't take over this office. Just last year several black students occupied the office of the Arts and Sciences dean, and the fool sat there making phone calls while they stood around him with signs protesting the lack of black professors.

DAVID: Are there any?

STRAND: What?

DAVID: I haven't come across any black professors —

STRAND: There is a proper way to do things — renting a bullhorn and letting your hair grow long is not one of them. Now I have no problem with you . . . your color.

DAVID: But you don't think I belong here.

STRAND: I happen to think you don't belong here because you hurt the academic integrity of this university. If the level of discussion in the class happens to be brought down by a question or two you decide to ask, then we all pay a price. Ultimately, you pay the biggest price because you will never get the answers you're looking for at a pace that's slow enough for it to make a difference in your life.

(Sally enters.)

SALLY: Oh, hi.

DAVID: Hi.

STRAND: As soon as I'm done we can go — you two know each other?

SALLY: Yes.

DAVID: No.

SALLY: Right. Hi. I'm Sally.

STRAND: Do you mind?

SALLY: What's your name?

STRAND: Sally.

SALLY: I'm just asking. *(To David.)* Have we met?

DAVID: What do you mean?

SALLY: You look familiar. No. I'd remember, wouldn't I? Well. Good luck. I'll be right outside.

(Sally exits.)

STRAND: Where were we?

DAVID: I was looking for advice.

STRAND: Lay off her.

DAVID: What?

STRAND: You're here, Mr. Jackson. You've been given a chance. Do your work as well as you can but don't get involved in all that other stuff. Don't get swallowed up by the moment.

DAVID: You're going to change your mind about where I belong, Professor.

STRAND: Where did your father go to college?

DAVID: He didn't.

STRAND: Your mother?

DAVID: No, sir.

STRAND: My father was the first in his family to go to college. He went to a state school in Illinois. I followed by going to Colgate, then Korea, and returning to finish at the University of Illinois. My daughter — Sally — goes to this university. Each generation does better than the last. You are the first to go to college, Mr. Jackson. Congratulations. But you belong in a different school. These people who have brought you here have brought you here under false pretenses. You're not a student here. You're someone's project. These COSEP people are meeting legal requirements, assuaging their guilt, and trying to change the world.

DAVID: Robert Owen?

STRAND: Yes. Exactly. Insane. Softheaded. Sentimental. Good luck, Mr. Jackson.

(David turns to go.)

Sally has a lot of interesting friends. She wanted to join the International Red Cross when she was seven. I brought home a little ambulance with little figures. The normal fare. The driver. The medic. The victim — of course she ripped him apart and made him limbless almost immediately. That one soon became her favorite. Watch that she doesn't rip you apart, Mr. Jackson.

(David exits.)

SCENE SEVEN

The present. An empty art gallery. Jackson is looking around. Student enters.

STUDENT: Hey. Man. What are you doing?

JACKSON: What?

STUDENT: What are you looking at? The walls are empty. Dude. There's nothing on the wall. Hey, guy. Hey! White paint. And it's not art. Hey. Are you high? Hey, man. What's wrong? You're not looking at art. It's Dutch Boy. Solitude.

JACKSON: I just want to look around. Do you mind? Thank you.

(Student exits.)

(Lights shift.)

(1968. A gallery. Several of Sally's pictures are up. They are under the

caption: A Study in Oppression. The pictures are of David in various stages
of undress. However, his face is never clear. Also, there are some smaller pho-
tographs. Objects. David's pillow for one and his underwear lying carelessly
on the floor.)

(Sally enters followed by Strand.)

SALLY: I can't believe you're here.

STRAND: You invited me.

SALLY: So. You missed my recital.

STRAND: Sally, you were eight years old. When are you going to let that go?

SALLY: I learned early on not to expect you to do the right thing. *(Pause.)* OK.
Look. Let's start over. *(She takes a deep breath.)* I can't believe you're here.

STRAND: You invited me.

SALLY: No. No. No.

STRAND: What?

SALLY: You're supposed to say you wouldn't miss it for the world.

STRAND: Of course, I wouldn't miss it. Your photographs are causing a bit of
a stir.

SALLY: Other students in the class have their photos up, but mine get all the
attention.

STRAND: Interesting pictures, Sally.

SALLY: Are they good? Oh, forget it. I don't know why I ask you. I don't care
what you think. A lot of people — smart people — have told me they're
good.

STRAND: Then I must be a very smart man.

SALLY: What?

(He smiles.)

STRAND: I think they're wonderful. Now what is this business I hear about
your going to the ghetto to take the pictures?

SALLY: The ghetto. What a sensational word.

STRAND: Sensational or not, it's dangerous.

SALLY: Whatever.

STRAND: No. Listen. I'm concerned. Who is he anyway? And why is he just
wearing underwear? It's slightly embarrassing.

SALLY: Oh, don't be so old-fashioned.

STRAND: You missed his face.

SALLY: Huh?

STRAND: He has no face.

SALLY: I cropped it out on purpose.

STRAND: Why? What's a picture without a face?

SALLY: Art.

STRAND: And in this one — is that some kind of bra over his face?

SALLY: Yes.

STRAND: Why couldn't he have covered the rest of his body.

SALLY: Dad, why can't you just like them? Not everything has to have an explanation.

STRAND: Where is the wine?

SALLY: What?

STRAND: I tried to be nice.

(Strand exits.)

(David is there.)

DAVID: I can't believe you did this.

SALLY: I had to.

DAVID: Why?

SALLY: I brought one into class. It was such a great picture.

DAVID: Why would you do that?

SALLY: I just wanted one other person to see these photographs. To tell me that they were good.

DAVID: An entire class, Sally.

SALLY: Smile.

DAVID: What?

SALLY: Dad is looking over here.

DAVID: Get rid of them.

SALLY: The professor asked me where I got it. The one question I was not prepared to answer. It never occurred to me he might ask. I couldn't just say it was you. That we had just had sex. You were so freaked out about even giving me your room number. You didn't want to lose your scholarship. And then my professor just started to talk. And I let him.

(A light on Dr. Lending, photography professor.)

LENDING: This is a familiar figure near bus depots and train stations. His almost nude body demonstrates his few possessions or perhaps simply a lack of self-esteem. In your photograph we are confronted with the past, with slavery and the price this generation of black men has had to pay for it. There is hope in the photograph — hope that perhaps for this exhausted man the worst is behind him. Is it? We are left with a question. Congratulations.

(Lights off on Lending.)

SALLY: He just assumed you were some homeless guy. He asked me if I had shot others. I brought them in. Oh, god. You're not mad at me, are you? I mean, you're mad but not really mad, right?

DAVID: Take them down.

SALLY: When the time is right, I plan to confront them with the truth.

DAVID: The time is right right now.

SALLY: I'll tell them. See, I fooled you. I fooled you because you wanted to be fooled. You had this young man walking among you and you refused to see him for who he was. Instead, you chose to believe the photograph because it represents something that's familiar, obvious.

DAVID: I don't want them up.

SALLY: Trust me. The truth has never helped anyone get anything.

DAVID: And you said you want to be a journalist. You're a very scary girl.

SALLY: I'm not a girl, David. Or have you missed the whole point of the sixties.

DAVID: What's going to stop me from telling the truth?

SALLY: Nothing I suppose. Nothing at all.
    (Pause.)
    Oh, David, I think I'm in love with you.

DAVID: Then just do this for me.

SALLY: Nothing is going to happen.

DAVID: I'm not a liar. I don't like to lie.

SALLY: Just . . . look . . . let's talk about this later before Daddy gets suspicious.
    (Sally exits.)
    (Henry enters. He gets close to David who is looking at one of the photographs.)

HENRY: Interesting pictures.

DAVID: Shit man. You scared me.

HENRY: I like art.

DAVID: Good for you.

HENRY: Have you checked out some of the other photos? Not as interesting. Do you think photography is art?

DAVID: I don't know . . . I don't really —

HENRY: What do you think of these pictures?

DAVID: What do you mean?

HENRY: Any good?

DAVID: Yeah.

HENRY: Really?

DAVID: What do you want?
    (Henry whispers.)

HENRY: I got a gun.

DAVID: For what? I don't want to know. Good for you, that's all I have to say.

HENRY: It's for you, man.

DAVID: No, thank you.

HENRY: You screwing the professor's daughter. How is that going?

DAVID: How do you know that? You watching me?

HENRY: We got Howie on you.

DAVID: Who's Howie?

HENRY: You haven't heard of Howie? Howie who-can-shoot-a-gun-really-well. He transferred here from West Point.

DAVID: He's pointing a gun at me?

HENRY: He's pointing a gun at Western Thought. You happened to be hiding right behind it.

DAVID: What the heck is he doing at a university?

HENRY: Trying to fight for what we should have — what's ours. An education. More shelf space for the kinds of books we should be reading. Equal rights. Look at the numbers — look at how few of us there are. Anyway, he just happens to shoot a little better than most of us. Not that we're bad. Point blank we can do just about anything, and this is quickly getting to be a point-blank situation.

DAVID: And guns are the answer?

HENRY: They ain't the problem.

DAVID: I'm not here to get involved with guns.

HENRY: You're already involved.

DAVID: What?

HENRY: Moment you were born you were involved. It's about time you learned that. Let Howie teach you.

DAVID: Stop talking about this Howie guy for a moment.

HENRY: Violence ain't all bad, David. Sometimes a good explosion is what you need to wake everyone up.

(Henry takes out a gun.)

DAVID: What's the gun for, Henry?

HENRY: I have come to save your sorry ass. Oh, David of the ghetto. Look at those pictures. Any brother who looks at them pictures knows it's you. You let a white woman photograph you. Now she's the one telling your story — no chance you going to tell it. We got to change that. You see, David, it's who shoots the pictures, writes the book — let one of them do it none of us stand a chance.

DAVID: What are you going to do?

HENRY: Henry here will take care of you. Howie isn't going to let her get away with this.

DAVID: Who is Howie?

(Henry looks at the gun. He points it at David.)

DAVID: Don't do that. Hey, I said don't —

HENRY: No different than a camera, is it?

DAVID: It's not funny.

HENRY: You're probably used to it by now.

DAVID: Stop it.

(Henry fires the gun. It's a water gun.)

HENRY: It's a toy, Negro.

DAVID: You're sick.

HENRY: Look how scared you got and it wasn't even real. Now imagine if it were.

(Sally enters.)

SALLY: Hi.

HENRY: Interesting pictures you took. You're Sally, right?

SALLY: You like them?

HENRY: My relationship to them is a little more complicated than that.

(Henry exits.)

SALLY: Weirdo.

DAVID: They know. I work with him. He knows. They all know.

SALLY: I'm not going to allow anyone to intimidate me.

DAVID: Take them down.

SALLY: No.

DAVID: Don't do this.

SALLY: Up until I met you I would have taken a step back. I would have let them bully me. But now — this is my work. Where are you going?

DAVID: I have to go for a walk. I need to think about this.

(He exits almost bumping into Jackson. Lights shift.)

(Another part of the gallery. Lending, the photography professor is there. Henry enters.)

HENRY: Hello there.

LENDING: Huh?

HENRY: I said hi.

LENDING: Hello.

HENRY: Just thinking about this business of taking pictures. They did this for your class?

LENDING: Yes. Actually there's a program right at the entrance that explains the process, the class and —

HENRY: I don't read.

(Pause.)

(Henry laughs.)

HENRY: You think I meant it. Like I didn't read. Like I didn't know how to read.

(Lending laughs.)

LENDING: No. No. Of course not.

HENRY: It's OK if you assumed —

LENDING: There are other rooms — other pictures. You'll get a sense of everything that the students are doing.

HENRY: What does it take? If I want to do this? If I want to do this next semester.

LENDING: You're thinking about taking my class?

HENRY: Yeah. I guess. I mean, do I have to have a camera?

LENDING: What?

HENRY: To take the class.

LENDING: You're thinking about taking photography but aren't sure if you need a camera.

HENRY: Yeah.

LENDING: Yes. Unfortunately — what's your name? *(Pause.)* Unfortunately, you do need a camera to take photography.

HENRY: Uh-huh.

LENDING: Was there another question?

HENRY: What if I just want to model for you?

LENDING: What?

HENRY: Take my clothes off.

LENDING: Why would you want to do that?

HENRY: I have a beautiful body.

LENDING: I'm sure that — well, it's important that you're proud of who you are. I'm proud of what you have accomplished just to get here.

HENRY: You mean crossing the street and not getting run over. You think I'm that stupid.

(Pause.)

LENDING: Let's pick this up another time. Why don't you swing by my office.

HENRY: I was looking at those pictures. The ghetto ones. A Study in Oppression.

LENDING: There are other rooms with other pictures.

HENRY: Kind of boring, aren't they?

LENDING: Your opinion. Which, of course, you're entitled to.

HENRY: Really? I'm entitled to something? Good. Anyway, this ghetto exhibit. Wow. That's all I have to say.

(Lending turns to go.)

Actually, I have more to say.

LENDING: You want to walk over to the next room —

HENRY: I like this room. Suddenly, there's no one here except us. Funny, right? Anyway, I had to stand in line just to get in. Never seen people in line just to get into the ghetto. Most folk running the other way.

LENDING: This is different, I suppose.

HENRY: You ever been to the ghetto, Professor?

LENDING: I can't say I've spent a whole lot of time —

HENRY: Any time?

LENDING: No.

HENRY: Let's just say I've been to the ghetto, Professor. I've lived there. That ain't the ghetto.

LENDING: Please don't do anything foolish.

HENRY: What?

LENDING: I'm just saying. It's a difficult time for everyone.

HENRY: For you?

LENDING: For the community.

HENRY: Are there any black photography students in your class?

LENDING: This semester?

HENRY: No. Ten years from now! What do you think I'm talking about? I'm talking about the present, Professor, because I might not be around for the future. Ever have to live with that possibility?

LENDING: Unfortunately, this semester —

HENRY: Is that your camera? Can I see it?

LENDING: Careful with it.

HENRY: The thing about photography is that people tend to believe what they see. They don't bother checking up whether things are true or not. That's my job. I'm a fact-checker! That's my purpose.

LENDING: Can I have —

HENRY: Now, what do I do when I discover someone has been lying? That's when it gets tricky. I can't take care of business all by myself. Luckily, I can get other people involved.

LENDING: Just. My camera. Please.

HENRY: Smile, Professor.

LENDING: Please.

HENRY: Smile.

LENDING: The camera.

HENRY: Not until I get a smile out of you.

(Lending smiles. Henry shoots a picture.)

I think I'm ready to teach your class.

(Henry hands the camera back to Lending.)

Enjoy the picture, Professor.

(Blackout.)

SCENE EIGHT

Night. David walks through the dark campus. It's very cold. He comes up on a student.

MARK: It's over here.

DAVID: What is?

MARK: You waiting for the test results? Over here. Professor Ryan throws out the answers from that window over there.

DAVID: Oh.

MARK: I thought I was the only fool to be out in this weather. Everybody went down to Phoebe's to get drunk. How did you do?

DAVID: What?

MARK: On the final? You OK? Suffering post-test delirium? Bio 121 does that. (Mark yells up to the window.) Come on! We're freezing down here.

DAVID: How did you do?

MARK: I did OK. I guess. I don't know. Mark.

DAVID: David.

MARK: I've never seen you in lecture.

DAVID: Really?

MARK: I'm not always there. I can't get up for it.

DAVID: Yeah. Eight thirty is kind of early.

MARK: Class is at ten thirty.

DAVID: Right. I don't know — I just get —

MARK: You don't even know what time class is? You're really lost. I hate to see what you got on this test.

DAVID: I didn't . . .

MARK: What?

DAVID: I'm not wearing thermal underwear.

MARK: Hey, man. What do you want me to do about it?

DAVID: I should go.

MARK: All right. All right. (*He yells back up at the window.*) HEY. WE GOT SOMEONE OUT HERE NOT WEARING THERMAL UNDER-WEAR.

DAVID: Stop that.

MARK: HE'S FREEZING. YOU HEAR? NO THERMAL UNDERWEAR.

> (*Suddenly, a shadow is seen at the window and papers are thrown out with the test answers.*)

MARK: It worked. It worked.

> (*Mark grabs one of the papers and starts checking his answers. After a moment he sees that David is just standing there watching him.*)

MARK: Hey. These are it. What are you doing?

DAVID: It's all right.

MARK: Come on. You were waiting for them.

DAVID: I know I didn't pass —

MARK: Don't say that. Just check the answers before you say that.

> (*Mark gives David a piece of paper. They're both checking the answers on the piece of paper.*)
> (*Pause.*)

How did you do?

DAVID: I can't remember what I put for some of these. And you?

MARK: Let's go get drunk.

> (*Blackout.*)
> (*Lights up almost immediately. The two are drinking in a park.*)

MARK: Mitosis. Who's going to remember that five years from now. My point is who cares. What matters — I mean what are you going to do with your life. And I'm not just asking that because I'm drunk. I mean, I don't want to get all serious or anything but is it going to matter. This test, I mean. It matters in that I met you and we're drinking because twenty years from now the only thing I'll remember from this class is tonight — it's you.

DAVID: Why do you say that?

MARK: Say what?

DAVID: That you'll remember me.

MARK: You want me to forget you.

DAVID: You don't even know me.

MARK: I'll remember this kid standing out in the cold not wearing thermal underwear but desperate to know if he was right or not. You want some more.

(They drink.)

Parthenogenesis — heck I can't even pronounce it, much less define it. Do you know what it is, David? *(Pause.)* You're not in the class.

DAVID: What?

MARK: You're not in the class, are you?

DAVID: I don't always go.

MARK: You're not in it at all.

(Pause.)

DAVID: No.

MARK: Why did you lie to me?

DAVID: It was easy. I'm good at it.

MARK: You're not that good. You got caught.

DAVID: Can I have some more of that?

(Pause. Mark gives him the bottle.)

MARK: David? Or is it some other —

DAVID: No. David.

MARK: Be glad you're not taking the class.

DAVID: It's that hard?

MARK: It's that boring.

(They drink.)

DAVID: I want to be an astronaut.

MARK: What?

DAVID: You asked me before what I wanted to do with my life.

MARK: Are you lying now?

DAVID: I'm starting to think the only place I belong is up in space.

MARK: We're Earthbound, David. All of us. They're talking about the Moon but they won't get there.

DAVID: I think they will.

MARK: If you make it, hold up a sign from up there. Say hi.

DAVID: What do you want to do?

MARK: I haven't even thought about it.

DAVID: You were the one that asked me —

MARK: I knew you were different.

DAVID: How? I mean other than the obvious . . . .

MARK: Obvious what?

DAVID: Obvious.

(Pause.)

How am I different?

MARK: You stopped to wait for the answers to a test you didn't even take.

DAVID: I'm confused.

MARK: Good. Most people are. They just don't know it. You think Johnson isn't confused. Why do you think he's running back to Texas.
(*Pause.*)
My brother died in Saigon. The dumbest reason too. He screwed this Vietnamese girl and her brother wanted him to marry her. He said no. He got a shot in the head for it. He never even saw combat. I'm not going over there even if I have to fail this class over and over again.

DAVID: You wanted to fail?

MARK: I didn't bother opening the book for this one.

DAVID: So you didn't really care if —

MARK: I cared enough to fail. I love this school because I'm safe here. I've never felt safe anywhere — not after I turned sixteen anyway.

DAVID: This is it. This is why I came here.

MARK: What are you talking about?

DAVID: Just to sit somewhere and talk.

MARK: With a failure and a drunk.

DAVID: This is the most ordinary extraordinary moment I've had since I got here.

MARK: I think you're drunk.

DAVID: I feel safe right now. This is college, isn't it?

MARK: Look around.

DAVID: This is what it feels like for you all the time, right?

MARK: Yeah. What do you mean?

DAVID: Well it's not so safe for some of us.

MARK: I know.
(*Pause.*)

DAVID: I'm going to take bio next semester.

MARK: I'll be there.
(*They laugh. Suddenly it starts to snow.*)

DAVID: Oh, my god. Perfect. I've never seen snow before.

MARK: You're kidding me.

DAVID: No, really.

MARK: We'll be buried in it till spring.

DAVID: That's fine. That's what I want.
(*Lights shift.*)
(*Henry enters.*)

HENRY: Going home for break?

DAVID: Looking forward to getting away.

HENRY: Problems are still going to be here when you come back.

(Blackout.)

END OF ACT I

ACT II
SCENE ONE

The present. Professor Pryce addresses the class.

PRYCE: It started with an act of vandalism. The photographs of an African American individual identified as a homeless man were defaced early one morning toward the end of the fall semester in 1968. The photographs had been taken by a white student who also happened to be the daughter of a prominent professor. She arrived one day only to discover that the photographs had been ripped and torn. The impression was at once violent and appropriate. What the general university population did not know at that time and what many African American students did know was that the pictures were not of a homeless man but a student who was attending the university. It always comes down to a difference of perception. One that continues to exist even today.

(Lights shift.)

(It is a cold winter day in Ithaca. People rushing to and from classes. Everything is in motion.)

(Jackson spots a Young Man. He is played by the same actor who plays David.)

JACKSON: Hey, wait.

(Jackson catches up to him.)

YOUNG MAN: What do you want, man?

JACKSON: I want to talk.

YOUNG MAN: Not interested.

JACKSON: You have a girlfriend?

YOUNG MAN: Now what business is that of yours?

JACKSON: You're a freshman?

YOUNG MAN: Yeah. So.

JACKSON: What's it like now?

YOUNG MAN: Huh?

JACKSON: What's it like to be here? You want to go for a cup of coffee?

YOUNG MAN: Try that shit on someone else because whatever you selling, I ain't buying.

JACKSON: I'm a student here.

YOUNG MAN: Really? You're on the forty-year plan?

JACKSON: No. I just started.

YOUNG MAN: Lay off the drugs, brother. Someone your age shouldn't be touching the stuff.

(Young Man exits.)

(He transforms into David.)

(David enters his room. Sally is there. She is wearing a red wig.)

DAVID: Who let you in?

SALLY: Janacek. Told me to make myself comfortable. He's really come around.

DAVID: Are you kidding me? My roommate?

SALLY: As if that's not proof this COSEP thing is working. I think he's getting used to the idea of us.

DAVID: Really?

SALLY: Not a chance. The door was open. I walked in and lay down on your bed. I've missed you so much. Your blankets have the sweetest smell — sandalwood. I think you fall in love with the way people smell just as intensely as the way they look.

DAVID: Sally.

SALLY: Welcome back! Did you go down to get your textbooks yet?

DAVID: You're wearing a red wig.

SALLY: I told you one day I'd change. New semester, new color. What do you think?

DAVID: You're planning to walk around like that for the rest of the semester?

SALLY: I have other colors. Frankly, I think we need to start over and I thought changing hair color was one way of doing that. Things at the end of the semester . . . they got out of hand. And . . . . Well . . . We had the biggest snowstorm right after you left. I was home for days. It's funny, all the kids go home for break. All I do is walk five blocks east, three north, and there I am . . . 221 Comstock. How was your mom?

DAVID: First thing out of her mouth, What have they done to you up there?

SALLY: She'd heard about the exhibit?

DAVID: No. She thought I was too skinny. Got down to the business of feeding me. You know what's weird, I spent most of my time home too.

SALLY: You were thinking about us?

DAVID: I saw some friends from high school, but after a while we ran out of things to say to one another. Or I ran out of things I could say to them.

SALLY: What grade did my father end up giving you?

DAVID: I'd rather not talk about it.

SALLY: I know anyway. I looked at his grade book. Why did you sign up for the second part of the class?

DAVID: He can't make me go away.

SALLY: He doesn't care.

DAVID: I care.

SALLY: Look, forget about my father. I'm sorry I even brought it up. I just . . . let's try to make this work. Intense obsession/passion/love . . . whatever you want it call it . . . it usually never makes it past the semester break; but the fact is I'm here and you're not kicking me out, which you have every right to and now I'm a redhead and I think things are going to be OK and please say something.

(Pause.)

DAVID: This can't work out.

SALLY: Of course, it can.

DAVID: I think you should leave.

SALLY: David.

DAVID: I really do think you should go.

(Pause.)

SALLY: The night the pictures got slashed.

DAVID: What about it?

SALLY: I couldn't fall asleep. I went for a walk. It was snowing that night. The first snow of the year. Kind of beautiful. I sat on the steps near the quad thinking about showing up at your room. Surprising you. I wanted to surprise you. I knew I wouldn't see you for some time. I wanted to make love to you again. *(Pause.)* I saw two people running away from the arts building. They were laughing. I walked in. And there it was, the pictures ruined. *(Pause.)* Do you know who did it?

DAVID: I didn't do it.

SALLY: Then who did?

DAVID: I don't know, but I never wanted those pictures up.

SALLY: It's obvious now.

DAVID: Where are they now?

SALLY: They're ruined.

DAVID: I'm sorry.

SALLY: Those pictures are a part of me — and maybe it's because I had just given myself to you. Or maybe because in you I found what we are all looking for. When I look at those pictures I'm there too.

DAVID: Your prejudices.

SALLY: Maybe. My love is there too. You can't deny that. Everything is up there. It's hard to let that go. It's hard to let you go.

(They kiss.)

DAVID: You should leave.

(She tosses him the red wig and exits.)
(Lights shift.)
(Lending and Sally.)

SALLY: I want the pictures back up.

LENDING: Someone is trying to send you a message.

SALLY: I don't care.

LENDING: I have a responsibility to the students of this university — to their safety. Someone had a very strong reaction to those pictures.

SALLY: That's all it takes for you to take art down? Put them back up, Professor.

LENDING: Is there something I should know?

SALLY: What do you mean?

LENDING: There was a student at the exhibit. He threatened me.

SALLY: What did he look like?

LENDING: Tall. Not too . . . well. Not skinny but. He had this kind of grin. He was. I don't know what else to say.

SALLY: You don't remember anything else about him?

LENDING: No.

SALLY: Nothing?

LENDING: He was . . . black. I'm sure about that.

SALLY: Are you?

LENDING: Of course, I am. I wouldn't make that kind of accusation. I'd rather not say anything. The university doesn't have to know. I don't want trouble. For anyone.

SALLY: I want them back up.

LENDING: Sally, there are rumors that perhaps your subject — that maybe you might have made a mistake.

SALLY: What kind of mistake?

LENDING: That he is, in fact, a student. That perhaps you weren't completely honest — which is OK. Many people would argue that all photography is a lie, but just between us . . . .

SALLY: Professor, I never lied. You were the one who originally suggested —

LENDING: You agreed with me. *(Pause.)* You know who did this.

SALLY: One followed me the other night. He didn't show his face. They're trying to bully me.

LENDING: In two years you'll be out of here. This is my home. I can't let you put those pictures back up.

SALLY: My father is on the tenure committee, Professor. Funny . . .
(Pause.)

LENDING: When are you going to give me a new set of prints?

SALLY: I want to put them back up, as is.

LENDING: They're damaged.

SALLY: It's a conversation now. Originally it was just a one-sided view, my view. My lens.

LENDING: A conversation?

SALLY: I use light and shadow, and he — they — whoever —uses violence and destruction. That's their language. Everyone's taking sides. At least, what's happening with my pictures is that one side is talking to another. I'm not about to let anyone — including myself — get in the way of that conversation.

(Sally goes.)

(Blackout.)

SCENE TWO

Strand's office. David enters.

STRAND: These are not office hours.

(Pause.)

DAVID: I know.

STRAND: Well? *(Pause.)* I have work to do.

DAVID: I've been thinking about this — about what to do?

STRAND: What do you mean?

(David takes a step forward.)

Why don't you come back later.

(Pause.)

DAVID: I want to talk to you about some of my ideas for the paper.

STRAND: Is that all?

DAVID: You're scared of me.

STRAND: No.

DAVID: Is the university a frightening place?

STRAND: That's a very big question. I'll say yes. Simply because I believe you have a point to make — however wrong that point is it has now become my job to entertain it.

DAVID: Why is it frightening?

STRAND: Oh, let's just say that it's taking people to a very dark place — a dead end — where the light of education is not able to reach.

DAVID: I want to write about Robert Owen.

STRAND: Mr. Jackson.

DAVID: In the context of today — what's happening today. By creating the right kind of environment — not so much that the COSEP program is changing my character — it is. But what Owen did not anticipate is how the character of the exploiter changes — or fails to — when it comes into contact with the exploited.

STRAND: The exploiter. Oh, now come on.

DAVID: I'm wondering how much COSEP has really changed this university. I'm wondering how much I have changed you. Perhaps in ways you're not even aware of.

STRAND: It's provocative, I won't deny you that. But we left the Utopian Socialists behind last semester.

DAVID: Aren't you listening to me? What I want to write has to do with you.

STRAND: I'm not a historical figure. I'm a professor. So I suggest you write about a historical figure — one closer to the end of the nineteenth century, which is after all what the class is about.

DAVID: That's what I've come to understand. It's taken me a while, but I understand it now. You are history. I am history. We're both historical figures caught up in a historical moment.

STRAND: You're not listening. This is the twentieth century and therefore as far as my class is concerned, it does not exist. You have signed up for the second part of this class, which surprised me considering our . . . difficulties in understanding one another. I admire your tenacity, Mr. Jackson, but that doesn't mean I will accept some poorly researched paper that is more social criticism than history. Now I have work to do.

DAVID: All of this will make sense if you give me a moment.

STRAND: I don't have the time —.

DAVID: *(Overlapping.)* I have this guy telling me I got to pull all of Western Thought off the shelves in the library —

STRAND: Your tuition does not cover the right to ramble on in my office.

DAVID: — other people telling me the government is set to exterminate us; got a roommate who avoids me — fine with me. Some other person trying to convince the world I'm someone else. And you. You're talking about high standards. The failure of this university to preserve the highest of standards. So there is the environment I find myself in. Everyone pulling. I'm disjointed. I'm part of some kind of social experiment. They offered me an education. Good. Except this experiment hasn't been thought through. I feel isolated. Alone. And not welcomed by many . . . including you.

STRAND: That's a personal essay, which will do you some good in the more accommodating world of the arts where anything goes. But this is history. Hard facts. Nothing less than the truth.

DAVID: The truth? The truth is you had a problem with me since that first day. You never gave me a chance. Never understood my contribution to this university.

STRAND: You sit in the back row and say nothing. I don't recall your ever raising your hand.

DAVID: Professor, you can't have it both ways. You never wanted me to participate. I listened. I took notes. I did as much as I could.

STRAND: You've convinced yourself of that.

DAVID: I am a part of this university. I didn't know that — I wasn't sure those first few weeks but I am now. This social experiment was never done just for me.

STRAND: No?

DAVID: It was for you. For my roommate. I am part of the modern world. A university has to reflect that world. This university is trying. It's doing a lousy job but it's trying. You're not even trying.

STRAND: Are you lecturing me, Mr. Jackson? Are you taking over this office? Are you locking me in? Are you about to stage a sit-in? Is violence in your future? Should I be afraid? I don't need to listen to you any further.

DAVID: Owen understood if he didn't change, the world would blow up in his face. You still don't get that, do you?

STRAND: Are you done?

(David nods yes.)

When we first met I asked you to try to be a scholar — to stand above all the junk happening here.

DAVID: I don't know if that's possible.

STRAND: I've been able to.

DAVID: I think you're wrong.

STRAND: You're about to take the poison that is the modern university. You'll feel powerful. You'll feel like you can do something but it's temporary. What I'm offering you is timeless. Four years is a very short time to spend joining political organizations, marching, demonstrating . . . but it will feel good. You'll feel important. Relevant. Don't be seduced by the times. You have a lot of things going on in your head right now. Take a deep breath and just do what is necessary — what is expected of you.

(David hesitates. He starts to go.)

I bet you anything in the world, Mr. Jackson, that you haven't noticed the roundels outside of Franklin Hall. They're there for us to admire — sculpted heads of famous electrical scientists. Volta happens to be my favorite. Do you know what I'm referring to? No. Maybe you should be less interested in the present and more interested in the past.

DAVID: All I'm trying to do is get to a place from which I can start to look up.

STRAND: Good luck.

(*Blackout.*)

SCENE THREE

Professor Pryce.

PRYCE: The students felt isolated here because they had been promised many things: knowledge, stability, and the love and respect of one of this nation's leading institutions. Instead, they found themselves being stared at, never quite respected or listened to; they found heartache. They were given the keys to the master's house only to find out that there was yet another door past the front door. As the spring of 1969 approached the small but vocal African American population on campus started to react to the pictures. Small but vocal. That's important to remember.

(*Blackout.*)

SCENE FOUR

Café. Jackson is studying. Jeff enters with a laptop bag.

JEFF: Here.

JACKSON: You're late.

JEFF: Yeah. I know but . . . .

(*Jeff removes the laptop from his bag.*)

JACKSON: What are you doing?

JEFF: I Googled you.

JACKSON: What?

JEFF: I Googled you. On the computer. Just to see what would happen. I did it out of curiosity. I was bored last night. No pot. I decided that I was going to Google everyone I know. Except everyone I know is like twenty and they don't have a past. Except Cara — this girl I know from Psych.

She's got her own site. Pictures of herself all over it. She's an amateur nudist. Anyway, I spend like five minutes on the site and I get distracted — as you could imagine because I am young and I do have hormones; but as I said I am young and five minutes is enough. Soon I'm bored again and then I remember you. I type in your name. Go ahead. Do it. Type in your name. David. David Jackson.

JACKSON: I don't have a Web site.

JEFF: Try it.

JACKSON: Jeff —

JEFF: You are on the Web, David. Shouldn't you have let me know that you were at that takeover?

JACKSON: You must have me confused me with someone else.

JEFF: I knew you'd say that. So I Googled images of you. To see if there would be any. *(Jeff Googles Jackson.)* There you are. That's you. So now, David, I'm beginning to feel like a total asshole. Here I am — we were friends . . . I thought. I know nothing about you. I mean. Look at this picture. You're holding a rifle.

JACKSON: That was a long time ago.

JEFF: So? What does that mean? You forgot? How many times does one take over a fucking university building?

JACKSON: In the sixties, often.

JEFF: How many times does one do it using guns? Why are you even showing up to class at this point? You know what happened. You were there. You lied to me and the funny thing is . . . I'm not sure why.
(Pause.)

JACKSON: This is feeling a little too familiar.

JEFF: What is?

JACKSON: Forgive me for being a little cautious but I get nervous when white people take an interest in me.

JEFF: Something happened to you, man, but that's the past.

JACKSON: It doesn't go away. I was hoping that by coming back, I could put it behind me.

JEFF: Let me help you. Tell me everything. Tell me the truth.

JACKSON: No. Thank you. I've been down that road before.

JEFF: What?

JACKSON: You wouldn't be the first white person who tried.

JEFF: So now I'm some white guy.

JACKSON: That's what you're always going to be.

JEFF: What the fuck do you mean? We were friends, right? No. We weren't. Now I know. I don't like being lied to.

JACKSON: How can I even tell you the truth when I'm not even sure what happened.

JEFF: Try. OK?

JACKSON: There was a girl named Sally. I let her take some pictures. And I've spent a long time trying to run from all that.

(Jeff closes the laptop.)

JEFF: I want to know everything.

(Lights shift.)

(Sally is walking across the quad. David approaches her.)

DAVID: What the hell are you doing? Why are the pictures still up?

SALLY: People are looking.

DAVID: What?

SALLY: People are looking at us. Or you don't care anymore. What happened to that shy young man?

DAVID: And this thing about a conversation in the ghetto? Have you gone nuts?

SALLY: That's what it is.

DAVID: You should expect more troubles.

SALLY: Another conversation, you mean?

DAVID: I wouldn't call it that. We don't like it.

SALLY: Who is we?

DAVID: There are some of us —

SALLY: We now includes you?

DAVID: Yes.

SALLY: And by we I suppose you mean —

DAVID: My friends.

SALLY: Your new friends.

DAVID: It's bitter cold out here, so please. Pictures. Down.

SALLY: You're a hard man to get hold of.

DAVID: This semester is different.

SALLY: You didn't want anything to do with me.

DAVID: I come home early. I lock myself in. I don't want to see anyone. I have a lot of work to do.

SALLY: I came by your room a few times.

DAVID: I know.

SALLY: You didn't open the door. Did you think it would end so easily? Do you think I'd give up that fast? The pictures are up and if that's the only way

I keep what is us alive, if that's the only way I can keep you in my life . . . if that's the only way we can be public, I will keep them up.

DAVID: You have to stop.

SALLY: Your new friends say so.

DAVID: I say so.

SALLY: Not without some help from them.

DAVID: They have nothing to do with this.

SALLY: You were the one who brought them up.

DAVID: To warn you.

SALLY: You know most guys wouldn't need the help of some political organization to break up with someone. That's very clever of you. To tell you the truth, David, I haven't heard that one yet. That one is going to spread. The College Republicans made me do it! The Afro American Society forbids me to! Forgive me for being just a little upset.

DAVID: You're wrong.

SALLY: You're the one who's wrong. If it isn't me in your life, then you have someone else telling you who you are, what you are.

DAVID: What?

SALLY: I made you self aware. People can spend four years at a university and not know who they are. It only took a few pictures to show you. Until I put those photographs up you didn't even know you were black.

DAVID: You have no idea what my life has been.

SALLY: Oh, no?

DAVID: How dare you assume something like that. Just because there are things in my life — things I've chosen to ignore. To turn my back on. Wrongly. That doesn't give you the right to say that I don't know what the color of my skin — when everything . . . From what hospital I was born in, what school I had to go to — why I'm sharing some room with some kid I haven't seen in weeks because he can't stand me — for you to say I didn't know I was black until those photographs — those ridiculous fucking photographs — made even more ridiculous because you have kept them hanging after this . . . Take the pictures down or you're going to get hurt. I'm not going to get in the way of it either.

SALLY: This is not going to end here in the middle of the quad.

DAVID: Your choice.

SALLY: That's right.

DAVID: Do what I say, Sally.

SALLY: Everyone comes to college and they discover things about themselves: they discover that the world is unjust, they become idealistic — we're going to change the world . . . in four years! That kind of thing. But all that happened to me when I was twelve. You realize, David, that I've been living here my whole life. I've seen things people hoped for not happen, things people didn't even imagine would ever happen happen. I wouldn't trust your new friends just as I wouldn't trust someone who is only here four years. It's all a matter of perspective, something four years doesn't allow for.

DAVID: Why did you come after me? From the beginning. I want to know.

SALLY: I liked you.

DAVID: What did you think would happen? Did you care about me?

SALLY: Of course, I cared. I still do.

DAVID: Why were you attracted to me?

SALLY: The usual things. Unhappy childhood. Need for attention. The war.

DAVID: You don't ever answer me straight.

(Pause.)

SALLY: When I first met you I fell for you hard because you were unique. You were experiencing college in a way few people do. You were out to learn. To take it all in. You weren't here to immediately fix the world. That's rare today. Now you're just another ordinary person threatening to have his way.

DAVID: That's all I want to be. Ordinary. Allow me to be that for the rest of the year.

SALLY: I also saw your color, David. It's beautiful — I mean, it was beautiful the moment I saw you, but it's not like I haven't found other things beautiful . . . what I'm trying to say is that when I was lying next to you in bed — you'd fallen asleep and I did the silliest thing; I checked if you were still breathing. I was so in love with you at that moment. And it occurred to me that we would end up together for the rest of our lives. It's funny how idealistic one becomes right after sex. So I grabbed the camera because I wanted to preserve that moment. I wanted to show the world. So I brought it into class and the world just assumed a different thing. A horrible thing. An ugly thing. And I was too afraid to tell them the truth. I'm confused. Really, really confused. And I don't know what to do. David, I'm not sure how to tell you this.

(David walks up to her. He's about to hug her then notices where he is standing — out in the middle of the campus. The campus is in motion. They stand there not able to touch.)

(Lights shift.)

(Henry and David in the cafeteria.)

HENRY: A white baby? A white baby?!

DAVID: Shh.

HENRY: A WHITE BABY?! No. You're fucking kidding me.

DAVID: I haven't told anyone.

HENRY: Shit, man. You know just how ugly white babies are?

DAVID: It's not about what the kid looks like. And the problem here is he ain't going to be totally white.

HENRY: All right. All right. Henry here is going to take care of you.

DAVID: How?

HENRY: First thing, I'm going to have a talk with Howie.

DAVID: Howie? What does Howie know about this?

HENRY: What do you want me to do, man? This is a little over my head.

DAVID: Howie is not the answer to all my problems. In fact, I don't want my problems taken care of.

HENRY: What?

DAVID: I just want someone I can talk to — someone who is going to listen to me. I have no idea how things got to this point. She's got a baby in her and I'm some kind of homeless man hanging on some wall, and I'm close to failing some history class that happens to be taught by the father of the woman who is pregnant who took my picture — get the fucking circle? I can't think.

HENRY: Then it's time I take you to meet Howie.

(Lights shift.)

PRYCE: The students who took over the Straight that year were there for a variety of reasons. They each had a specific reason for being there but what united them, what kept them together — and mind you, at some point during the takeover they snuck guns in, so they were prepared for the worst. They didn't know how the standoff would end, so they were risking their lives — what kept them together was an understanding that some fundamental wrong had been done to them. Some were able to articulate what it was; others were simply able to feel it.

(Lights shift.)

(Jackson and Jeff. Jeff is working at the computer.)

JACKSON: Anything?

JEFF: Just some images. He's holding two rifles.

JACKSON: That was Howie all right.

JEFF: What do you remember?

JACKSON: He was willing to die. Not just him, of course. We took a vote. Some of us wanted to burn the building down if they raided it. We decided against arson by four, five votes. It was close.

JEFF: What did you vote for?
(Lights shift.)
(Lending's office. Lending and David.)
DAVID: Professor?
LENDING: Yes?
DAVID: I wanted to talk to you. It's about the exhibit.
LENDING: I'm rushing out but maybe later —
DAVID: It's about the conversation.
LENDING: Well, yes. That's one of the photographers. I'm slightly embarrassed about that, but I believe in artistic freedom.
DAVID: It's not a conversation.
LENDING: I agree. However, if that's what she chooses —
DAVID: Professor, you have to take those pictures down. *(Pause.)* Those pictures are of me. *(Pause.)*
LENDING: You're the student.
DAVID: Yes.
LENDING: Why did you lie?
DAVID: She did.
LENDING: You both did.
DAVID: I want my life back.
LENDING: You should have thought about that earlier. It's not possible right now.
DAVID: Why?
LENDING: This will soon pass. I want us to heal. It's one lie — one white lie so that we as a community don't implode. No one will remember this next year. The semester is almost over. I promise you — .
(David walks away.)
(Lights shift.)
JACKSON: I voted to burn the building down.
(Blackout.)

SCENE FIVE

Professor Pryce.

PRYCE: I have the list of the demands that were presented to the university administration during the takeover in 1969. Allow me to read this in their own words.

The demands of the African American Society are as follows. The black studies program everyone keeps talking about, no more talk, we want it to start next semester. And we want the right to approve who is going to run the program. We want a commitment for more African American professors and administrators. And while you're at it, how about some more white janitors — a demand that has not yet been met. And we want a new judiciary system. A system where our voice is as strong as any other voice. Oh, and we don't want any of us going to jail for this takeover — this is a political act not a criminal one. We want our frustration to be acknowledged.

(Lights shift.)

(Henry and David on a roof. They're holding guns.)

HENRY: No one out there yet. The rain is keeping people away. Wait until they hear about it.

DAVID: I don't know what I'm doing here.

HENRY: You wanted your pictures down. I arranged that. What's your problem?

DAVID: It's finals in two weeks.

HENRY: It's finals right now. We don't get what we want, it's over. Hey. I think that guy over there is from CBS.

DAVID: Local.

HENRY: So. I bet he probably knows Cronkite.

DAVID: Henry.

HENRY: Keep your eye out there, man. Any moment the national guard is going to come and try to take us.

DAVID: I called my mama. Told her I was willing to die. You should of heard her go off on me. You're the first she kept saying. The first. The first to go to college. Never mind taking over buildings, joining secret organizations, never mind all that, keep your face buried in your work. I explained to her I couldn't; as much as I tried I kept being pulled. She wouldn't hear of it. So she made me promise I would not participate.

HENRY: You lied to your mama?

DAVID: I had to.

HENRY: What kind of man are you?!

DAVID: Good question? What kind of man am I? Who am I? College is supposed to be about discovering yourself. It isn't about voting to burn a building down. I don't understand why I did that.

HENRY: It also isn't about screwing a white girl while blacks are getting beat up all across the country for the right to simply be themselves. It isn't about letting her put your pictures up. It isn't about getting your color mixed with hers. You have shown a complete lack of judgment. Now get yourself together.

DAVID: I looked over at you when we voted. You didn't raise your hand.

HENRY: You got me mistaken —

DAVID: No. I looked carefully. I wanted to know — I was sure I knew what you would do.

HENRY: Arson ain't my thing.

DAVID: You're all talk.

HENRY: I don't like fire. You have trouble controlling it.

DAVID: Anger.

HENRY: Huh?

DAVID: Same thing.

HENRY: Are you angry? It's about time.

DAVID: I'm angry in that before I stepped on campus I knew exactly who I was — where I was headed before deciding to come here.

HENRY: You were headed nowhere.

DAVID: The local college maybe — a job back home. That's somewhere. Now I'm standing guard having just voted to do something I would never have thought to do.

HENRY: You come to college to grow into someone — you just experiencing some growing pains.

DAVID: And you? What do you really want to get out of this, man?

HENRY: All you have ever wanted to do was study, stay outside the fight. All I've ever wanted you to understand is that that's not possible for people like us. Am I scared? Yes. I don't want to set this building on fire. I don't want to die, but then you have to understand that for a lot of people in this world we are not yet alive. Now hold that rifle like a man.
(Blackout.)

SCENE SIX

The present. Afternoon. An older Strand is gathering his papers getting ready to go home. His back is to the door. Jackson enters.

STRAND: I'm afraid you'll have to come back next Tuesday. Office hours are over for this week.

JACKSON: Professor.

(Strand turns around.)

STRAND: Yes?

JACKSON: Professor, I was wondering if I could have a word with you.

STRAND: Are you faculty?

JACKSON: It's a testament to what we did that it's so easy to get us confused now.

STRAND: I'm sorry?

JACKSON: I'm actually a student here.

STRAND: You are? I only teach one class now — you're not in that class. Next semester I'm retiring. I know I've said that before, but this is it; so therefore, I'm not exactly sure what you want from me.

JACKSON: Professor, I was a student of yours.

STRAND: You're a student now?

JACKSON: Yes. But once . . . A while back as well.

STRAND: You took my class?

JACKSON: Nineteenth Century European History.

STRAND: I haven't taught that class — what did you say your name was? My red book. It has every class I've taught since I first got here. What year?

JACKSON: I took your class the fall of '68, the spring of '69.

(Strand looks at him.)

David Jackson, Professor. I was part of that COSEP program. You remember me?

STRAND: You left after the end of the school year.

JACKSON: Yes.

STRAND: Here we are. David Jackson. D. I believe I was generous that spring semester.

JACKSON: I want to challenge that grade.

STRAND: What do you mean?

JACKSON: I believe other things got in the way of you being able to judge me properly.

STRAND: That was over thirty years ago, Mr. Jackson.

JACKSON: It's never too late.

STRAND: I'm afraid it is. The way the system works —

JACKSON: The system doesn't work for me. It never has. I've decided to go outside the system for this one. I want you to simply change the grade in that book.

STRAND: It wouldn't be an official —

JACKSON: I don't need it to be official. I don't think you do either. That book is enough for me.

(Pause.)

STRAND: How old were you when we first met?

JACKSON: Eighteen.

STRAND: That's young, isn't it?

JACKSON: Yes.

STRAND: I was also young. That was probably not apparent then but it's true. In fact, this university, this country was young. It was dealing with problems, with issues it had never dealt with before. When my grandson — yes, I have a grandson — when he used to play in the backyard, he'd come in with scratches all over his body. In time, those would heal. One or two are permanent. This university has been permanently scarred. That takeover demonstrated to us — the guardians of knowledge — that we were doing something fundamentally wrong. Some of us listened immediately. Others like myself did not. However, scarred we were . . . we continue to be. I'm changing your grade, Mr. Jackson. Not because I believe I gave you the wrong grade. I'm changing your grade because I do not trust the judgment of someone living in young times and the memory of someone as old as I. Is that to you're satisfaction?

JACKSON: I don't need my grade changed.

STRAND: Then why did you come?

(Pause.)

JACKSON: I cried in this office.

STRAND: You weren't the first.

JACKSON: I hated you . . . and I wanted you to love me. How embarrassing. This room . . .

STRAND: Well, it'll be someone else's office next year. Things do change, don't they?

JACKSON: There's an Africana Studies program.

STRAND: There you go.

JACKSON: We fought hard for that.

STRAND: Perhaps. Or perhaps it would have happened anyway.

JACKSON: I'm taking a class in the department. "Taking the Journey Home."

STRAND: It sounds interesting enough.

JACKSON: It deals with the concept of home — not just a space that we inhabit at the moment but something that is forever present in our lives. For example —

STRAND: I don't need one, Mr. Jackson. You can walk me out if you'd like but I do have to get home.

(Strand starts to get his things together.)

JACKSON: How is she?

STRAND: Listen. Falling water. You can hear the natural sound of the campus at this time of night. There was a period when that sound — you couldn't hear it over all the shouting. If this were a game, who has won? You have your program, more black students than ever, and I have the sound of falling water again. As with everything else, I believe it's a draw.

JACKSON: Does she ever . . .

STRAND: She does volunteer work at the local shelter. She has her own darkroom and every once in a while she takes out her camera. However, she has a son and a mortgage, so she now has her sight on things more immediate to her own well being. As for the younger generation, those here on campus, they have inherited the right to wear sweat pants to class. I had a student come into class wearing sweat pants — on the buttocks, in big block letters, the phrase: experience this. Let's go.

(Lights shift.)

JEFF: I got this off eBay.

JACKSON: What is it?

JEFF: The 1969 yearbook. But there's no mention of the takeover. It's as if it didn't happen. One of the most important events in the history of the university and it's not even in the yearbook.

JACKSON: The takeover happened too late in the semester. We have our memory — which is not always right — and Google, which is wrong most of the time.

JEFF: So how did it end?

JACKSON: The administration finally settled. All along there was talk that they were going to call the National Guard but they didn't. They lost face, but no one died.

JEFF: So that's it. You leave the building — everything behind?

JACKSON: Just as we were getting ready to, Howie stops everyone.

(Lights shift.)

(Howie is on stage.)

HOWIE: No one move. It isn't over until we walk out. And we're walking out with our guns. None of this bullshit peaceful resolution because what we have we're willing to use, and if we aren't using it today it's because things went our way; but if tomorrow comes and there is no real change, then tomorrow we pick up our guns again and use them for real. And I'm not just talking about tomorrow or the next day. If I have to come back ten years from now, I'm willing. So we are walking out with our guns because the world just has to see we are armed. And, hell, don't we all look good like this?

(Lights off on Howie.)

JEFF: So that's how it ended.

JACKSON: There was a picture of it in the *Times*. It won the Pulitzer. I was in it. All my fight to take those pictures down and suddenly I'm frozen in time — again in someone's picture. I'm holding a rifle. I'm kind of in the back but there I am. My first year in college.

(Blackout.)

SCENE SEVEN

David's room. He's there packing. Sally enters.

SALLY: Hey.

(He continues packing.)

Haven't seen you for a while.

DAVID: Yeah.

SALLY: Impressive. The takeover. I wanted to be inside with you. To take care of you. Then I realized you didn't want to have anything to do with me. *(Pause.)* Look, I'm sorry I had to . . . I was really scared. I guess I'm not as brave as I thought I was. Or maybe I'm not yet ready to be a mother. I should have talked to you first. I know that hurt you. I know a lot of things I did hurt you. Look at me, David.

(He does.)

I'm sorry.

(He continues to pack.)

I love the end of the semester — everyone out in the quad wearing shorts for the first time in God knows how long. It's a little sad too — this last burst of activity and then in a week the place will be empty. I guess you're not doing a summer session this year. They're kind of fun — professors tend to be a little more loose, a younger lot. People like my father, they don't teach in the summer. You need help with that?

(Sally sits on the suitcase while David zips it up.)

So you got what you wanted. They're hiring some black professors — starting a program next semester. Not bad. Look, the first year is always the hardest.

DAVID: That's what they say.

SALLY: And I know this one was particularly hard but . . . Soon you come back for what you think will be forever and suddenly you're up there getting your diploma.

DAVID: I'm not coming back.

SALLY: You always feel that way at the end of the first year. You think, I have to do this again. But that's why you have the summer — work on your tan — or whatever — and before you know it, you'll be ready to come back.

DAVID: I'm not going to be ready. This is not the place for me.

SALLY: Don't say that.

DAVID: I'm telling you how I feel.

SALLY: David.

DAVID: The first day I got here I looked out from that window over there and I thought everything was golden. It was a little after six at night and the sun was burning itself out. Students were walking to dinner in groups, as freshman tend to do. A professor was getting into his car, slowly, you know, as if he had all the time in the world. A father was saying good-bye to his daughter. I wanted to know what he was saying to her, in way of advice. I wanted advice. And in the distance there was a rally, people screaming out in anger, but I was so far away from it I heard what I thought was laughter. And I laughed because for a moment I thought I had arrived at this perfect place — a kind of place one could only imagine. For a moment everything made sense and then it all unraveled.

SALLY: Where are you going to go?

DAVID: I'm going to try to find a place where it all makes sense.

SALLY: This is 1969, David. Nothing makes sense.

DAVID: Move, please.

(She gets up off the suitcase.)

SALLY: Take some time off and then come back. Let the decade run out and then come back. You need to finish this, David.

DAVID: Someday.

SALLY: I have nightmares, David. I wake up and I'm pulling my hair. Something was pulled out of me. Not literally. I mean. Yes. But. Something was pulled out of us. Please. Figure out a way of putting it back.

(Jackson appears.)

JACKSON: Sally?

SALLY: *(To David.)* Yes?

JACKSON: I don't think my life can ever be put back together again.

SALLY: *(To David.)* Don't say that.

(Jeff appears.)

JEFF: *(To David.)* You look new.

JACKSON: Huh?

JEFF: *(To David.)* Like a new man.

JACKSON: I'm old.

JEFF: *(To David.)* Not inside. *(To Jackson.)* Hey, I think we should take another class together. I like this arrangement.

JACKSON: I do too.

DAVID: *(To Everyone.)* Good-bye.

(David exits. The others remain on.)

END OF PLAY

EVERYTHING WILL BE DIFFERENT
A BRIEF HISTORY OF HELEN OF TROY

Mark Schultz

> For beauty is nothing but the beginning of terror which we are
> still just able to endure, and we are so awed because it serenely
> disdains to annihilate us.
>
> — Rainer Maria Rilke
> *Duino Elegies*

> Ugliness is beauty at rest.
>
> — Jean Genet
> *The Miracle of the Rose*

PLAYWRIGHT'S BIOGRAPHY
Mark Schultz is a founding member and artistic associate of Theater Mitu, a member of Rising Phoenix Rep, and co-ordinator of MCC Theater's Playwrights' Coalition. Recent plays include: *Everything Will Be Different* (Soho Rep & True Love Productions) for which he won the 2005 Oppenheimer Award; *Gift* (Rising Phoeniz Rep / NY International Fringe Festival); *Last* (Rising Phoenix Rep / WAX); *The Place Where* (Chashama); and *Still* (Rising Phoenix Rep / Blue Heron). *Everything Will Be Different*, was produced in the U.K. by the Actors Touring Company with Theatre Royal Plymouth under the title *A Brief History of Helen of Troy*. With Theater Mitu he has performed, composed, dramaturged, and written. His play *Passion* was featured in Francis Ford Coppola's *Zoetrope* magazine. He holds an M.F.A. in playwriting from Columbia University.

ORIGINAL PRODUCTION
Everything Will Be Different was first produced by Soho Rep with True Love Productions at Soho Rep (46 Walker Street, New York, NY.) on April 7, 2005, with the following cast:

CHARLOTTE	Laura Heisler
HARRY	Christopher McCann
HEATHER	Naomi Aborn
GARY	Geoffrey Nauffts*
FRANKLIN	Jason Jurman
FREDDIE	Reynaldo Valentin
Director	Daniel Aukin
Lights	Jane Cox
Costumes	Kim Gill
Set	Kip Marsh
Sound	Shane Rettig
Assistant Director	Kendall O'Neill

*Bill Coelius played the part of Gary after April 23

CHARACTERS

CHARLOTTE: fifteen or thereabouts
HARRY: her father
FRANKLIN: a friend
FREDDIE: Franklin's cousin
GARY: a counselor
HEATHER: a friend

PLACE

Various

TIME

Present

APPRECIATION

Mark Schultz wishes to thank: MCC Theater, MCC Theater's Playwrights' Coalition: Stephen Willems, Josh Hecht, Robert LuPone, Bernie Telsey, Will Cantler; Lucy Thurber, Rami Metal. All of the actors who helped develop this piece, especially Susan O'Connor. Daniel Aukin and all at Soho Rep. Theater Mitu and Rising Phoenix Rep. Val Day. Erich Erving, of course . . .

EVERYTHING WILL BE DIFFERENT

A BRIEF HISTORY OF HELEN OF TROY

PROLOGUE

Harry and Charlotte sitting. Eating.
Silence. Eating. Silence.
Charlotte looks at Harry who is eating very slowly. Concentrated.
Eating.
Charlotte reaches her hand across the table, slowly, still eating. Just as she is
about to touch Harry, he rises.

HARRY: It's good soup, honey. It's good. It's. Really.

It's good. Nice.

(Pause.)

You can't. Keep. Needing. So much. OK? You can't. So stop it. OK? Stop
it. Just stop it. We're fine. Let it go.

(Pause.)

Want some bread? I think the news is on.

*(Beat. Harry crosses off. Charlotte's arm is still outstretched. She does not
move.)*

A BRIEF HISTORY OF HELEN OF TROY IN FOUR PARTS
PART ONE

The title of the scene is read or projected.
Sudden bright spotlight on Charlotte. She reads from a paper, as if giving a
book report of some sort.

CHARLOTTE: Um. My report is on Helen of Troy? So. Um. It's called. Helen of Troy.
Um. So.
Helen of Troy was the most beautiful woman in the world and I love her. I just love her. Everyone loved her. Everyone wanted her. Everyone wanted to have her. And they would have done anything for her. Even die. A hundred times maybe if they could. If she asked them. And she would. And they would. And it would be very very sad.

I think of what it must have been like when she first came. To Troy. How everyone must've been so happy. And joyful. How the air must have felt bright. With love. How she must have shined. Waving and smiling at everyone as she passed by them. Everyone gasping at how beautiful she was. Wanting her. Loving her. Needing her. And everyone. Not knowing. How short. How really really short the time was. Before Death would come. With a hundred thousand arms. To steal her back.
(Heather is illuminated suddenly.)
HEATHER: Charlotte?
CHARLOTTE: Mama?
HEATHER: No. She's dead. But I'm here. Wanna go out somewhere?

1

(Lights snap on. Charlotte center. Surrounded by packed bags. Harry, her father, in the doorway. Smoking. Calmly. A long pause.)
CHARLOTTE: Nothing you can say. By the way. Just to let you know. In case you're wondering. If you, I mean, if you thought. Anything. Don't. OK? That's all. I'm decided. These are my bags and I'm leaving and it's decided and you can't say anything. OK? You can't.
HARRY: Right.
CHARLOTTE: I am determined.
HARRY: OK.
CHARLOTTE: And I would say, I love you, Daddy. But I'm not sure I do. Anymore. So.

HARRY: Oh. Sure. Yeah.

CHARLOTTE: So this is good-bye.

HARRY: Right.

(Beat.)

CHARLOTTE: I am so resolved. I am so ready. There is a world and I will see it. And you won't stop me. I will have adventures. I will be like an explorer. I will make new friends. I will fall in love. I will be like Christopher Columbus or Francis Drake or like Magellan or whatever. Because there is a world and I am determined. And when I come back? If I come back? No one will recognize me. I will be like a movie star or like a famous person and no one will recognize me and I will see through everyone. I will see through everyone. Even you. I will look right through you and you will look at me, and you'll think to yourself who the hell is that and I'll just smile at you. I'll just smile and I'll mumble something like profound or something really famous like a famous something like what someone famous would say because that's who I'll be because I'll know a lot more, I'll know a hell of a lot more when I come back. Or maybe I'll just say, "Fuck you" because I can see through you. Fuck you. Under my breath. To the wall. To the fucking wall. I'll see through you to the fucking wall and you won't even know that you're nothing to me. And I'll say fuck you and you'll think Is she talking to me? and you won't even know.

You are a ghost to me. And I don't care. Everyone a fucking ghost. Everyone. And I'm the only one. I'm the only one who means more than you or anyone else.

(Beat.)

HARRY: Honey?

CHARLOTTE: What.

HARRY: Where is this coming from? Do I need this now? Do you think I need this now? I don't think I need this now.

CHARLOTTE: This is the truth. Daddy.

HARRY: The truth. OK.

(Beat.)

I'm gonna tell you.

CHARLOTTE: What.

HARRY: You're not very pretty. I mean, you know you're not very pretty. Right? I mean, not like your mom. Right? OK. And those — that acne? That's what it is. It's acne. You have acne. People don't like acne. Famous people? They like pretty. They hate acne. I'm just telling you. That's the truth. That's the real world. So you know. These are the breaks. I like your luggage. It's a really nice pattern. Francis Drake was a pirate, and Christopher Columbus was an asshole. Right? I mean, you know. You're just not very pretty, honey.

CHARLOTTE: I know.

HARRY: OK. So you know. Truth. So.

CHARLOTTE: So.

HARRY: Stay. Don't do this.

(Beat.)

CHARLOTTE: Can't stop me.

HARRY: OK. But. Honey. No one will love you. Is what I'm saying. Not like you want. It's the God's honest truth. It's really the truth. And I hate to be the one, you know I do, I hate to be the one. To tell you. But there's no love for you. Not out there at any rate. Not like what you'll find here. Your mother and I

CHARLOTTE: Dead.

HARRY: Sure she's dead.

CHARLOTTE: She's dead.

HARRY: OK. She's dead. You're right. When you're right. You're right. I, then. I feel you're making a mistake.

So stay. I forgive you. I'll help you unpack. We'll have dinner. Honey, I forgive you. I don't feel hurt. You wanted attention. That's fine. You can bake us a cake or something. We'll have cake or something. It'll be nice.

CHARLOTTE: I don't want cake.

HARRY: Something else, then.

CHARLOTTE: Don't want anything else.

HARRY: Important thing is together. Whatever we do, we'll do it together. And it'll be special. I love you. And this is real love. Your mother wouldn't want you to leave.

CHARLOTTE: She's dead.

HARRY: Yeah, I know.

CHARLOTTE: Don't bring her into it.

HARRY: Fine. She's out of it.

(Beat.)

That her luggage? I really like that pattern.

CHARLOTTE: I don't know.

(Beat.)

HARRY: Who let you use your mother's luggage? That's not your luggage.

CHARLOTTE: It was here. I used it.

HARRY: That's not your luggage. Right? That's your mother's luggage. Who let you use your mother's luggage?

CHARLOTTE: I just used it.

HARRY: Who let you? That's the question. Someone give you permission? Did I give you permission? Did your mother? She's dead, by the way, before you answer.

CHARLOTTE: She would have wanted me to have it.

HARRY: You're a liar. And you're lying to yourself. And that's the truth. And you're ugly and you're an ugly liar and OK. Just get your stuff out of the bags.

CHARLOTTE: What?

HARRY: Get your stuff out of the bags. Who gave you permission?

CHARLOTTE: What?

HARRY: Who gave you the fucking permission? Get your stuff out of the bags.

CHARLOTTE: But I'm all packed.

HARRY: I don't care. I don't *care*. They're not yours. They are not yours to take. Take what's yours and leave the fucking bags. You want me to help?

CHARLOTTE: But she doesn't need it.

HARRY: That's not the point. You know that's not the point. That's not the fucking point. Get your clothes and whatever the hell — how much shit do you have anyway? Get your *fucking shit* out of your *mother's* bags. You don't think I know she doesn't need it? That is not the *point*.
(*Beat. Harry suddenly lunges for and rips into the luggage. Charlotte tries to restrain him.*)

CHARLOTTE: Daddy!

HARRY: You will not. You will not. You will not.
(*They fight over the luggage, bags and clothes flying. Harry is bent on destruction. The debacle ends with clothes covering the stage, the luggage emptied, the combatants exhausted.*)

HARRY: You have so many clothes. Where did you get all these clothes?

CHARLOTTE: You ruin *everything*.

HARRY: These your mother's clothes?

CHARLOTTE: I *hate* you. You're a *monster*.

HARRY: I forgive you, honey. But you are so grounded right now.

CHARLOTTE: I *hate* you.

HARRY: You're a fucking *liar*. Truth? You want truth? You *lodestone*. You *weight*. You empty fucking *burden*. You worthless ugly fucking pimple-faced fucking *adolescent* you are a *liar*. And you are *grounded*. You are so *fucking* grounded. You hate me? You love me. Clean up this mess.

CHARLOTTE: I'm still leaving.

HARRY: No. Honey. You're not. *(Pause.)* So OK. I love you and I forgive you and I'm not happy with you right now and I want you to clean up this room and make us some cake that we will eat together because that is what we are. To each other. And you will never leave. You will never leave. You will never never never leave. Right? Do you hear? Clean this up. The news is on.

CHARLOTTE: I had plans!

HARRY: Over. Done. Gone. No more. I will ruin you. To keep you. If I have to.

(Charlotte cries.)

HARRY: You are *not* the only one who suffers. Right? OK? You are *not* the only one.

So. Put your mother's clothes away. And don't touch them. Ever again. OK?

2

(Soft light. Charlotte's room.)

CHARLOTTE: He's like obsessed.

HEATHER: He is.

CHARLOTTE: He's like really obsessed. I can't go.

HEATHER: You can't go?

CHARLOTTE: I can't go. Wherever.

HEATHER: So like he locks the door? Like he won't let you out?

CHARLOTTE: He yelled at me and he tore up my luggage.

HEATHER: What?

CHARLOTTE: He yelled at me and he tore up my luggage. He called me ugly.

HEATHER: Your dad?

CHARLOTTE: Yes.

HEATHER: You're just a little challenged is all.

CHARLOTTE: I am not ugly.

HEATHER: You are not ugly.

CHARLOTTE: I know. I want him to die. Do I have acne?

HEATHER: I don't even know what that is.

CHARLOTTE: Acne?

HEATHER: No. You don't. Wait. Yeah.

CHARLOTTE: Yes?

HEATHER: Yes.

CHARLOTTE: God. I want him to die.

HEATHER: He lets you out for school, right?

CHARLOTTE: Maybe. I don't know. It's the weekend. And I'm like grounded forever.

HEATHER: He has to let you go to school.

CHARLOTTE: I don't know. I can't do anything.

HEATHER: He has to let you go to school. That's like, illegal if he doesn't. It's so illegal.

CHARLOTTE: I know. Is every dad like this? Is your dad like this?

HEATHER: No. Like he's weird and all? But he lets me drive? And I don't have a license or anything. And sometimes like I'm all: Can I borrow your credit card? And he's like: Why? And I'm all: So I can buy some clothes? And he's like: Sure. And I totally use his credit card. I love him.

CHARLOTTE: That's like perfect.

HEATHER: He listens to Neil Diamond. That is not perfect.

CHARLOTTE: I like Neil Diamond.

HEATHER: No one likes Neil Diamond.

CHARLOTTE: I guess you're right.

HEATHER: I know I'm right.

CHARLOTTE: Heather? What would I do without you?

HEATHER: I don't know. Rot?

CHARLOTTE: Probably. *(Beat.)* I always wanted my name to be Caroline. Like Sweet Caroline.

HEATHER: There are so many better things to want.

CHARLOTTE: I guess.

HEATHER: Trust me. There are.

CHARLOTTE: Like what?

HEATHER: Like love. And fame. And a nice outfit. And a massage. And power. And power. And love. And love. And love. Also love.

CHARLOTTE: If I ever get out of here.

HEATHER: You'll get out.

CHARLOTTE: I will be so loved.

HEATHER: You will be.

CHARLOTTE: Everyone will want me.

HEATHER: I want you.

CHARLOTTE: Do you?

(Beat.)

HEATHER: You know what you need? You need to like do something for you. Like go to a spa or something. You so deserve it. We should go. My dad'll pay.

CHARLOTTE: You're such a good friend.

HEATHER: I know.

CHARLOTTE: I love you Heather. *(Beat.)* We can do anything, can't we? Like everyone says You can do anything. But that really means something with us, doesn't it?

HEATHER: It does.

CHARLOTTE: It so does.

(Beat.)

HEATHER: Hey I'm really sorry about your mom.

CHARLOTTE: I know.

HEATHER: It's just so sad.

CHARLOTTE: I know.

HEATHER: Are you sad?

CHARLOTTE: Yeah.

HEATHER: Me too. She was so pretty. She was like, the best mom.

CHARLOTTE: I know.

HEATHER: With like the cupcakes? And the chicken pot pie? Oh my God, I loved your mother's chicken pot pie. It was like. Not even chicken. But. More than chicken. Or something. I don't know. It was just really good. I wish she was my mom.

CHARLOTTE: I know.

HEATHER: I wish my mom would die? 'Cause she's worthless? And that somehow, like in the next world or the afterlife or whatever, she would meet your mom, and like, send her back.

CHARLOTTE: Me too.

HEATHER: But it always happens to the beautiful ones Charlotte.

CHARLOTTE: What?

HEATHER: Early death.

CHARLOTTE: Really?

HEATHER: Of course. Everything beautiful dies. Only the ugly things stick around. That's why, if I live past thirty-five? I will be so upset.

CHARLOTTE: That is such a good point.

HEATHER: I know.

(Beat. Heather stares at Charlotte.)

CHARLOTTE: What?

HEATHER: Nothing. Just. Sometimes when I look at you? I can see her. This beautiful thing. Sort of hiding. And lost. In you.

CHARLOTTE: Really?

HEATHER: You just need to let it out is all.

CHARLOTTE: Really?

HEATHER: Definitely. We just need to focus.

CHARLOTTE: Oh my God. I will. I so will.

HEATHER: Good.

CHARLOTTE: You're the best, Heather.

HEATHER: I know.

> (Beat.)

> Hey Charlotte? I gotta go, OK. I have a date. With a really hot guy. And I gotta go.

CHARLOTTE: You're so lucky.

HEATHER: I know.

CHARLOTTE: He's cute?

HEATHER: Of course.

CHARLOTTE: You're so lucky.

HEATHER: I know. He has a brother. They're twins.

CHARLOTTE: You're so lucky.

HEATHER: I know. I gotta go.

CHARLOTTE: OK. Go.

HEATHER: Gone.

CHARLOTTE: Bye.

> Bye.

> Good-bye.

3

(Stark lighting change.)

CHARLOTTE: I'm not pretty. Yet. I know. I don't have. Whatever. Going for me. I'm not a model. I don't use product. I don't believe in product. I think I'm natural. I have natural beauty.

FRANKLIN: This is what you tell yourself.

CHARLOTTE: It's what I know.

FRANKLIN: Natural beauty.

CHARLOTTE: Shut up.

FRANKLIN: What? OK. That is so relative. What — natural beauty? There is nothing special about natural beauty.

CHARLOTTE: You work at the Cinnabon store. You put frosting on like I don't know. Shit. That's you. What do you know about natural beauty? OK, I *am* natural beauty.

FRANKLIN: I have a job.

CHARLOTTE: I know.

FRANKLIN: I am a responsible individual. Is all.

CHARLOTTE: OK.

(Pause.)

CHARLOTTE: You wanna. Have sex?

FRANKLIN: Charlotte?

CHARLOTTE: Yeah?

FRANKLIN: No.

CHARLOTTE: Why not?

FRANKLIN: I'm waiting for marriage.

CHARLOTTE: So?

FRANKLIN: So I'm waiting for marriage.

CHARLOTTE: Whatever. That is so lame.

FRANKLIN: Marriage is special, Charlotte.

CHARLOTTE: Are you Mormon or something?

FRANKLIN: No.

CHARLOTTE: Since when are you all religious?

FRANKLIN: I'm not.

CHARLOTTE: Isn't your brother like a junkie or like in prison or something?

FRANKLIN: Yeah.

CHARLOTTE: You are not a good boy.

FRANKLIN: Am too. I work.

CHARLOTTE: For Cinnabon.

FRANKLIN: Yeah?

CHARLOTTE: OK. I'll bet you want me.

FRANKLIN: No.

CHARLOTTE: I'll bet you're gay then.

FRANKLIN: No.

CHARLOTTE: So let's have sex. I am so hot right now.

FRANKLIN: Charlotte. I don't even really like you.

CHARLOTTE: So. You don't have to like me to fuck me. Aren't you curious?

FRANKLIN: No.

CHARLOTTE: You're such a liar. OK. This is the plan. You fuck me. And then we have an affair. And then we run away together. And then I dump you. And you're devastated. And I fuck my way to fame and stardom. I fall in love with someone beautiful and you're still devastated.

FRANKLIN: I don't like that plan.

CHARLOTTE: But you want it. Tragedy is so beautiful. Your life can be so tragic if you just let it.

FRANKLIN: Charlotte. I gotta go to work.

CHARLOTTE: Everyone thinks they're really really important? But no one really is. I think you should remember that.

FRANKLIN: You are so weird.

(Freddie enters. Beautiful. Letterman's jacket.)

FREDDIE: Franklin. Fucker. What time is it?

FRANKLIN: Four

FREDDIE: Yeah four. Car's waiting, asshole.

FRANKLIN: Shit. Sorry.

FREDDIE: Right shit sorry.

(Quick beat.)

Hey.

CHARLOTTE: Hi.

FREDDIE: What the hell you doing over there, Franklin? You coming?

FRANKLIN: Coming.

FREDDIE: Jesus.

(Freddie exits.)

CHARLOTTE: You know him?

FRANKLIN: Yeah. Cousin.

CHARLOTTE: He's wonderful.

FRANKLIN: Shut up, Charlotte.

4

CHARLOTTE: So like, seeing as I'm made for sex? I'm gonna be in porn.

GARY: Huh?

CHARLOTTE: I'm gonna be in porn? Like when people fuck you and stuff on camera?

GARY: I'm not sure that's a viable career goal.

CHARLOTTE: What?

GARY: Charlotte, I'm not sure that's a viable career goal. Like for living. Like a goal for what people do. What you want to do.

CHARLOTTE: It's what I want. I've read about it. I've done a lot of research. Porn is like a very nicely paying industry. And it is an industry. It's not like some flash in the pan sort of thing like some Internet thing or I don't know. It's been around. A while. There are videos and magazines. And if you're a woman? People love you. And they want to have sex with you. And they fantasize about you? And that's what I want.

GARY: Have you considered maybe something else maybe?

CHARLOTTE: No. I think porn and I are a great match.

GARY: Charlotte?

CHARLOTTE: Uh huh?

GARY: I don't agree with you. And I think you're being unrealistic. And I think you're being unrealistic.

CHARLOTTE: You said that twice.

GARY: It's for emphasis.

CHARLOTTE: Um what is realistic? OK? What does that mean anyway? I don't think you know what is realistic. I don't think you know what I can do. What I'm capable of. Do you give this advice to everyone? You're being unrealistic? What if I said, I want to be a doctor. What if I said, A doctor. Or what if maybe I said I want to be the president. Like *your* president. And you'd vote for me and everything. What if I said that? Would that be realistic? More realistic? 'Cause I don't even know what that means. So tell me.

GARY: Um. Charlotte. Um. Maybe. It's best to consider. For what you want to be? It's good to think about what you like to do. And not like what you think you like to do. And when I say do, I mean something fulfilling. Something reliable. Something you're interested in. Something like can lead to a job. A profession. Something solid. A teacher maybe. Like that. Do you like math?

CHARLOTTE: I like fucking?

GARY: Do you like math?

CHARLOTTE: I like fucking?

(*Beat.*)

GARY: I don't believe you, Charlotte.

CHARLOTTE: What?

GARY: I don't believe you.

CHARLOTTE: OK. What?

GARY: You heard me.

CHARLOTTE: That is so inappropriate.

GARY: In what way is that inappropriate.

CHARLOTTE: How do you know? OK? How do you know? You don't know. Can you read my mind? Can you like read my mind and tell I don't like fucking? I was made for sex. OK? That's like a fact. That's like gravity. OK? And I don't get you. You're supposed to be supportive. Right? You're supposed to support me. And help me. So help me be a porn star.

GARY: I am a guidance counselor.

CHARLOTTE: Guide me.

GARY: No. I am a guidance counselor. Not a corruptor of minors. There is life.

There is real life. There is a world. And there are rules to this life, this world, and one of them, albeit perhaps an unspoken rule, one of them is that little high school girls do not receive help from their guidance counselors in becoming porn stars. Or whatever. I am not your pimp. Or john. Or whatever it is these people, those people are called. This seems, to me at least, this seems obvious. This seems very. This is something you can take for granted.

CHARLOTTE: When I'm famous? You will be so sorry.

GARY: Maybe.

CHARLOTTE: No. You will be. You will think to yourself, God. I should have just helped her and everything. I should have just helped her realize that dream. That goal. I could have become like, her inspiration. Like the wind beneath her wings or whatever. I hate that song. But it's over now. Now you're gonna like in the future when I'm famous you're gonna be sad. I will be so beautiful. Like my mom. You seen my mom? No. 'Cause she wouldn't even look at you. And now she's dead and don't even try to comfort me.

I'm gonna be beautiful. And you're gonna want me.

GARY: Charlotte?

CHARLOTTE: No. OK? No. It's over. It's over. You're gone. OK? You're through. You and me are over.

GARY: Charlotte?

CHARLOTTE: You hurt me. OK? You *hurt* me. You're supposed to help me and you hurt me. But OK whatever. Whatever doesn't kill me makes me I don't know something. But it's a good something. I have dreams. Needs. I am a star. OK?

(Pause.)

GARY: I'm sorry about your mom.

CHARLOTTE: Shut up.

(Pause.)

GARY: You have any hobbies?

CHARLOTTE: No.

GARY: Nothing?

CHARLOTTE: No.

GARY: Skills?

CHARLOTTE: No.

GARY: Like can you operate a I don't know a copy machine? Something?

CHARLOTTE: I was made for sex. Not copying.

(Beat.)

GARY: I can't. No.

(Beat.)

Go home, Charlotte. Please. Go home.

5

HARRY: Got you something.

CHARLOTTE: Not talking to you.

HARRY: Something nice. Think you'll like it.

CHARLOTTE: Not talking to you.

HARRY: I know. You say that. Take it anyway.

(Harry gives her the gift.)

HARRY: Please. It's not gonna hurt you. It wouldn't hurt you to open it.

(Beat.)

Please. Just make me happy.

(She hesitates. She opens the gift. A very stupid and vastly inappropriate stuffed animal.)

HARRY: It finishes the set, right? The set I got you. It finishes the set. Right?

CHARLOTTE: What is it?

HARRY: It's a — one of those things. That you liked. The magic pony things. I don't know. Didn't you have a magic pony collection or something?

CHARLOTTE: No.

HARRY: Didn't I get you a magic pony something?

CHARLOTTE: No.

(Beat.)

HARRY: You wanna. Start a magic pony something?

(Beat.)

CHARLOTTE: No.

(Beat.)

HARRY: I thought.

(Beat.)

I'm trying, Charlotte.

CHARLOTTE: Daddy? How old do you think I am?

HARRY: Charlotte.

CHARLOTTE: Am I like, eight years old? Do I look like eight years old? I don't even know what this is. Magic pony? It's like. I don't even know. Do eight year olds even get this? Maybe if I were like four, I could look at this and be all, Oh my God, a magic pony or whatever. But right now? I don't even know what this is.

(Beat.)

HARRY: Please.

(Beat.)

CHARLOTTE: Oh God, Daddy. I love it. It's great. It's such a great little fucked-up magic pony. Or whatever the hell it is. I love fucked-up magic fucking ponies for little four year olds. This is great. I can start my collection now. God Daddy. This is so fucking thoughtful.

(Silence.)

HARRY: I keep wondering what I did to deserve this. I keep thinking to myself, asking myself, in what way, in what crucial way did I fail in order to get this. In order to have this.

I don't know what to do.

Never mind.

(Pause.)

CHARLOTTE: Mom always knew what I liked. What I wanted. Anything. She always knew.

HARRY: What's that supposed to mean?

CHARLOTTE: Nothing. I don't know. I'm not talking to you.

(She exits. Leaving Harry alone.)

6

(The lights for this scene become warm, inviting.)

HEATHER: This is for your hair. It has placenta? Which is like dead vagina or something? So it's really gross? But it's good for you, so don't think about it. And this has a bronzer, so I just want you to use this like once a week or something, 'cause otherwise you'll turn orange and look all retarded or sick or something, so once a week. And this is a whole line of products I use which are like aromatherapy? So they smell good? I like the sage. It's for mental clarity which you are so going to need, Charlotte.

CHARLOTTE: Thanks, Heather.

HEATHER: I want you to be focused. This is your mission. This is like Mission Impossible or whatever, but it is totally possible. You OK?

CHARLOTTE: There's just so much.

HEATHER: Of course there is. Nothing worthwhile is ever easy. Start slow. Just use like the daily mask or something. It refreshes *and* rejuvenates.

(Beat.)

It's OK to be overwhelmed at first. But it shouldn't be a habit, Charlotte. Beauty should be your habit. You have to get over this product aversion or whatever. Product is your friend. Read the label and apply. Easy.

CHARLOTTE: I'll try.

HEATHER: Try hard.

CHARLOTTE: I will.

HEATHER: Hard, Charlotte. This is so important.

CHARLOTTE: I will.

(Beat.)

Thank you, Heather.

HEATHER: What are friends for?

CHARLOTTE: I would be so lost.

HEATHER: I know. But you're not. Not now. And you won't be.

(Beat.)

CHARLOTTE: My mom? She would always say. Before she. Died and all. She would say: Charlotte you're so pretty. You're just so pretty. I am so lucky to have such a pretty. You know. Daughter. Or whatever. And it was nice. And I was. Happy. It made me happy.

And I didn't believe her, you know. I thought, oh that's like mom talk or whatever that's what every mother says, my child's so beautiful or whatever and you could be like the Elephant Man and your mom would still be all, oh you're so pretty. So I never believed her. But it made me happy. Because it seemed. I don't know. Possible? Maybe? When she said it.

And you're just so beautiful, Heather. And popular. And smart. And just like. Beautiful. And I want. So much. I mean. Why are you even my friend? It's like. I don't know.

HEATHER: Charlotte?

CHARLOTTE: You're just so beautiful.

HEATHER: Shhh. Listen to me. You are so pretty. OK? You are just so pretty. I am so lucky to have such a pretty friend. And this is the truth. When we're done? Everyone will know how pretty you are. And everyone will say: Look at her. Look at Charlotte. How beautiful she is. Like her mother. Just like her mother. And everyone will want you so hard. The whole world will ache for you. Will kill for you. Will love you. Finally. And again. And again. And again. Everyone will suffer. For love. For you.

(Beat.)

CHARLOTTE: The daily mask?

HEATHER: Read the label and apply. Easy.

7

(Stark lighting change. Harry dumbly staring at something. A bottle in hand. Largely off balance. Sort of teetering. But not falling. Long pause. Charlotte bounds in.)

CHARLOTTE: So? How do I look?

HARRY: What? Huh?

CHARLOTTE: How do I look?

HARRY: Oh.

Where did I put the. The thing. The. Remote control. You. Um.

CHARLOTTE: Daddy.

HARRY: You talking to me again? That's so nice.

CHARLOTTE: How do I look?

(He turns slowly to look at her. Still wavering.)

HARRY: Um.

That's a. Real. Nice dress.

CHARLOTTE: It's new. I got it today.

HARRY: Oh. Nice. And. That. Lip gloss or something, honey? Is that lip gloss?

CHARLOTTE: You noticed?

HARRY: Oh. Yeah. Sure. Sure. Shiny. It's. Great, honey. It's. Really. It's. Almost. It's. Pretty. Almost. Honey. It's great. Um.

And the. Oh wow. The makeup. Huh. Great.

But you know. You should. You should really return the dress, honey. It's. Nice. But. You should just return the dress.

CHARLOTTE: Daddy.

HARRY: You should just return it. It's. It's not for you. That's all.

CHARLOTTE: But I like it. You said it was pretty. It goes with my eyes. The salesgirl said it went with my eyes.

HARRY: Well, you know. She's lying. And. Um. You should just return it. It's. For someone else. Really.

Can you. Um. Help me find the remote?

CHARLOTTE: Daddy.

HARRY: It's really important. Honey. And. I can't find it.

CHARLOTTE: I like. This dress.

HARRY: That's really good. That's really. Really great. But you can't wear it. You're not like your mom. You know. You're not. Nice clothes. Um. You can't wear them, honey. And I know. I know you're trying. But. It's just not. Working. Um.

So yeah you should wash your face, honey. It's better. Go wash your face. I don't wanna. You know. You should wash your face.

CHARLOTTE: Daddy?

HARRY: You look. Stupid. Charlotte. You look stupid. Just. You look stupid. And it's sad. Don't try.

'Cause you're not your mother. Right? You're not your mother. You shouldn't try to look like your mother. I mean. What are you trying to do? Look like a ghost? Like a dead ghost? Like a ghost? You trying to scare me? Is this a joke?

So don't do it. You can't do it. You shouldn't do it.

But could you help me? Find the remote? I mean. How many times. Do I need to ask. Is it so hard?

(Long pause. Harry simply stands, wavering. Charlotte looks at him.)

CHARLOTTE: I wish. You. Were the one.

(Charlotte leaves.)

HARRY: Yeah. Well.

(Pause.)

WHERE'S THE FUCKING REMOTE?

8

(Softer light.)

CHARLOTTE: Um. Considering my skills? And my love and compassion for all of the people in the world? Like all of the people? But especially the children? I think, I really think my real calling is to be a nun. I really think that. Or an anthropologist. Or something. Like that. Because I have such a beautiful and wonderful mind. I do. And I would hate to waste it on just anything, you know, I would hate that. And I think it's important that I serve the world in some real capacity. I mean, service. Something like service. In service. I so want to serve.

GARY: You've considered, I don't know. Have you considered porn?

CHARLOTTE: Um. What?

GARY: Have you considered porn? Sex for money? For other people? That sort of service? Was that a consideration you may have had?

CHARLOTTE: Um. No.

GARY: 'Cause I really think it's something, you know, something to consider. It's not outside the realm of possibility. It's really not. And it pays nicely. I have a lot of research, I've done a lot of research on the subject and women are really, they're really treated I mean it is a profession for women, men too I guess, who want to serve. People who want to serve. I think you should consider it. I mean it's not like being a nun or anything but they're very similar and I think when you give it some thought, I think you'll come to see a lot of the real benefits of working in adult entertainment.

CHARLOTTE: Really?

GARY: I mean this impulse, it's really nice, this impulse for the mind and everything and for others. But you're such a beautiful little girl. I mean I really think it would just take a haircut maybe and a facial or something. And you're set. You're set.

CHARLOTTE: I have really good grades.

GARY: Well, I think, in this situation, I think your achievement is really secondary to your, well, your beauty. Your beauty. Charlotte. I mean that with all sincerity and it shouldn't really be wasted in a career in which it's um meaningless. It's an option.

CHARLOTTE: OK.

GARY: And I guess what I'm saying is that, if you consider this option, if you give it a little thought beyond the just, you know, that's interesting, if you give it a little thought, I guess what I'm saying is that I support you in this decision. I'm behind you. I really am.

CHARLOTTE: You're joking with me.

GARY: No.

CHARLOTTE: Is this a joke?

GARY: No.

CHARLOTTE: You're like, this is not. Happening. You don't say this. You don't say this to students. To me. To girls. You don't say this.

GARY: I say what I feel. What I think is best for the student. There's nothing wrong with that. And for you, I think porn is such an obvious choice. You shouldn't neglect it as an option is all I'm saying. And. You know. It would make your mother proud.

CHARLOTTE: Really?

GARY: Definitely. Parents are happy. Happi*est*. When their children succeed. You can succeed where, maybe, they haven't. Or couldn't. I mean, your mother was so pretty Charlotte. I'm sure porn would have been a serious a very serious option for her. Something. You know. On her career radar which. For whatever reason. You know. You can fulfill the dream

CHARLOTTE: Um.

GARY: Don't second-guess yourself. You have something so uniquely special, Charlotte, I don't really know what it is, a charisma maybe, or maybe it's just a look, or I don't know but you have something special. You shouldn't just let it, you know, you shouldn't just let it go. You shouldn't take it for granted. Use it.

CHARLOTTE: Um.

GARY: No. Use it. OK? Use it.

CHARLOTTE: Um.

GARY: Use it. OK?

(Beat.)

CHARLOTTE: OK.

GARY: Alright.

CHARLOTTE: Yeah.

GARY: OK.

CHARLOTTE: Great.

GARY: Great.

CHARLOTTE: Um. How do I start? Where do I start?

GARY: Interested?

CHARLOTTE: I mean. Yeah. Sure. Why not?

GARY: Why not? Sure. OK. Yes. I have a camera.

    (Beat.)

    Right? It's a Polaroid camera. It's not very good. It's about twenty years old. I photograph birds. In trees. I like ornithology. I have many photo albums.

    (Beat.)

    Do you like birds?

CHARLOTTE: Sure.

GARY: You wanna see my photo album? Do you know where I live?

    (Beat.)

CHARLOTTE: I love you.

A BRIEF HISTORY OF HELEN OF TROY IN FOUR PARTS
PART TWO

Stark lighting shift. The title of the scene is read or projected.

CHARLOTTE: Helen had a daughter. Hermione. Who is not talked about. A lot. But she's there. Or not there. Not in Troy. She's home. In Greece. Doing. Whatever it is. Little Greek girls do — when her mother goes. When she leaves. When she's taken. And sometimes I think about her. Sitting in a room maybe. And her dad. Menelaus. In the next room. Crying. Sometimes I think about her. And I wonder what she thought. How romantic, maybe. To be swept away like that. How romantic. How exotic. Troy. What a place. When I grow up, that's where I'll go. What an adventure. Maybe that's what she's thinking.

Or maybe she starts getting angry. At the men who took her. At the beautiful city over the ocean, made more beautiful just by the fact that her mother is there, being worshipped and adored by so many grateful people.

Or maybe she thinks, Why didn't she take me with her? Is she ashamed? Didn't she love me? Why would she leave me behind?
And maybe she decides, somehow, to bring her back. And to punish the world, really punish it, for taking her.

Maybe that's how the war really started. A little girl. Alone in a room. And her dad. Menelaus. In the next room. Crying.

9

(Charlotte is showing Franklin Polaroids.)

CHARLOTTE: There's this one. This one is my favorite. Oh my God, I had to hold that pose for like I don't know, forever. Isn't that hot? Being a model is hard. But so worth it. There are so many rewards. This one has like perfect light. Doesn't it look like I'm glowing? I am so glowing. I look good.

FRANKLIN: He is not taking pictures.

CHARLOTTE: He is taking pictures. This one's nice.

FRANKLIN: He is not taking pictures.

CHARLOTTE: He is so taking pictures. He has a camera.

FRANKLIN: I have a camera. I'm not taking pictures.

CHARLOTTE: You're not him. OK? You're not an artist. Or a professional. Or anything like that. You don't know what it's like. To find *real* beauty. You don't know what *real* beauty is.

FRANKLIN: He's a guidance counselor.

CHARLOTTE: People have day jobs, alright?

(*Beat.*)

You like this one?

FRANKLIN: No. And anyway, I *am* an artist. I draw.

CHARLOTTE: Everyone draws.

FRANKLIN: I draw well.

CHARLOTTE: Everyone draws well.

FRANKLIN: No they don't.

CHARLOTTE: Yes they do. That is so subjective, Franklin. I draw all the time. You are so pretentious. I'm an artist because I draw. That is so pretentious. My little brother draws.

FRANKLIN: You don't have a little brother.

CHARLOTTE: Whatever. If I did, he would draw. All the time.

FRANKLIN: Lemme see you draw.

CHARLOTTE: I don't have to draw. I'm a model.

FRANKLIN: You're such a liar, Charlotte. You are *not* a model.

CHARLOTTE: And you are *not* an artist. Franklin. So whatever. I know what I am. These would look so hot in black-and-white.

(*Beat.*)

You don't care.

FRANKLIN: No.

CHARLOTTE: What is wrong with you? Everyone likes these pictures. I even showed my dad. He is so proud.

FRANKLIN: You did not. That's disgusting.

CHARLOTTE: What's disgusting? Beauty? That I'm really beautiful?

FRANKLIN: You are not beautiful.

CHARLOTTE: You're a *liar!* This is proof. Proof. I am beautiful. I am so fucking hot. Do you see how hot I am? I am so fucking beautiful and this is proof. Anyway you're just jealous. Someone loves me. A grown person loves me.

FRANKLIN: Mr. Smith?

CHARLOTTE: Gary.

FRANKLIN: He's gay, Charlotte.

CHARLOTTE: You're gay, Franklin.

FRANKLIN: He is so gay! How can you not see that he is so gay?

CHARLOTTE: You really are jealous. Gay Franklin. OK, why am I showing you these?

FRANKLIN: I have no clue.

CHARLOTTE: Give them back.

FRANKLIN: I haven't touched them.

CHARLOTTE: Whatever. You're so *gay*.

FRANKLIN: Charlotte.

CHARLOTTE: Franklin.

FRANKLIN: I am not gay.

CHARLOTTE: Have you told your brother? The one in jail?

FRANKLIN: Charlotte.

CHARLOTTE: I bet he'd kick your ass.

FRANKLIN: You don't know what you're talking about.

CHARLOTTE: I bet he'd kick your ass. Or rape you. They rape each other in prison like all the time. I saw it on *Nightline* or something. He could teach you how to take it, Franklin.

FRANKLIN: I am so gonna hit you.

CHARLOTTE: Whatever gayboy. I'm a girl. People don't hit girls.

FRANKLIN: I'M NOT A FUCKING FAGGOT!

CHARLOTTE: Sorry, Franklin, but it's like. OK. You don't go out with anyone. You don't have any friends. You're not interested in my pictures.

FRANKLIN: They're *ugly!*

CHARLOTTE: You are such a faggot. That is like proof you're gay. And anyway, you say you're an *artist*. That's *your* word. Not mine.

FRANKLIN: You said Mr. Smith was an artist.

CHARLOTTE: He takes pictures. You draw. The difference is so clear.

FRANKLIN: Everyone draws.

CHARLOTTE: You draw *well*.

FRANKLIN: I'm not gay.

CHARLOTTE: Then fuck me.

FRANKLIN: Huh?

CHARLOTTE: Prove it. You're not gay. Fuck me and I'll believe you. You know you want to. If you're not gay. I'm ready.
(*Pause.*)

FRANKLIN: You are so gross.

CHARLOTTE: Gayboy.

FRANKLIN: Shut the fuck up Charlotte I mean it.

CHARLOTTE: Then fuck me.

FRANKLIN: No.

CHARLOTTE: Your brother would fuck me. After all the cocks he's sucked in prison. He'd want me so bad.

FRANKLIN: Stop talking about my brother.

CHARLOTTE: I don't care if you're gay, Franklin. People can be gay.

FRANKLIN: I'm not gay. I don't have to prove it. I know it

CHARLOTTE: Whatever. You're so predictable. Defensive. Something to hide. Whatever. You'd fuck me if you were straight.

FRANKLIN: That is so gross.

CHARLOTTE: I hope your mom doesn't cry when she finds out.

FRANKLIN: Don't say that.

CHARLOTTE: That's like so sad when the moms cry? Or your dad. God. If my dad cried like your dad's gonna cry. I hope he doesn't hurt you. I'll bet that's what you're afraid of, 'cause you're like such a pussy?

FRANKLIN: Please don't say that, Charlotte.

CHARLOTTE: I hope he goes easy. That's all I'm saying. Cinnabon man. Gayboy. Faggot.

FRANKLIN: Charlotte.

CHARLOTTE: God and I bet you want your cousin. I bet you like jerk off thinking about your cousin Freddie. Right? How hot he is? That is so obvious. Wow. *You* are so disgusting.

(He punches her in the face.)

FRANKLIN: LIAR. LIAR. CUNT. LIAR.

(He runs away.)

CHARLOTTE: OW! YOU'RE GONNA RUIN MY FUCKING CAREER!

10

(Harry. Disheveled. Probably sobering up. Watching TV. The news. Barely audible. Long pause. Charlotte enters.)

HARRY: Hey honey.

(Beat.)

News is on.

(Beat.)

Watch the news with me? There's cake in the. Fridge.

(Beat.)

You OK?

(Beat.)

What did I do? I do something bad again? Honey —

CHARLOTTE: No.

HARRY: Good. 'Cause I'm tired.

CHARLOTTE: No.

HARRY: Good.

> (*Beat.*)
>
> Watch the news with me?
>
> (*Beat.*)
>
> What's with your face?

CHARLOTTE: Nothing.

HARRY: Someone hit you?

CHARLOTTE: No.

HARRY: Looks like someone hit you.

CHARLOTTE: No one hit me.

HARRY: Looks like it.

CHARLOTTE: Drop it daddy.

HARRY: OK.

> (*Beat.*)
>
> Sit down. We'll watch the news.
>
> (*Beat.*)
>
> You just gonna stand there?

CHARLOTTE: Maybe.

HARRY: Cake in the fridge. Wanna get us some?

CHARLOTTE: I wanna talk about Mom.

HARRY: What?

CHARLOTTE: Tell me about Mom.

HARRY: Not right now, honey. Get some cake.

CHARLOTTE: Why not? You're so mean sometimes.

HARRY: I'm just. Real tired, sweetie. I don't want to talk about it.

CHARLOTTE: You loved her?

HARRY: Yes. God. Just get some cake.

CHARLOTTE: What was she like? With you?

HARRY: We're not talking about this right now.

CHARLOTTE: Did she love you?

HARRY: We're not talking. About this. Right now.

CHARLOTTE: What did she look like naked?

HARRY: Charlotte what are you trying to do?

CHARLOTTE: Nothing.

HARRY: Not now. OK? Not this. Anything else fine. But this. No.

CHARLOTTE: You never want to talk to me.

HARRY: That is *not* true.

CHARLOTTE: Then let's talk about Mom.

HARRY: No. No. Something else. OK?

CHARLOTTE: What was it like kissing her?

HARRY: Stop it Charlotte.

CHARLOTTE: Did you like kissing her?

HARRY: Now. Charlotte.

CHARLOTTE: Did you like when she touched you?

(Beat.)

Daddy?

(Beat.)

How did she touch you? Did she like when you touched her? Was it nice?

(Long beat.)

Can you show me?

(Long pause.)

HARRY: Go to your room.

CHARLOTTE: Please?

HARRY: Go to your room.

CHARLOTTE: Daddy?

HARRY: I AM WATCHING THE FUCKING NEWS. Charlotte. I am watching the news. I am not talking about your mother. I am watching I AM WATCHING THE FUCKING NEWS DO NOT TALK TO ME ABOUT YOUR MOTHER.

(Pause.)

CHARLOTTE: If you teach me. I can be. Just like her.

(Beat.)

Wouldn't that be nice?

(Pause.)

HARRY: You are. An evil. Little girl.

CHARLOTTE: Who cares? I won't tell.

HARRY: Why now? Of all times. Why do you need to make it so hard for me to love you? Why do you need to do this?

(Beat.)

Do you want me to hate you?

(Beat.)

Go to your room.

(Beat.)

This didn't happen.

(Beat.)

We'll start over.

(Beat.)

Hi honey. How was your day? There's cake in the fridge.

(Beat.)

Hi.

(Beat.)

Sometimes people need space. And. Sometimes. It's really unfair. When other people. Need. So much. From someone. Who just needs space.

(Beat.)

OK? We've talked about this. Right?

(Beat.)

I miss your mom.

CHARLOTTE: I know.

(Long pause.)

HARRY: Go to your room.

11

(Warm, beautiful light. Charlotte's bedroom. Freddie enters. Bare chested. Football in hand. He's beautiful.)

FREDDIE: Um. Hi.

Charlotte.

Um.

OK I know this is awkward and everything. Me just coming here and all. Like this. I mean I know I just really met you and everything. But I've seen you. Really. And I just gotta. I had to come and tell you. You know. And.

This is embarrassing, I know. And I don't mean it to be. It's not supposed to be. I mean. But. Jesus, it's cold out, right? Anyway there's like a million things I wanna tell you right now, Charlotte. And I just. I don't know. Like. You have such a cool room. I really like your bedspread.

Um.

This is usually the other way around.

OK I've seen you. And. You are so. Pretty. I think. I mean. I think you're pretty. Right. Um. So I'll just come out and say it. OK. I think I love you. Charlotte. I really do. And. It's not like this happens every day. You know. For me. I don't just like fall in love with people. It's hard. And I've really fallen for you. And I know it's stupid and like. Stupid and everything. But. I wanna know if maybe we can go out and be like boyfriend girlfriend or something I don't know. 'Cause I'm really. I'm. In love. With you. And it's hard. Keeping it inside. All the time. And I came here to say that. And ask you. You know. If we can maybe. Go out sometime. And. Eat something. Or. Watch a movie. Or I don't know. I got a great entertainment system at home. I could show you. DVD. Surround sound and everything. It's really cool. But. You know.

We could go out and. Maybe I could touch you. And. Maybe you'd let me kiss you. I mean if that's OK. Is that OK? 'Cause I really love you. I really wanna be with you. It's so important to me right now. I really. Just had to come and tell you. I couldn't wait. Um.

Shit I gotta get back to practice. Um.

Okay. I love you. Please love me.

Oh. And. I'm really sorry. About your mom. Being dead and all. That sucks.

I gotta go.

12

(Stark lighting change. Gary is reading a letter.)

GARY: This is interesting. This is really interesting. I'm not sure what it means.

CHARLOTTE: You know what it means.

GARY: No. I'm not sure I do. Which is why I said it. I'm not sure I know what this means. Is there. Maybe you know?

CHARLOTTE: Don't play stupid.

GARY: Um. OK.

(Beat.)

How about I play perplexed? I am perplexed. I am very very perplexed. I use this word *perplexed*. And I'm worried. Charlotte. "Thank you for seeing me." You wrote this, right? These are your words. "Thank you for seeing me. I had a great time. You're the best. The pictures are awesome. You're a great lover. I would totally do it again. You have a nice penis."

(Beat.)

And you sign it. That's. Here. Your signature. Right?

(Beat.)

Um Charlotte when did we have a great time? When did you see my penis? What are these pictures?

CHARLOTTE: You are so mean. And I hate you.

GARY: I don't know what you're talking about.

CHARLOTTE: Why are you denying it?

GARY: I wish I knew what I was denying.

CHARLOTTE: You took pictures.

GARY: I took no pictures.

CHARLOTTE: You did. You love bird-watching. You had a camera. Have a camera. You have a camera you use to take pictures. The Oriole is my favorite bird, you said. But there aren't many orioles around here. Why don't you get undressed? You said that. You told me to get undressed. I was *in* your *house* and you *told* me to get undressed.

GARY: I did not.

CHARLOTTE: You did! You liar! You did! And you took pictures. Wow you are so beautiful is what you said. Wow. Can I touch you? And you did. You touched me. My arms. My legs. My breasts. You touched my breasts. And your hand.

GARY: No. Charlotte.

CHARLOTTE: And your penis and it was wonderful. You were wonderful. And you loved me. Hard. And we needed each other and it was very very romantic with the birds singing and the pictures and wet between us and the love the real real love and you were like so beautiful and. Massive. And. I loved you.

GARY: We did not have sex, Charlotte.

CHARLOTTE: We made love.

GARY: We did not have sex. We did not make love. You are a little girl. Guidance counselors do not have sex with little girls.

CHARLOTTE: You had sex with me!

GARY: I did not have sex with you. Lower your voice.

CHARLOTTE: You promised me. You promised love. And fame. And a career. You said I would be *famous* that you would make me famous. That people would love me. You said that and I believed you. You said that.

GARY: I did not say that.

CHARLOTTE: You said that.

GARY: I did not say that.

CHARLOTTE: You said that! You said that! You said it and you said it and you said it.

GARY: Are you trying to blackmail me? What are you trying to do? What do you want?

CHARLOTTE: I am a porn star. I told you. You said you would help me. So. Help me.

GARY: We've been through this.

CHARLOTTE: No. No. You will not like dismiss me or whatever. You will not dismiss or like ignore what we have. What we had. I have the pictures. I have the pictures.

GARY: What pictures? I took no pictures. I don't even have a camera. What pictures? I hate birds. They scare me. I hate nature. I don't have a camera. I don't use a camera. Who uses a fucking camera? I don't use a camera.

CHARLOTTE: I wasn't gonna tell anyone. You think I was gonna tell someone? Like about our love? Or like our passion or whatever?

GARY: Do you want me to lose my job?

CHARLOTTE: No.

GARY: Do you want me to be fired? To go to prison? To live in prison? Do you want me to go to jail? Why would you write something like this? Why would you do this?

CHARLOTTE: I wrote it because it was true.

GARY: Are you crazy? Are you fucking nuts? This is not true. This was never true. I never did this. I would never do this. I love my job. This is a joke.

CHARLOTTE: This is not a joke.

GARY: This has to be a joke. All this is a joke. Tell me you want to be a doctor. Tell the truth. You want to repair old TVs or be like a computer programmer or something. I will work for you. I will work *with* you. Let me work with you.

CHARLOTTE: You loved me. You photographed me.

GARY: No! No no no. No! Emphatically. No. No. Understand. No. No. No.

CHARLOTTE: Why don't you love me anymore?

(Pause.)

GARY: OK. You need help. You need a lot of help. And I am not sure. No I am positive. In fact I am positive. I know I am not the one to be able to give you this help. I am a guidance counselor. You need a doctor. I can help you find one. I'm picking up the phone now.

CHARLOTTE: No.

GARY: No what?

CHARLOTTE: Don't.

GARY: You need help.

(Beat.)

CHARLOTTE: It was a joke.

GARY: It was a joke.

CHARLOTTE: I was joking.

GARY: This was a joke.

CHARLOTTE: Yes.

(Pause.)

GARY: Jesus, Charlotte. Why can't you want normal things? Like everyone else? There's a world of good stuff to want. There's a world of good for you if you want it. People will help you to it. I can help you to it.

CHARLOTTE: I was made for more. Some of us were made for more.

GARY: Maybe.

CHARLOTTE: I know it.

> *(Pause.)*

GARY: Well. OK. Be that as it may.

> *(Beat.)*
>
> You cannot write letters like this. And just. Hand them to people. You cannot carry letters like this in school. This is what happens. It's hard. I know. But don't do it. Ever again.
>
> *(Beat.)*
>
> I mean, on a certain level, I'm flattered. I'll be honest. But no more. OK? OK? OK.
>
> *(Gary begins to rip up the letter.)*

CHARLOTTE: What are you doing?

GARY: I'm sorry?

CHARLOTTE: What are you doing, that's my letter.

GARY: I'm ripping it up.

CHARLOTTE: But that's my letter give it back.

GARY: Charlotte it is not your letter, you gave it to me.

CHARLOTTE: That's my letter give it back.

GARY: Charlotte, it's wrong. We agreed it was wrong. Didn't we agree?

CHARLOTTE: *You* said it was wrong. Not me. Give it back.

GARY: Charlotte. It was wrong for you to write it. It was *wrong* for you to write it. OK? It belongs in the trash. 'Cause there are boundaries, Charlotte, proper boundaries. What is appropriate and what is not appropriate. Right? I mean this is like Social Etiquette 101, like basic social etiquette, how people live and interact and work with each other and make good things happen in the world. And this is not appropriate. Right? This is not appropriate. I need you to understand that this is not appropriate. And it is wrong. It is so wrong. It is wrong.

> *(Beat.)*

CHARLOTTE: Franklin says you're gay.

GARY: What?

CHARLOTTE: He says you're gay and that you touched him. Abused him. Molested him. He said you like drew the blinds. This very office. And that's why he's gay. He blames you. You destroyed him. This desk.

> *(Beat.)*

So OK. This is how the story goes. You love me. You admit it. And I still
get to ruin you. OK?

(Pause.)

GARY: No. Charlotte. Wrong. Get out.

(He throws the remaining scraps of the letter away.)

The title is read or projected.

CHARLOTTE: The slaughter lasted ten years. Fighting for ten years. For the most beautiful woman in the world. How bright she must have been. In the midst of all that blood and death and horror. How much brighter she would have seemed. Confident. Unafraid. Strong. In the center of all that darkness. And I think. Maybe the darkness comforted her. Maybe she knew it had come to take her home. Maybe she looked out at all the dead bodies, the fighting men, the weeping women and children, and saw her daughter. In her room. Alone. And maybe, looking at the black storm clouds, the war machines, the funeral pyres blazing through the night, maybe she whispered, Hermione, my daughter, I love you too.

So maybe the darkness fed her. And nurtured her. And taught her. How to shine. So much brighter. And maybe she loved the darkness for giving her this chance. This opportunity. To be so much more beautiful than she ever was before.

And at the end of the war, that's why everyone wanted to kill her. That's why everyone wanted to punish her. For being so beautiful. For setting the world on fire. For loving that radiant darkness. Because it loved her. So mercilessly.

And that's why everyone started to hate her.

(There is a long silence.)

13

FREDDIE: Hey.

CHARLOTTE: Hi.

FREDDIE: You're staring at me.

CHARLOTTE: What?

FREDDIE: You keep staring at me it's fucking creepy.

CHARLOTTE: Sorry.

FREDDIE: Yeah sorry. You OK? I help you with anything? There something you need or I don't know. You need something?

CHARLOTTE: No. Yes.

FREDDIE: I know you?

CHARLOTTE: Yes.

FREDDIE: How do I know you?

CHARLOTTE: Franklin?

FREDDIE: I don't know what that means.

CHARLOTTE: Your cousin?

FREDDIE: Yeah?

CHARLOTTE: I'm his friend.

FREDDIE: Oh yeah right.

CHARLOTTE: His best friend.

FREDDIE: Yeah. Yeah yeah.

CHARLOTTE: I'm his friend.

FREDDIE: Stupid. Yeah. That makes sense. What's your name?

CHARLOTTE: Charlotte.

FREDDIE: Like Charlotte's Web or whatever?

CHARLOTTE: No. Just. Like Charlotte.

FREDDIE: Fucking hated that book. Freddie.

CHARLOTTE: I know.

FREDDIE: Right. So. How come you guys don't hang out?

CHARLOTTE: Huh?

FREDDIE: How come you and Franklin don't hang out?

CHARLOTTE: We hang out.

FREDDIE: Really?

CHARLOTTE: Yeah.

FREDDIE: Haven't seen you around but that one time you know. Which I for-
     got right? I thought he was like a loser or something. No friends or.
     Whatever.
     (Beat.)
     Well good. He's got a friend.

CHARLOTTE: We hang out.

FREDDIE: Great. Good to know. You in love with him?

CHARLOTTE: No.

FREDDIE: Why not?

CHARLOTTE: 'Cause I'm not.

FREDDIE: You wanna be?

CHARLOTTE: No.

FREDDIE: Good for you. He's a fucking loser.
     (Beat.)
     Yeah so I've noticed there's nothing left to talk about. Right?

CHARLOTTE: I don't know.

FREDDIE: So you should maybe do something else.

CHARLOTTE: No. I don't know.

FREDDIE: Yeah you should go do something else.

CHARLOTTE: Like what?

FREDDIE: I don't know. Go find Franklin. Do. Whatever it is. The two of you do. What do you do?

CHARLOTTE: Talk. Mostly.

FREDDIE: You suck his dick?

CHARLOTTE: No. That's gross.

FREDDIE: Yeah. Whatever. Probably. So go home. Where do you live?

CHARLOTTE: Couple blocks away.

FREDDIE: That's great. That's so close.

CHARLOTTE: Yeah.

FREDDIE: Yeah. OK. So go home.

 (*Beat.*)

CHARLOTTE: You. Want to come with me?

FREDDIE: I'm sorry?

CHARLOTTE: You. Want to come home. With me?

FREDDIE: What?

CHARLOTTE: I have ice cream.

FREDDIE: Huh?

CHARLOTTE: You like ice cream?

FREDDIE: Ice cream?

CHARLOTTE: Or cake. I have cake.

FREDDIE: What are you talking about?

CHARLOTTE: We could watch TV. We could have cake and watch TV and stuff.

FREDDIE: At your house?

CHARLOTTE: Yeah.

FREDDIE: I don't even know you.

CHARLOTTE: You could get to know me.

FREDDIE: Why?

CHARLOTTE: Because I'm fun. And I'm pretty. And I have a nice house. Big TV. And I like you. And we could be friends. Like really really good friends. And you're beautiful. And. I could go down on you. If you want.

FREDDIE: You could go down on me?

CHARLOTTE: It could be fun. I've been practicing.

FREDDIE: You've been practicing.

CHARLOTTE: Every day. I know what I'm doing.

FREDDIE: You crack me up.

CHARLOTTE: Why? I'm serious.

FREDDIE: No I believe you.
> *(Beat.)*
> I have a girlfriend.

CHARLOTTE: So?

FREDDIE: She's my girlfriend.

CHARLOTTE: Whatever.

FREDDIE: I'm just saying.
> *(Beat.)*
> How many blocks?

CHARLOTTE: Five.

FREDDIE: Huh. You swallow?

CHARLOTTE: Sure. Whatever.

FREDDIE: Right.
> *(Beat.)*
> So you'll just blow me.

CHARLOTTE: Yeah.

FREDDIE: Just like that.

CHARLOTTE: Yeah.

FREDDIE: Right. You're a good kid, Charlotte. Let's get some cake.

CHARLOTTE: Really?

FREDDIE: Yeah.

CHARLOTTE: Really?

FREDDIE: Yeah. Let's go.

CHARLOTTE: Wow. OK.

14

(Soft light.)

HEATHER: So is it true? Oh my God is it? Wow. That is such a coup. That is such a big coup. You're like, I don't know. You're my hero. That's awesome. I'm totally jealous.

CHARLOTTE: He's so cute.

HEATHER: Hot.

CHARLOTTE: Hot.

HEATHER: He is hot. Oh my God. Do you love him?

CHARLOTTE: I think so.

HEATHER: Why?

CHARLOTTE: I don't know.

HEATHER: You don't have to.

CHARLOTTE: I know.

HEATHER: Wait on love. OK? That comes later. I know what I'm talking about. You'll only hurt yourself.

CHARLOTTE: OK.

HEATHER: Trust me.

CHARLOTTE: OK.

HEATHER: Did you suck his dick?

CHARLOTTE: No.

HEATHER: Good. It is so overrated.

CHARLOTTE: We just started going out.

HEATHER: Whatever. Look at you all shy. There is no need to be shy. OK. When he starts to love you like a lot? He'll totally want you to suck his dick. And that's normal and everything? But make him wait. It is no fun.

CHARLOTTE: OK.

HEATHER: I know what I'm talking about.

CHARLOTTE: You're the best.

HEATHER: I know. You've seen him naked?

CHARLOTTE: Heather.

HEATHER: That is a totally valid question. Don't Heather me. You sound like my dad. You should really see him naked. Not my dad. Your guy. Size him up. Make sure he's like. OK. And not. Retarded or whatever.

CHARLOTTE: He's not retarded.

HEATHER: Whatever. You need to know. This is important. Has he kissed you?

CHARLOTTE: Not yet.

HEATHER: Are you really going out with him?

CHARLOTTE: Heather. Yes.

HEATHER: 'Cause it sounds like he's your brother or something. I mean, what have you done? Have you done anything? Have you like gone out or whatever? Have you held hands? I mean, Charlotte. Going out does not mean like repartee. You know. Or whatever. Dating is not a conversation.

CHARLOTTE: I know. We're going slow.

HEATHER: Going slow? You could not be going slower. Charlotte. Take control. Bull by the horns. Hand jobs are fine at this stage. And fucking's OK too I guess. But draw the line at blow jobs. I am so serious.

CHARLOTTE: I will.

HEATHER: Not until you're ready. You'll just hurt yourself. Anyway it takes time to develop good blowing skills. Maybe you should practice. Like find someone to practice on?

CHARLOTTE: Like cheat on him?

HEATHER: It is not cheating. OK. It is practice. It's like when you practice anything. You're not cheating the final whatever. Performance. Or audience. Or. Whatever. It is just not cheating.

CHARLOTTE: OK.

HEATHER: The world is not so cut and dry, Charlotte. This or that. There is so much in between.

CHARLOTTE: I know.

HEATHER: So act like it. OK?

CHARLOTTE: I will.

HEATHER: Don't just say it.

CHARLOTTE: OK.

HEATHER: No one is going to wait for you to be what you are. OK? And no one is going to care about you if you *aren't* what you *are*. So you have to be gorgeous *now*, Charlotte. Or you never will be. Your eyes look really nice today

CHARLOTTE: Thanks. That is so profound. About the being and stuff.

HEATHER: I know. I'm like the Dalai Lama or whatever. But without like all the bad clothes and the shaved head and the Third World country.

CHARLOTTE: You're like my sister, Heather.

HEATHER: Isn't it fun?

CHARLOTTE: I want so much for us.

HEATHER: I know. Me too. Oh my God. I almost forgot. I brought you something from Mexico?

CHARLOTTE: What is it?

HEATHER: It's a peso. Which means you can't really do anything with it? But it's from another country. And I thought of you.

CHARLOTTE: It's beautiful.

HEATHER: I know. Isn't it pretty? With the bird?

CHARLOTTE: Yes.

HEATHER: I thought of you. How you couldn't come. 'Cause of your dad?

CHARLOTTE: I know. He's horrible.

HEATHER: The beaches are so pretty. And everyone is so friendly. They're all like full of love or whatever. And they'll do anything for a dollar. Or even a peso. But I saved that one for you. I was gonna buy a monkey with it? Or a cucumber? Or a boy? But my daddy wouldn't let me. So I saved it for you.

CHARLOTTE: Thank you.

HEATHER: You should let me do your hair. You are so pretty, Charlotte. I'm so jealous.

(Beat.)

Can I kiss you?

CHARLOTTE: What?

HEATHER: We should totally have like a lesbian moment right now.

CHARLOTTE: Heather?

HEATHER: What?

> *(Beat.)*
>
> It was a joke.
>
> *(Beat.)*
>
> We should move to Mexico. Everyone is free in Mexico. You can do what you want. And the weather's nice. And there are pyramids. And jungles. And scorpions. And parrots? No one cares what you do. Everyone's a criminal anyway. It's where real life is. And real love. And we could live there. Together. Just us.
>
> *(Slowly, awkwardly, they move to kiss each other.)*

HEATHER: Can I?

> *(Beat.)*
>
> I think your acne cleared up. That's so cute. Do you use the product now?

CHARLOTTE: Yes.

> *(They kiss.)*

CHARLOTTE: I'm so. Happy. With you. Heather.

HEATHER: Me too.

> *(They kiss.)*

CHARLOTTE: I think I'm gonna vomit.

HEATHER: It's OK. Just means you're excited. It's good.

> *(They kiss.)*

CHARLOTTE: I gotta pee.

HEATHER: Hold it.

CHARLOTTE: I can't.

HARRY'S VOICE: *(Offstage.)* Charlotte?

HEATHER: Then don't.

> *(They kiss.)*

HARRY'S VOICE: Who're you talking to?

HEATHER: I love you.

> *(Harry enters. The lights instantly become cold. Stark. Charlotte wets herself.)*

HARRY: Charlotte, who are you talking to?

CHARLOTTE: What?

> *(Beat.)*
>
> WHAT?

(Beat.)

WHAT!?

(She screams. Frustration. Shame. She runs off. We hear her crying. Beat.
Slowly, Harry, in whatever way he can, cleans the floor.)

HARRY: *(More to himself.)* It's OK. It's OK. It's OK.

(To Charlotte offstage.)

It's OK. I cleaned it. It's clean.

CHARLOTTE: *(Offstage.)* I HATE YOU.

(Beat. Harry nods his head slowly. He exits.)

15

FREDDIE: You've gotta stop it.

CHARLOTTE: What?

FREDDIE: Following me. You've gotta stop it.

CHARLOTTE: I'm not following you.

FREDDIE: And the phone calls.

CHARLOTTE: I don't call you.

FREDDIE: Stop fucking calling me, Charlotte.

CHARLOTTE: I don't call you.

FREDDIE: I have caller fucking ID. It's embarrassing.

CHARLOTTE: Whatever.

FREDDIE: So stop calling.

CHARLOTTE: Fine.

(Beat.)

FREDDIE: You are fucking annoying you know that? Like some yipping fucking dog or something. Like a fucking vulture cock Chihuahua. Hovering
and yipping and fucking yipping and hovering and begging begging begging. Freddie can we go out now. Freddie can I suck your cock. How
'bout I suck your cock? Jesus Charlotte. Get a fucking life.

CHARLOTTE: But we're going out. We're like dating and everything.

FREDDIE: What?

CHARLOTTE: You said we were dating.

FREDDIE: I never.

CHARLOTTE: You meant to.

FREDDIE: What the fuck?

CHARLOTTE: You meant to say that we were dating.

FREDDIE: I said Thank you for the mediocre fucking blow job Charlotte is what I said.

CHARLOTTE: Whatever. My version's better.

FREDDIE: That's bullshit. That's crazy fucking bullshit I have a girlfriend. I *have* a *girlfriend.*

CHARLOTTE: So what?

FREDDIE: So she's my *girlfriend.* I'm dating her. I fuck her. And she's not a fucking ugly Chihuahua cock vulture or whatever you are. Suck Franklin's dick. Get him off. He needs it. Date Franklin.

CHARLOTTE: Franklin's gay.

FREDDIE: He's what?

CHARLOTTE: He's gay. And anyway he's not my boyfriend.

FREDDIE: He is not gay.

CHARLOTTE: He's a queer homosexual.

FREDDIE: Motherfucker.

CHARLOTTE: Yeah.

FREDDIE: Motherfucker.

CHARLOTTE: And he like fantasizes about you?

FREDDIE: That's great.

CHARLOTTE: Yeah he told me. He has this fantasy of you all naked and sweaty and everything? Like after practice? I am not joking. And he goes down on you? And you fuck him? And the sun on the horizon and everything? And he is so gay. But I don't think Franklin swallows. *I* swallow. So he's gay and I can't date him but you're my boyfriend anyway so it doesn't matter.

FREDDIE: Fucking pervert.

CHARLOTTE: I know. It's so sad. But I'm here. I'm teaching myself better form? Like with my lips? So look. I can cover my teeth with my lips now. It'll be so much better.

(Beat.)

FREDDIE: Jesus you're so fucking disgusting.

CHARLOTTE: I'm just nasty. There's a difference. You like nasty. So let's go home. Oh my God there is so much cake at home.

(Freddie spits on Charlotte.)

FREDDIE: No.

(Beat.)

CHARLOTTE: That's OK. That's OK. You can do that. That's OK. I don't mind.

(He spits on her again.)

FREDDIE: No.

(Beat.)

You're horrible. You're ugly. You're like a walking cancer you're so fucking ugly. Don't touch me. I see you near me again, I see you hovering in the corner, I hear the fucking phone ring, I will kill you I will murder you you horrible fucking bitch.

CHARLOTTE: I'll tell.

FREDDIE: What.

CHARLOTTE: You let me go down on you. You made me swallow.

FREDDIE: Everybody goes down on me. And everybody swallows. Big. Fucking. Deal.

CHARLOTTE: You love me.

FREDDIE: Right. Fuck off. I got practice.

(Freddie walks off.)

CHARLOTTE: You love me. You fucking love me. YOU CAME IN MY MOUTH YOU *LOVE* ME. You *love* me.

(Freddie is gone.)

CHARLOTTE: Everybody loves me.

16

(The sound of the television. The news. Charlotte desperate and frustrated.)

CHARLOTTE: I'm going. This is it. No jokes. I'm not gonna sit around here and wait. For whatever. To happen. I'm gonna go and make it happen. I'm gonna leave. I'm gonna fucking get out of here.

So I'm going to Mexico, Daddy. I'm gonna live in a pyramid in Teoti whatever. Where the Aztecs lived. And no one can stop me. And I'll live there and the parrots will feed me and tell me stories. And I'll grow strong and people will worship me and sacrifice babies to me and everyone will be ashamed of themselves. Everyone will be so fucking ashamed. And jealous. Of me. I'll be so beautiful. And I'll marry God in the Aztec pyramid. God as a blood red sun. And we'll fuck like monkeys to the sound of the chattering jungles and make God babies and repopulate the world with beautiful God babies and everyone else will go. Everyone else will have to go. Including you.

And everything will be different. And really really different.

So I'm going. Don't try to stop me. Complain. Whine. I don't care. I HAVE MY OWN FUCKING LUGGAGE THIS TIME. I bought it myself. I even have a peso. You can buy the world with a peso if you know who's selling

    I'm taking the car. All the way down.

    You won't stop me.

    (Pause.)

HARRY: Fine.

CHARLOTTE: What?

HARRY: Go. Fine. Go. Get out. Whatever. Go. Get lost. Get out. Do what you want. Leave. Get out. Go. Go. Go. Go.

    (Beat.)

    Bye, honey.

    (Pause.)

CHARLOTTE: Wrong answer. That is the wrong answer. THAT IS THE WRONG FUCKING ANSWER. WRONG. WRONG WRONG WRONG WRONG YOU WORTHLESS. WRONG.

    (Charlotte runs off. Long long pause. Harry begins beating himself on the head violently with the remote control for some time, after which he throws the remote at the television. Pause. The sound of the TV.)

HARRY: Honey?

    (Long pause. Then suddenly to the television.)

    SHUT UP. SHUT UP. SHUT UP. SHUT UP. SHUT UP.

    (Long pause. The sound of the TV. Harry alone.)

17

    (Franklin in Charlotte's bedroom. He looks horrible — beaten and bloody.)

CHARLOTTE: What are you doing here?

FRANKLIN: Hi.

CHARLOTTE: Franklin, what are you doing here?

FRANKLIN: Saying hi.

CHARLOTTE: Hi.

    (Beat.)

    So why are you in my room, Franklin?

FRANKLIN: I'm ready.

CHARLOTTE: What?

FRANKLIN: You've got a great room, Charlotte. It's really great. I like your bedspread. Looks nice.

CHARLOTTE: You OK?

FRANKLIN: Yeah I'm OK. You wanna sit on the bed and I'll stand here and we'll talk for awhile?

CHARLOTTE: No.

FRANKLIN: So I'm ready is all. I just needed some time to be ready is all and now I'm ready so. Here I am. I'll sit with you on the bed if you like and we'll get comfortable. And we can start.

CHARLOTTE: Did someone hurt you?

FRANKLIN: Fell down some stairs. It's nothing. I'm really OK. You don't have to be concerned or anything. Sit on the bed. We can talk. Or we can get started. Or whatever. However it goes.

CHARLOTTE: You should go home. Or to a doctor. Or somewhere.

FRANKLIN: I'm OK. It's nothing.

CHARLOTTE: No but you're being really creepy? So you should probably go home.

FRANKLIN: Later.

CHARLOTTE: I'll call my dad.

FRANKLIN: Your dad's here? That's great. Maybe I can meet him.

CHARLOTTE: Dad?

(Beat.)

CHARLOTTE: Dad?

FRANKLIN: Maybe he's tired or something. Maybe he went to get something from the store. I can stay and meet him maybe. Sit on the bed.

CHARLOTTE: This is my house Franklin. And you shouldn't be here. No one invited you.

FRANKLIN: So I figure that it's really important. For me to do this. I guess. I mean, I figure that I'm probably in love with you. Or will be most likely. With enough time. Given a little time. I could be a real good husband. Maybe we could get married. Married people learn to love. Sometimes slowly, but they learn. I'm a good learner. Fast learner. I'd learn faster. Why won't you sit on the bed? Please sit on the bed. Please make this easy.

CHARLOTTE: Go home. Take a shower.

FRANKLIN: That's funny. I look dirty? I guess. Probably.

(Beat.)

You talked to Freddie?

CHARLOTTE: I didn't talk to Freddie.

(Beat.)

FRANKLIN: Some things are just really hard? Some things are hard to get your mind around? And you need to work them out is all. You need to see what they mean if they mean anything. And maybe they *don't* mean anything. Maybe they don't really. And maybe they're just hard things to understand. Sometimes these things are just. Really hard to figure out. Confusing. Maybe. Even.

(Beat.)

I don't know what I'm saying. Funny, right? What am I saying, right?

(Beat.)

You shouldn't have talked to Freddie.

CHARLOTTE: I'm sorry.

FRANKLIN: So maybe we can start now.

(Beat.)

I don't know what to do. You know what to do?

CHARLOTTE: Go home.

FRANKLIN: I climbed in your window. That was hard. I climbed in your window and I'm here and it was hard getting here. Coming to this place. And you want this. You've said it. You want this. So now you have it. You can have it. I give it to you.

CHARLOTTE: I don't want it anymore.

FRANKLIN: Why is it all so hard with you? Why is everything so hard? Just be nice to me. Please be nice to me.

(Beat.)

CHARLOTTE: But. You're supposed to want me. Like really want me. You're supposed to be beautiful. And tender. And like come to me all beautiful and tender. And kind. And you're supposed to say things to me. Pretty things like what lovers say. Like what people who love each other say. To each other. And that's what you're supposed to do.

FRANKLIN: I know.

CHARLOTTE: So do it.

(Beat.)

FRANKLIN: Maybe —

CHARLOTTE: No. You have to do it. So do it.

FRANKLIN: Maybe later.

CHARLOTTE: No.

FRANKLIN: Maybe sometime later OK? Not now. Maybe later.

CHARLOTTE: No. No. No no no. You can't do this.

FRANKLIN: What did I do? What did I do, Charlotte? How did I do this? How could I want this? Why would I want this?

CHARLOTTE: I didn't mean. For this. Like this.

FRANKLIN: But you did.

CHARLOTTE: No.

FRANKLIN: You did. Charlotte. Look at me.

(Beat.)

You did. And now you have to make it better. Now you have to fix it.

(Beat.)

So make it better. Please just make it better.

CHARLOTTE: No.

FRANKLIN: Charlotte?

(Pause.)

CHARLOTTE: I'm scared.

FRANKLIN: Me too.

(Pause. Decision.)

CHARLOTTE: OK.

(Beat.)

Hi.

FRANKLIN: Hi.

CHARLOTTE: *(A grossly inadequate apology by way of an equally inadequate fantasy.)* You look so. Handsome. Today. Franklin. Thanks for coming to my room. Thanks for saying hi. Thanks for. Loving me. Or trying to. At any rate. I'm sorry.

(Beat.)

FRANKLIN: What do I do?

(Charlotte crosses to Franklin. Slowly gets on her knees. Undoes his pants. All very awkward. She starts to blow him. Franklin begins to cry.)

FRANKLIN: Fuck you. Fuck you. Fuck you. Fuck you. Fuck you.

A BRIEF HISTORY OF HELEN OF TROY IN FOUR PARTS
PART FOUR

The lights take us out of the room for this. The title is read or projected.

CHARLOTTE: And just like that. You know. Just like that. The war is over. And it's over. And it's *lost*. And it's like all the light going out of the universe all at once. All the stars going out. This feeling. That it's over. And that it's lost. And that there's nothing. Nothing. Anymore. To be done.

Because. She's still there. In spite of everything. She's still there. Standing on the bloody beaches of Troy. Surrounded by all the screaming seabirds hovering and swooping over all the dead soldiers, all those bodies. Thronged by masses of women who've been sold into slavery, and ringed by all the little bodies of all the little children who've been thrown from all the city walls left standing. At the heart of the crushed and broken and miserable world. There's Helen. More beautiful than ever. Radiant in the midst of every horror. Smiling at catastrophe.

And on the other side of the world. Still alone. Still in her room. Her daughter. Hermione. And she screams. She screams. From her dark little room. Across every sea, over every fucking ocean separating her from her mother. She screams. WHAT IS TAKING SO FUCKING LONG? WHY THE HELL AREN'T YOU BACK YET? WHAT MORE DO YOU WANT? You need to be *here*. *Now*. With *me*. *Now*. I love you. And Helen. Her mother. The most beautiful woman in the world. She smiles. And whispers. Thank you. I love you too. Thank you. But no. I can't. I'm staying.

And she walks away. Across the beach. To the waiting arms of an army some say will kill her. Others say will take her away. But you know. Either way. She's never really coming home. Not again. Not ever. Not to you.

And there you are. Alone in your room. Watching her leave. And all you have. All that's left. Is this longing. This horrible aching longing. That you reach out to. That you cling to. That you learn to call your friend.

(Long beat. Then a cry of anguish.)

COME BACK!

(Beat.)

Please. Come back. Please. Please. Come back. Come back. Please. Come back.

18

(The lights bring us back to the room. Franklin and Charlotte finish getting dressed in silence. They don't look at each other. The silence is considerable. They're both incredibly self-conscious. Silence. Franklin moves to the window to leave. Stops. Turns.)

FRANKLIN: I think. Charlotte. You know. I think that. Maybe beauty is the thing that's always leaving. That's always being lost. That you always have to say good-bye to. You know. And what's hard is that, for all the good-byes, its never gone for good. It just keeps leaving. And leaving. And leaving. And you just have to keep letting it go. And that's life. I don't know. I don't know what that means, really. But. I think I hate you. I think I really hate you. So. Um. Please don't ever come near me again.

(Franklin exits. Charlotte stares after him, finishes dressing in silence. Remains still. Pause. Feels something in the bed. Investigates. Discovers the ugly stuffed animal from her father. Looks at it. Unnaturally calm. Stoic. Pets it. Places it next to her. Remains still. Pause. There is a feeling that something horrible may happen, a calm before a storm.)

(She looks for the phone. Finds it. Holds it. Picks up the receiver. Sets it down again. Beat. She disconnects the phone. Picks the receiver up again. Puts the receiver to her ear. Does not dial. She is beginning to break. She struggles with composure throughout.)

CHARLOTTE: Um. Heather? Um. Hi. Um. Hi. Heather? Um. Everything's OK. It's really OK. Um. I just had to call. And. Um. How was your weekend? Good. I hope. I would love to have visiting cousins from Czechoslovakia. That would be. So fun. I think. You're so so wonderful. I don't think. I don't know. Um. I think maybe it would be good. Maybe. If I didn't see you. Anymore. For a while. Maybe for just a little while. 'Cause I think. Maybe. For just a while. I should maybe try. Um. Try stuff without you? Please don't be mad. I don't want you to be mad. It's not like. Please don't be mad. I've. I just have to think through a few things. And I think I could do that better if maybe you weren't around. For a while. For a long time. Probably.

And I know. I know. I know what you're thinking. I'm a loser. I'm such a fucking loser. I'm an ugly fucking stupid fucking ugly fucking loser. And you're right. You are so right. And I can't do it on my own. And people will hate me. And laugh at me. And I'll be lost. I know. I'll be lost. Without you. I know it. You are my life, Heather. You are everything. I want. And I wish. I could keep you. Close to me. And this is so hard. This is so hard. Please don't yell at me. I feel like I'm dying. I love you so much.

I'm gonna try to make it to Mexico. To see you. One of these days. I figure you'll probably move there. Soon. But I'll visit. It just might take longer for me. This way. To get there. Without you. But I think it'll be better. I think . I hope it'll be better. This way. But so hard. You made me feel so beautiful, Heather. Thank you. And good-bye. Good-bye.

(She hangs up. Picks up the receiver again.)

CHARLOTTE: Heather?

(She hangs up. Picks up the receiver. Listens.)

CHARLOTTE: Mama?

(She sets the receiver down slowly.)

CHARLOTTE: *(Almost a whisper.)* Daddy?

(Beat. She bursts into tears, really crying, and crying. She searches for the stuffed animal. Clutches it to herself. Stumbles to the bed. Climbs in. A flood of tears. She cries herself to sleep.)

19

(Charlotte asleep in her bed. Harry hovering nearby. A drink in his hand. A long long pause.)

HARRY: OK. OK. OK.

Hey honey. Shhhh. Sleeping. I know.

OK.

I'm trying. I am.

OK.

(He crosses to the bed.)

Tiptoe. Tiptoe. Tiptoe.

(Sits on the bed. Sets his drink on the floor.)

Shhh. Easy. Shhh.

OK.

Where to start.

Um.

This is hard.

(Long pause.)

It was.

Like sweetness. Like every sweetness. Every joy. Every.

Happiness.

How beautiful she was.

(He touches Charlotte.)

And I would. Like this. Or this. Sometimes. Or.

God.

Stupid stupid stupid.

(Pause.)

OK.

I miss you. So much. I see you all the time. I don't know what to do. What do I do?

Helen Helen Helen Helen Helen

It's good to see you. It's good you've made it back. I'm glad you made it back.

Helen.

Is this the face that launched a thousand ships? Funny.

It is. Yes. God yes. It is. It is. It is.

I love you.

(Charlotte stirs. Harry rises.)

HARRY: God.

CHARLOTTE: Daddy?

HARRY: Nothing. It's nothing. Nothing.

CHARLOTTE: *(Sitting up.)* You OK?

(Pause.)

HARRY: Your mother's dead, Charlotte. She's dead. She's really dead. And I don't know. What. I don't know. I don't know.

Please don't. I'm sorry. I didn't. Mean. I wasn't.

God.

CHARLOTTE: Daddy.

HARRY: What?

CHARLOTTE: It's OK.

(Beat.)

HARRY: I wouldn't hurt you.

CHARLOTTE: I know.

HARRY: I wouldn't.

CHARLOTTE: I know.

(Pause.)

HARRY: Can I. Hold you?

(She opens her arms. He sits on the bed and holds her. She holds him.)

HARRY: Please. Don't not love me.

CHARLOTTE: OK.

HARRY: OK.

And. Please. Don't leave me.

CHARLOTTE: OK.

HARRY: OK.

Thank you. Thank you. I'm so sorry. Thank you.

(Harry begins to cry. Lights fade.)

END OF PLAY

STRING OF PEARLS

Michele Lowe

PLAYWRIGHT'S BIOGRAPHY

Michele Lowe is the author of *String of Pearls* (Outer Critics Circle Award nomination), *The Smell of the Kill* (Broadway debut), *Backsliding in the Promised Land* (Syracuse Stage), *Map of Heaven, Germany Surrenders,* and *Hit the Lights!* (book and lyrics). She recently completed two new plays: *Mezzulah, 1946* and *Good on Paper,* which was commissioned by the GeVa Theatre Centre. Michele has participated in the Eugene O'Neill National Music Theatre Conference, New York Stage and Film, and the ACT & Hedgebrook Women Playwrights Festival. Her work has been produced at Primary Stages, Vineyard Theatre, Intiman, City Theatre, Reykjavik City Theatre (Iceland), Berkshire Theatre Festival, Cleveland Play House, and Cincinnati Play House in the Park among others. For television she has written several episodes of *Little Bear* based on characters created by Maurice Sendak. Screenplays include *The Emergence of Emily Stark* and *Quitting Texas* for Avenue Pictures. Michele is a recipient of the Frankel Award. She is a graduate of Northwestern University's Medill School of Journalism. She is a member of ASCAP, the Dramatists Guild, and a Core Member of the Playwrights Center.

ORIGINAL PRODUCTION

String of Pearls was produced by City Theatre Company (Tracy Brigden, artistic director; David Jobin managing director) in Pittsburgh in October, 2003. It was directed by Eric Simonson; the set design was by Loy Arcenas; the costume design was by Michael Olich; the lighting design was by Thomas C. Hase; the sound design was by Dave Bjornson and the stage manager was Patti Kelly. The cast was as follows:

WOMAN #1 . . . . Rebecca Harris
WOMAN #2 . . . . Helena Ruoti
WOMAN #3 . . . . Sheila McKenna
WOMAN #4 . . . . Sharon Washington

String of Pearls was produced by Primary Stages (Casey Childs, executive producer; Andrew Leynse, artistic director, Elliot Fox, managing director) in New York City in September, 2004. It was directed by Eric Simonson; the set design was by Loy Arcenas; the costume design was by David Zinn, the lighting design was by D.M. Wood, the sound design was by Lindsay Jones and the stage manager was Emily N. Wells. The cast was as follows:

WOMAN #1 . . . . Ellen McLaughlin
WOMAN #2 . . . . Mary Testa

WOMAN #3 . . . . Antoinette LaVecchia
WOMAN #4 . . . . Sharon Washington

String of Pearls was commissioned and developed by The Cherry Lane Theatre, New York City, and received further development from New York Stage and Film, The Powerhouse Theatre at Vassar College.

Special Thanks to Matt Williams and Pamela Perrell.

CHARACTERS

(This is an ensemble piece for 4 women playing 27 roles.)

AMY: thirty-five, a research scientist living in Saddle River, New Jersey, in the present

BETH: thirty-nine, a housewife living in Saddle River,New Jersey, in 1969; the same actress also plays Beth when she is seventy-four

ELA: forty-two, a divorced mother of two living near Milwaukee, Wisconsin, in 1981

HELEN: forty, a political consultant living in San Diego, California, in 1982

STEPHANIE: forty-four, an architect/mother living in Boston, Massachusetts, in 1982

JOSIANNE: thirty, a Tunisian hotel maid living in Escondido, California, in 1982

DORA: fifty-three, a chaperone for the New York City Ballet living in Manhattan in 1983

VICTORIA: forty, a housewife living in Manhattan in 1995

ABBY: thirty-eight, a money manager living in Manhattan in the present

KYLE: forty-six, a mortician's assistant living in New City, New York in the present

CINDY: forty-five, a grave digger living in Nyack, New York in the present

HALLIE: Beth's housekeeper

ROBERTA: Amy's friend

BEVERLY: Poughkeepsie housewife

LINDA: Beth's daughter

WANDA: an old friend of Ela's

RANDY: another old friend of Ela's

DENISE: Ela's sister-in-law

ZOE: Stephanie's three-year-old daughter

AUNT PATTY: Josianne's aunt
ERICA: woman on the beach
JITTERS: twenty, a Latina art student going to Paris to study
FRENCH SALESWOMAN
GLORIA: Abby's mother
JEWELER
CHERYLE: school cafeteria worker living in the Bronx
KYLE'S MOTHER

THE BREAKDOWN:
WOMAN ONE: Amy, Wanda, Helen, Aunt Patty, Jitters, Abby
WOMAN TWO: Beth, Randy, Denise, Josianne, Victoria, Kyle's Mother
WOMAN THREE: Hallie, Linda, Stephanie, Dora, Cheryle, Gloria, Jeweler, Cindy,
WOMAN FOUR: Roberta, Beverly, Ela, Zoe, French Saleswoman, Erica, Kyle

STRING OF PEARLS

Music. The stage is bare, dark. Lights up on Beth, seventy-four.

BETH: *(To audience.)* My granddaughter Amy is marrying Kevin. She is living with me until the wedding. I have lived alone for thirty-five years. I am not used to seeing an extra plate in the sink or smelling sandalwood and vetiver in the hall or listening at night for someone's key in the door. I like it. I like it a lot.

(Hallie enters holding an open box.)

HALLIE: The caterer's on the phone for Amy.

BETH: She went to work. Did the florist call?

HALLIE: Not yet.

(Off the box.)

More books.

BETH: Which ones?

HALLIE: *The Life and Lyrics of Sir Edward Dyer* and *The Joy of Pickling.*

BETH: *(To audience.)* I'm thinking of doing some pickling.

HALLIE: Where do you want them?

BETH: Under the sink.

HALLIE: The sink?

BETH: What did I say?

HALLIE: *(To audience.)* She's not getting enough sleep. She stays up all night reading.

BETH: I'm not tired.

HALLIE: *(To audience.)* She's seventy-four.

(Hallie exits.)

BETH: I'm fine. I'm just excited.

(To audience.) Amy works at the hospital every night until midnight. I wait up for her. I don't mean to. Yes, I do.

(Amy enters holding her finger.)

AMY: Ow! I can't believe I did it again.

BETH: Kevin called — and so did Roberta.

AMY: Thanks Gramma.

BETH: It's so crazy around here.

AMY: I need a Band-Aid.

(Amy exits.)

BETH: Amy is a doctor of some reputation. She is developing a new heart made of pig guts with a team at Mt. Sinai. Amy's work is so complex, so demanding, so dangerous that the heart won't be ready for another ten years. And yet —

(Amy enters.)

AMY: Do you have any alcohol?

BETH: *(To audience.)* She can't sew.

(Beth exits.)

AMY: I am sewing my wedding dress by hand. I work each morning from four to six. It is only half done. I am terrified that when I walk down the aisle the dress will come apart and I will have to get married naked.

(Roberta enters.)

ROBERTA: Do you want me to give you a shower?

AMY: A bridal shower? No.

ROBERTA: I could make it small —

AMY: No.

ROBERTA: A dozen girls at my apartment —

AMY: No please Roberta.

ROBERTA: When you come over for dinner next Tuesday — ?

AMY: Yes?

ROBERTA: Act surprised.

(Hallie enters.)

HALLIE: Are you going to throw your bouquet?

ROBERTA: Are you going to write your vows?

HALLIE: Are you going to hire a band?

(Beth enters.)

BETH: Are you going to wear my pearls with your dress?

AMY: What?

(Hallie and Roberta exit.)

BETH: The pearls.

AMY: *(To audience.)* It is the first time she mentions the pearls.

BETH: The ones I gave your mother.

AMY: *(To audience.)* My mother died when I was six.

BETH: The ones she wore to her wedding.

AMY: I don't have them.

BETH: Are you sure?

AMY: Mom didn't give them to me.

BETH: Maybe your father has them.

AMY: I don't think so Gramma —

BETH: I'll call him.

(Beth exits.)

AMY: Gramma, don't —

> *(To audience.)* I am ignoring my father, I am barely speaking to my step-mother, I am enjoying my brother Jonathan for the first time in my life. Kevin and I don't want children. We don't want a kitchen or plants. We have agreed to spend our energies on our work and on each other.
>
> *(Beth enters.)*

BETH: Your father doesn't have them.

AMY: *(To audience.)* I have my mother's eyes, my mother's chin, and my mother's allergy to cats. I do not, however, have her pearls.

BETH: You need the pearls to get married.

AMY: The only thing I need to get married is Kevin. And the dress.

> *(Amy exits.)*

BETH: Amy retreats to her room. As the wedding draws near she speaks to me less, until the house is wrapped in silence. The replies flood the mailbox but she leaves them unopened. She reminds me of Ethan — absent, disconnected, nervous. Secretly I'm afraid she'll throw in the towel and elope.

> *(Beth exits.)*
>
> *(Amy enters.)*

AMY: Gramma leaves a pile of my parent's wedding pictures on my pillow. I see the pearls for the first time. White, shiny, round as marbles.

> *(Beth enters.)*

BETH: Maybe she loaned them to a friend.

AMY: Maybe she gave them back to you.

> *(To audience.)* Cruel. I know.

BETH: *(To audience.)* I clean out every closet, I open every box —

AMY: *(To audience.)* I hear her in the middle of the night —

BETH: *(To audience.)* I find my engagement ring. Too big for my hands. I'm shrinking, fading, turning to dust already.

AMY: *(To audience.)* I resolve to be nice to her.

BETH: Maybe your brother knows where the pearls are.

AMY: I do not need the pearls to get married!

BETH: *(To audience.)* She doesn't understand.

AMY: *(To audience.)* What do I say?

BETH: *(To audience.)* How to explain?

AMY: They're lost.

BETH: If I could find them for you.

AMY: It doesn't matter —

BETH: If I could start at the beginning —

AMY: You won't find them.

BETH: Beginning with the first . . .

AMY: *(To audience.)* Before they were my mother's they were hers.

BETH: First to receive them, first to wear them, first to give them away.

AMY: *(To audience.)* She was thirty-nine. August 1969.

(Amy exits. We hear audio from the Apollo 11 Moon Landing as the lights change.)

NEIL ARMSTRONG: *(Voice-over.)* "Houston, Tranquility Base here. The Eagle has landed."

CHARLES DUKE: *(Voice-over.)* "Roger, Tranquility. We copy you on the ground. You got a bunch of guys about to turn blue. We're breathing again."

(Beth is now thirty-nine. It is 1969.)

BETH: Ethan quit playing tennis after he broke his foot. He rarely rode his bike. He sat for hours in front of the television watching the moon land- ing. He'd do anything not to come to bed. At ten o'clock he'd call his mother in Poughkeepsie. At midnight he'd read an entire *Time,* or *Life,* or *Look.* I'd wait up for him, but it was no use. I'd pass out and by six the next morning, he was gone. Linda would see him waving to her as he went down the hall. If I woke up in the middle of the night and I touched his belly or his thigh, he'd grunt and roll over. So I'd go down- stairs and turn on Channel 9.

(Music up: Jimi Hendrix's "Are You Experienced?")

BETH: I'd see all these girls on the news half-naked, dancing, feathers in their hair, belts around the hips, shaking and swaying and all I could think was — these girls were having sex. Why wasn't I?

So after dinner one night, when Linda was out at a party, I tried to talk to Ethan about how I was feeling — but all that came out was "feather" and "halter top" and he didn't know what I was talking about. So I gave up.

Then came the invitation to his twentieth high school reunion. All of his friends from Poughkeepsie started calling and I guess they shamed him into it, because the next thing I knew, we were going, too. And when he gave me money for a dress, I took it as a sign. Maybe he wanted to look at me like he used to. Maybe he wanted to have some fun, some feeling, some attachment, like we used to.

I went to Bonwit Teller and bought a flaming red sleeveless Anne Klein and I did 100 sit ups every night for two weeks.

(Music up: "Goldberg Variations #6.")

BETH: The night of the party, he found this lovely station on the radio playing Bach and we glided, we swam up from Saddle River toward the country club, not saying a word, just the music between us.

When we got there the first people we ran into were Larry Bridges
and his new wife who turned out to be Ethan's girlfriend from Camp
Anawana — Beverly.

Beverly was exotic. She drank Brandy Alexanders. She danced. She
wore a red dress, too, but next to hers my dress looked brown — almost
grey. And she very clearly had something I did not. Beverly had a bosom.
It was a nice round bouncy bosom, a melonish kind of loveliness. I
wasn't jealous, I was more intrigued. How did one come to have such a
bosom? Was it her mother? Did she have sisters? Were they all involved
in the bosom business? Or was it just Beverly? I had never seen anything
so flawlessly round and so perfectly white in my life. They could have
been made of marble.

Ethan stood around and talked to the friends he had stayed in touch
with.

I said hello to a few people, but mostly I sat at the table, eyeing the
fruit cup, waiting for everyone to sit down so we could eat and go home.
The shine had quickly worn off the evening for me.

But not for Beverly. She was dancing, she was talking, she was getting around, and making friends with everybody. I lost track of her for a
while until she came up behind me, dumped me out of my chair and
dragged me over to the bar.

(Beverly enters.)

BEVERLY: He looks exactly the same.

BETH: Ethan?

BEVERLY: He still smolders.

BETH: *(To audience.)* I had never thought of Ethan in fiery terms before.

BEVERLY: Looking at him, you wouldn't know it — but he's not your average
kind of guy, is he?

BETH: *(To audience.)* What was she getting at?

BEVERLY: It just goes to show you — you only know the true nature of a person when you — well you must know.

BETH: *(To audience.)* No, I didn't know.

BEVERLY: Ethan's the first boy who ever gave me a pearl necklace.

BETH: *(To audience.)* Who was she kidding? He was from *Poughkeepsie*, his father was an accountant. Pearls? Come on.

BEVERLY: You mean he's never given you one?

BETH: Ethan gives me pens for Mother's Day. One year he gave me a broiler pan for my birthday.

BEVERLY: *(Intrigued.)* Well, you go right home tonight, and you tell him you want a pearl necklace. You demand that he give it to you. You insist. Besides, you look like you could use it.

(Beverly exits.)

BETH: We went home that night and I drank three cups of Maxwell House while he read *The Wall Street Journal.* When he finally came upstairs, it was after three — but I was up and pumping on twenty-two pistons. As soon as he got into bed, I jumped on top of him and said, Ethan Brown — did you really give that girl Beverly from Camp Anawana, a string of pearls?! And suddenly I felt him in between my thighs, get hard like a rock. And I — I started experiencing the most incredible tingling sensation around my chest.

So I said it again: A string of pearls Ethan, you gave it to her? And now he's so hard, I'm thinking Oh my god, oh my god, oh my god. And he looks right at me, right in my eyes and he whispers — You want a string of pearls?

And I think if *talking* about it is going to get him this hard, imagine what he's going to be like when he gives it to me.

So I say, OOOh, yes, Ethan. You bad boy, you never gave me a string of pearls. I want a string of pearls, give it to me. Wham! He rolls me over, pins me down and rips off my nightgown. His penis is coming out of his pajamas. He throws off his bottoms and pushes me down toward the end of the bed. And the whole time he's saying, You want a string of pearls? You want a string of pearls?

And I'm saying, Yes, Ethan, yes, gimme a string of pearls and the next thing I know he puts his penis between my breasts and whispers,

Squeeeeze it.

OH. OK.

So I squeeze my breasts around his penis.

Now I'm a 34 double A. The only time I ever used a bra was when I was pregnant with Linda. But something happened that night, I swear to God. I touched my breasts and they'd grown. I had mango breasts, beachy Gaugin breasts, breasts like you see in a Renoir painting or a B movie. I must have been a 40 D. Something — something miraculous was happening. He was growing, I was growing, and now he's pumping between my breasts and I'm getting so turned on and he's saying:

Yeah, yeah, yeah, oh, baby, oh, oh, oh, uh-hUH, baby, OH OH OHHH!!

And with no warning whatsoever he comes all over my neck. Then he leans over and whispers: "String of pearls."

(Lights up on Beverly.)

BEVERLY: When he did it to me I was fourteen.

BETH: Too young.

BEVERLY: Too messy.

BETH: Too surprising.

BEVERLY: Too much work.

(Lights down on Beverly.)

BETH: Two people in each other's arms. That night I fell in love with Ethan and myself — or whoever I thought I was: Barbarella, Kim Novak, Elizabeth Taylor. Surely we all shared something in common now. Finally, I could ask Ethan to put his hands in places I could not say before but could only point to.

And then we began to talk — about his work, about Linda, about the war. And pretty soon, he stopped calling his mother and his brother and he cut off his subscription to *Newsweek* and canceled *Time* altogether and we were really really happy . . .

And then out of the blue I get this . . . um, I get this call — the elevator man — the guy who comes in after hours — had found Ethan.

He'd already called the police and they'd told him to call me, so I drove down from Saddle River to Lenox Hill hospital in the city. They told me in the lobby it was an aneurysm and then they let me see him. I remembered picking out the shirt he was wearing at Lord & Taylor. It had been a Father's Day present from me to him, and he'd fought me on the color.

I went home with my little bag of Ethan . . . a clear blue bag with his wallet, his glasses and his aspirin, and another bag . . . and inside there was a blue box — square and velvet . . .

(Beverly enters with the box. Beth opens it and removes the string of pearls.)

There wasn't any occasion for it, our anniversary wasn't until October. It was the first time he'd bought me anything for no reason at all and he hadn't even been there to give it to me.

I put the pearls on when I got home. And I wore them to sleep that night and the next . . . naked except for Ethan's pearls. And that's how I slept for five years.

When my daughter Linda got married I put them in the box and gave them to her.

(Linda enters and Beth puts the pearls on her. Linda exits.)

(Beth exits.)

(Ela enters. It is 1981.)

ELA: I knew Linda. We weren't friends, but I knew who she was. She ran the book fair, the bake sale, and the Milwaukee March of Dimes Walk-a-thon. She was class parent two years in a row. They called her the Model Mother. No one could touch her. The rest of us were all failures compared to her. When I heard she was moving to Chicago I thought my God — it'll take six people to replace her.

(We hear the sound of a door opening offstage. Someone is trying to get her attention.)

ELA: *(Calling out.)* WHAT? No, Carly, you can't come in, dinner's not ready. Because I'm busy. It's not cold out. No it's not, it's above zero.

(The door closes.)

ELA: *(To audience.)* Her house sold fast. Too fast. And she wanted her kids to finish school here. That's how she and Amy and Jonathan came to live in my basement apartment. There would be just three of them down there. Howard, her husband, was already in Chicago. He planned to visit on the weekends. They paid me the whole six months up front which gave me an excuse to get rid of the last of Billy's things boxed in the basement.

(We hear the door open again.)

ELA: *(Calling out.)* WHAT? No Carly, not yet. Chicken fingers and baked beans. Well, then don't put your tongue on the mailbox.

(The door closes.)

ELA: *(To audience.)* The idea of someone not related to me living in my house was inconceivable to me — the way the idea of getting a divorce was inconceivable the year before. But you do what you do when you have to do it and like it or not it was done.

She asked me if she could take down the picture of Jesus on one of the basement walls and I let her. I'd had enough of church for the time being anyway. Just a lot of busybodies wanting to hear about Billy. I had no patience so I quit going.

The day Linda moved in, I hid all my jewelry in the freezer and put my silver in the attic. I changed the lock on the basement door and gave her a key; and I finally replaced the burned-out lightbulb on the stairs.

Then one day at school one of the mothers — somebody who's

never said a word to me in my life — pulls me aside and asks me if it's true — Does Linda Moser have cancer?

And I tell her:

I don't know. Why don't you ask her yourself?

And she gives me this look — and then flits off down the hall to ask someone else.

What's she asking me for?

Just because the woman lives in my basement apartment doesn't mean I know the intimate details of her life.

If Linda Moser has cancer that's her business.

That night around two in the morning, I go down to the kitchen for a Coke and I see Amy asleep at my table. I pick her up and carry her back down to the basement. I look around in the moonlight and I'm pleased to see the apartment looking so clean. I had picked the right tenant that was for sure. Then I laid Amy down in her bed . . .

(Lights up on Linda.)

LINDA: Can I have a glass of water?

ELA: *(To audience.)* And Linda woke up. She had a kerchief around her head but it was half off and there were patches of bald scalp showing.

LINDA: You want to see it?

ELA: See what?

LINDA: My head. I don't mind. I'll show you.

ELA: No. Thanks. No.

LINDA: It's not catching. You can't get what I have just by being in the same room with me.

ELA: I'm perfectly fine being in the same room with you.

LINDA: Then why are you holding your breath? *(Pause.)* Do you want to come to Atwater Beach tomorrow night? There's a group of girls from Shorewood going down there around eight —

ELA: That's not really my kind of thing.

LINDA: You might like it.

ELA: And I don't really know those girls.

LINDA: You might know some of them.

ELA: *(Lying.)* I'm sort of busy tomorrow tonight.

LINDA: Then just come for a while.

ELA: *(To audience.)* I knew I'd be doing her a favor if I gave her a ride. She could always get a lift home from one of her friends.

(To Linda.) Sure, I'll take you.

(To audience.) About a quarter to eight that night I look outside and

she's standing by my car wrapped in a blanket. So I take her to Atwater Beach.

(Lights change. We are at Atwater Beach. Wanda and Randy enter. Music up.)

RANDY: I'm going swimming tonight.

WANDA: Not me. Too cold.

ELA: *(To audience.)* I get her settled down in a lounge chair and I'm ready to leave when somebody hands me a drink and then a joint and then a bag of potato chips. I run into some girls I haven't seen since high school.

WANDA: Where've you been Ela Louise?

RANDY: She's too busy to come see us.

ELA: I didn't know you came here —

WANDA: Sure, sure —

LINDA: I had to twist her arm . . .

(Randy reaches for the joint.)

RANDY: Hey, twist your arm over here . . .

ELA: *(To audience.)* Somebody lights a few candles and the next thing I know it's ten o'clock and I'm drunk and there's this really young cop standing there with a megaphone telling us to disperse or he's going to arrest us.

By then we are two dozen mostly divorced women in various stages of menopause with seventy-two kids between us and we aren't going anywhere. Somebody threatens to pull the cop's pants down and he gets back in his car.

WANDA: He was cute.

RANDY: Aw, he's leaving.

WANDA: I think he's mad.

RANDY: He wasn't a real cop — was he?

(Randy and Wanda exit. Music out.)

ELA: *(To audience.)* We never see him again. About midnight, I gather up Linda and take her home. We sit on my sunporch for a while, too keyed up to go to sleep. I want to ask her about Howard, about Chicago, about —

LINDA: I taught Amy to swim at Atwater Beach. She was so little but she was so tough, so brave. I think she was just terrified but wouldn't let on. My father was like that. He got quiet when he got scared. Next time we go we should get there early . . . maybe bring dinner.

ELA: *(To audience.)* She was talking about next month now.

LINDA: You like roast chicken?

ELA: I don't know.

LINDA: You don't know if you like roast chicken?

ELA: I don't know if I'll go back next month.

LINDA: Oh come on. When was the last time you saw a policeman in his underwear?

ELA: I don't think he'll be back.

LINDA: You never know.

(*Linda exits.*)

ELA: She went down to bed and I didn't see her for a day or two. I thought about the beach — I . . . I didn't think I would go back. It wouldn't be the same. I'd probably feel uncomfortable. And then, a week later I get a phone call from my sister-in-law Denise.

(*Lights up on Denise.*)

DENISE: I heard about these Divorced White Witches from Shorewood who swim naked in Lake Michigan when the moon is full.

ELA: Where'd you hear that?

DENISE: I heard they got a man down there and did something to him.

ELA: Something good or something bad?

DENISE: How should I know? Divorced White Witches swimming naked under the moon? They could have done anything to him — anything.

ELA: What are you telling me this for?

DENISE: You're divorced.

ELA: So?

DENISE: Are you going to go down there next month?

ELA: I don't know, I was thinking about it.

DENISE: I'll go with you.

ELA: I'm taking someone.

DENISE: Swing by here and pick me up.

ELA: You're not divorced.

DENISE: So?

ELA: So call me when you find your husband fucking the babysitter in your living room.

(*Lights down on Denise.*)

ELA: When it was time for class pictures Amy went to school without her socks and Jonathan's shirt sleeves were dirty and frayed. The kids looked hungry. Then I caught Carly going downstairs with a frozen pizza. So I started bringing the three of them upstairs for dinner.

(*We hear the door open offstage.*)

ELA: (*Calling out.*) Carly take your mittens and your boots and your coat off right there! RIGHT THERE. Where's your hat? That was a brand new hat! Now you go right back out and find it. Well put them back on. You heard me. Now get OUT!

(*The door slams shut.*)

ELA: (*To audience.*) I was downstairs once when Linda's mother Beth called. Linda never told her how bad things were. She said she'd rather have a good conversation with her mom than a sad one. Howard came to see her but he couldn't sit long. It crushed him, she said, and she needed him to stay whole for the kids.

(*Linda enters.*)

It was happening so fast, taking over her body with such a fury . . . Then Linda asked me to open my house and a flood of her friends came to say good-bye. They came at all hours, day and night and finally I just stopped locking the door.

Soon the only thing that worked were her eyes — they were huge and getting bigger it seemed — you could see her soul pushing through them — trying to leave her body behind, struggling to get out into the air and breathe. She was expanding as she was dying, growing larger instead of smaller.

(*Linda puts the pearls on Ela.*)

ELA: About a week before she died, she gave me a blue velvet box that had belonged to her mom. It felt strange — I'd seen them on her so many times. When she put them on me, they were so flawlessly round and so perfectly white. I asked if she didn't think her daughter Amy should have them and she said, No, they're for you. For a job well done. And she explained, although very briefly, that her mother had gotten them from her father for the very same reason.

(*Linda exits.*)

(*Music up. Tiny white lights, insects in the night, flicker on and off around Ela.*)

ELA: The night after Linda died there was a full moon. We all met down at the beach, the Divorced White Witches of Shorewood, and we took off all of our clothes and we swam naked in the warm lake water. Soon the men came — dozens of them, silent and staring. And as we lifted ourselves out of the water lit by the July moon they bowed to us one by one and kissed our breasts and our hair and we turned them into fireflies that glowed once, twice and were gone. Then we made our way to the towels hanging from the trees and went home to our empty houses.

(*The moon begins to fade. The tiny lights flicker out.*)

ELA: When I started going back to church, I wore them. People would notice and say something nice. I kept the little box on my bureau. All the gold had rubbed off the bracelets and earrings Billy had given me but I didn't care. I had Linda's pearls. I wore them for almost a year rain or shine and then one Sunday — they were gone.

(Helen enters. She silently takes the pearls from Ela and exits.)

ELA: I tore the house apart — I cleaned out every closet, every shelf, every box in the house — I ripped up half the carpet with a staple remover 'til my hands bled. When Billy called I asked if he'd seen them. He was working in San Diego but had just come home to see Carly. No, he didn't remember seeing any pearls. When I told the Shorewood girls they cried. Some of them came over and we lit candles but it was no use. They were gone. That week some of them chipped in and bought me a little string of pearls at Marshall Field's. Tear drop pearls, you know. Nice. Nicest thing I own.

(We hear the door open offstage.)

ELA: *(Calling out.)* Did you find it? Well it's out there somewhere. No, no, come in, it's OK. The chicken's on the table. I'll go find your hat. No, no, you sit, I'll go. Because I'm your mother.

(Ela exits.)

(Helen enters. She wears a smart black suit and the pearls. It is 1982.)

HELEN: I met Billy at one of Mayor Wilson's parties. They were old friends and the Mayor thought he might give us a hand with the Republicans. Wilson was keen on getting the Republican Convention here. Billy had worked with the RNC all over the place and they liked having him around.

At the party Billy and I exchange phone numbers and he comes to my office the next day with a bottle of champagne.

Champagne? I say. Isn't that a little premature? We haven't even filled out the forms.

And he says Come here baby and I'll fill out your forms.

Oh my God it was so tacky you had to love it.

So Billy basically moves in with me — into my office, into my apartment, we're doing everything but chew each other's food. He's worthless in the office but the staff likes him and my gorgeous new Republican pitch-fuck is about the best looking thing in San Diego.

When he goes back to Milwaukee to visit his kid, I get a ton of work done. But I miss him, he's cute. Three days later he comes back with pearls.

(She takes them off and runs them over her teeth.)

They're real.

I wear them to work the next day. They actually go nicely with the little black St. John suit I bought in March. It was on sale so I bought two — one for me and one for my sister for her birthday. Stephanie wears sweatpants most of the time.

(Stephanie enters.)

STEPHANIE: *(To audience.)* Where the hell am I going to wear a suit?

HELEN: *(To audience.)* That's what most of her friends wear: casual clothing at all times of the day.

STEPHANIE: *(To audience.)* To a party for a five-year-old?

HELEN: *(To audience.)* I can't imagine what it does to her psyche.

STEPHANIE: *(To audience.)* To Mommy and Me/Music for the Wee?

HELEN: *(To audience.)* And I'm far too much in the public eye to even consider it.

(Lights down on Helen.)

STEPHANIE: *(To audience.)* I don't even get out of the car to go the bank. I hate telling people I'm an architect because the next question usually is: What are you working on? And, well, right now I'm working on potty training. I'm mothering. I'm dragging my three-year-old kicking and screaming out of playdates while she tells me what a horrible mother I am.

(Zoe enters.)

ZOE: I hate you!

STEPHANIE: Fine, but we still have to go home.

ZOE: I hate you, I hate you, I hate you.

STEPHANIE: Zoe, you love Mommy.

ZOE: No.

STEPHANIE: Yes, you do.

ZOE: Mommy?

STEPHANIE: What sweetheart?

ZOE: Do you like to make drawings?

STEPHANIE: Yes, Zoe, Mommy loves to make drawings. Mommy draws buildings. You've seen Mommy's buildings.

ZOE: Well, I'm gonna tell God to chop off your hands and pull out your eyes so you can never make another building again in your whole life no matter how much you cry.

STEPHANIE: *(To audience.)* And I think, silly Zoe, God's already done that.

(Zoe exits.)

(Lights up on Helen.)

HELEN: Did you like the suit?

STEPHANIE: Loved it.

HELEN: Did you try it on?

STEPHANIE: Yes, it looks beautiful.

HELEN: When are you going to wear it?

STEPHANIE: When you get married.

(To audience.) She's been engaged three times and she always keeps the rings. She says that the men insist and I say nobody insists you keep a $10,000 ring. She gets them appraised right away, then she breaks up with them. I'm not saying the two things are related. I'm just saying it's odd.

HELEN: (To audience.) I don't know how she ended up with her husband Andrew. (Pause.) Well yes I do know.

STEPHANIE: (To audience.) She never lets me forget that she dated Andrew first.

HELEN: (To audience.) Are you kidding — I gave him to her. I did everything but put a pink bow on his cock. I mean come on she was an architect, he was in commercial real estate. Strip malls. Tulsa. Cigar smoke in the car. They were perfect for each other.

(Lights down on Helen.)

STEPHANIE: Last fall, a couple Andrew and I know from Boston wanted to build a guesthouse and they called me. We had a meeting and they gave me a small retainer. That night, I went home, made the kids dinner, tucked them into bed and did thirty-four thumbnail sketches in eight hours. I woke the kids took them to school, came home and kept going until the school nurse called to say Dominic had broken his arm in gym. The next day Zoe came down with chicken pox. Then we had a flood in the basement, the dog got hit by a car, and the mommy gerbil ate all the baby gerbils.

I had both kids home on and off for two weeks while the babysitter was home visiting her sick father in El Salvador. He recovered. I didn't.

By the time I went back to my notes and house sketches an entire month had gone by. I looked at what I'd done and it made no sense. It was shit. I sent the check back to my friend and I never saw her again.

If my sister only knew . . .

(Lights up on Helen.)

HELEN: (To audience.) My sister has it so good she doesn't even know it. I'm days away from the convention pitch and I still don't have numbers from the Marriott or the Hilton and the people at United who swore up and down we'd get a 25 percent discount now say they'll only give us 15. And

Billy's still around. He hasn't had a single usable idea, not one original thought the entire time, but he keeps second-guessing our pitch every five minutes. The Mayor calls ten times a day, the printer needs the books by tomorrow, the convention committee wants to know if we can move up the time and Billy loses it. He yells at me, the son of a bitch screams at me in front of my own people — so I kick him out of my office. An hour later the Mayor calls and he tells me I'm off the team.

STEPHANIE: *(To audience.)* The last time I spoke to Helen she sounded depressed. She'd lost a big piece of business and she was actually crying on the phone. Andrew happened to be in San Diego and I asked him to go and see her. Maybe he could make her feel a little better.

HELEN: *(To audience.)* Stephanie calls me twenty times a day. Am I OK? Am I all right? Doesn't she have anything better to do?

STEPHANIE: *(To audience.)* Andrew travels two weeks out of the month. He's missed three vacations. They still haven't made him a vice president but they say it's going to happen this year. So he works every night and most Sundays. The kids fight when he's around just to get his attention. But when I complain to him, he says — Hang on. Hang on we're almost there. Keep your chin up, it's just around the corner. We're so close. And what I want to know is so close to what? Where are we going? Tell me about this mythical place that will erase the last seven years of my life. Because I'm so bored I'm going out of my fucking mind. That's where I'm going.

(Stephanie exits.)

HELEN: Andrew's in town. I meet him at the airport Hilton. He's going on and on about his business but I don't care. He looks good. And after his third gin and tonic he tells me he only wishes he'd met someone like me. Someone independent, someone who had more than diapers on the brain and I say, Well you could have had me.

And he says — Can I have you now?

The next thing I know, I'm paying the check and he's getting a room and we're chasing each other down the hall; I mean he is literally trying to tear off my clothes and just as we get inside the door, he rips my pearls off my neck — Billy the Asshole's pearls break all over the floor. I look over Andrew's shoulder and see myself hovering on the ceiling, watching as he rams himself into me for the seventeenth, eighteenth, nineteenth time — and the woman on the ceiling won't even look at me — she is so disappointed, so disgusted. And I know right then and there that I have pitched my last fuck.

(Stephanie enters. She holds up a pearl.)

STEPHANIE: *(To audience.)* I find a pearl in Andrew's pants while I'm cleaning out his pockets. He'd found it on the plane coming home. So I thread it onto a little string and when Zoe comes home from school, I give it to her and she goes wild for it. She and I get all dressed up and I take her to Antonio's for dinner. My butcher's there getting a pizza and when I say hello he has no idea who I am — me in my St. John suit.

And just as we sit down, I catch a glimpse of a beautiful woman and her little daughter in the mirror across the room — and it takes me a good two or three minutes before I realize — that's me in there. That's who I am. And while we're waiting for our dinners Zoe pulls six colored pencils and a little pad out of her purse and begins drawing. And when I ask her what she's making she says, "A building."

(Helen and Stephanie exit.)

(We hear the sound of a vacuum cleaner running over carpet. Suddenly something gets sucked up into it. The vacuum stops.)

(Josianne enters.)

JOSIANNE: I have two more rooms to clean on the fifth floor and then I can go home. I do not need the Hoover breaking down at this moment.

I open the bag of dirt and pour the dust into a towel, and there is a pearl. Hmm. I will give it to the front desk.

I start the Hoover again and again I hear something go up into the bag. I open the bag and now there are two pearls inside. I look down at my feet and I see six more. Now I'm on my hands and knees and I find twenty, thirty, forty-two more.

Someone will be missing such beautiful pearls. The guest will call the hotel when they get home and realize they are gone. I will bring them to Mrs. Lawrence the general manager. Perhaps she will give Albert and me a free dinner for returning them. She did it once for Sarah. Sarah found a thousand dollar in a drawer. But when I tell Albert on the phone about the pearls, he says to bring them home first. He wants to see them.

I finish cleaning the other rooms. Maria wants to have a drink but I tell her I'm tired and go home. There is a letter from my daughter Nina waiting for me. I have not seen her in twelve years. She is in Tunis with my aunt. I call her once a month.

(Lights up on Josianne's Aunt Patty.)

AUNT PATTY: Nina can't come to the phone.

JOSIANNE: Is she there?

AUNT PATTY: She's going out with her friends.

JOSIANNE: With a boy?

AUNT PATTY: She's your daughter, what can I tell you?

JOSIANNE: Lock her inside the house.

AUNT PATTY: You had Nina when you were fifteen! What do you expect?

JOSIANNE: *Ou est l'argent que t'envoye?*

AUNT PATTY: Gone.

JOSIANNE: Where?

AUNT PATTY: Where. Money goes. And it goes fast. You think you send so much?

JOSIANNE: Did you go to the lawyer?

AUNT PATTY: With what? He only sees the ones who can pay.

JOSIANNE: I'll send more money.

AUNT PATTY: Much more. We need more.

JOSIANNE: Tell her we'll be together soon. Tell her —

AUNT PATTY: I have to go. My program is on.

 (Lights down on Aunt Patty.)

JOSIANNE: Hello? Hello?

 (To audience.) I call back ten times but no one answers.

In the letter Nina says she has a boyfriend. A boyfriend. A *boyfriend.* Albert comes home smelling of beer and looks at the pearls. He turns them over in his hands. He makes a great show of knowing nothing.

Albert is my brother's friend. I know he tells my family what I do and where I go. I know he is watching me even when I can't see him. I have a cousin in Washington I want to see but he says no. It is too far.

He is the one who brought me to Mrs. Lawrence. She gives him my check. He gives me half, the rest he sends home to my aunt. *(Pause.)* He *says* he sends it home. And for that I have always given him what he wants.

He thinks we can sell the pearls in L.A. I tell him that is stealing. He tells me we have to go to L.A., we have to do this. He makes me think something bad will happen if we don't get rid of them. When I ask him for the pearls back he wraps them in his handkerchief and puts them in his pocket. Come and get them he says. I lock myself in the bedroom and pretend to go to sleep. Albert sleeps on the couch. All night I fix my hair, my nails, my face.

In the morning I put on my dress and Albert puts on his suit and we drive to L.A., to the beach, where the fancy hotels are. He parks the car on the street by the first hotel.

He takes the handkerchief out of his pocket and when I reach for it he slaps my hand away. He tells me to go to the beach behind the hotel he will meet me there. I want to go inside but he says no. He says I look like a whore. People do not buy pearls from women who look like me. I watch him go inside the hotel with the pearls. Then I follow him in. The hotel has a large and expensive jewelry store on the second floor. Bucheron it says in the window. Paris, Santa Monica, Hong Kong, Sao Paulo.

I go to the beach and I wait. It is very hot. I have no umbrella, there is no shade and I am very tired. I watch a woman and her little girl on the beach. The mother walks away. She gets a Coke, she buys some French fries. The little girl sits there waiting for the mother to come back. *Elle ne bouge pas.* The mother walks further away. She talks to a man, she listens to some music, she goes further down the beach. The little girl waits for her mama. Then someone comes — a man, a woman I can't see — and throws the little girl into the water. No one on the beach does anything. No one sees the baby drowning. Where is her mother? Where is her mother? *Where is her mother?*

(Erica enters.)

ERICA: Honey you're scaring all the kids.

JOSIANNE: That girl is drowning!

ERICA: Which girl?

JOSIANNE: In the water!

ERICA: Where?

JOSIANNE: I have to do something!

ERICA: But nobody's drowning —

JOSIANNE: Out there!

ERICA: There's only children playing. Look!

JOSIANNE: *(To audience.)* She's right. The children are all running back and forth in the water, the mothers are holding the babies in their arms.

ERICA: You want me to get you some water or something? I've got some grapes over at my blanket.

JOSIANNE: *(To audience.)* I see Albert coming.

(To Erica.) No, no. Thank you no.

(Erica exits.)

JOSIANNE: Albert shows me an envelope of money. Look, he says. Look. Six hundred dollars. The buyer for the whole company was leaving for Paris. He's taking them with him. Albert is very pleased with himself.

I kick him in the balls and I grab the money and I take his keys and I run back to the car. I get in and I drive. Two days and nights I drive and I don't look back until I reach the end of the world. I park and I get out.

Tacoma, Washington, is the ugliest place I ever saw but I stay and I find my cousin and I get a lawyer and I give her my $600 and I start to get my daughter here. And when she comes, I'm gonna put her in school and I'm gonna lock her up in my house and she's not gonna come out until the day I die.

(Josianne exits.)

(Dora enters. It is 1983. Music up.)

(Woman enters with a jewelry box. She opens it to reveal a strand of white pearls.)

DORA: Cultured pearl.

(Woman enters with jewelry box. She reveals a strand of black pearls.)

DORA: South Seas pearl.

(Woman enters with a jewelry box. She opens it to reveal a photograph of an eight-year-old girl.)

DORA: French Pearl.

(The Women exit except for Dora. Music out.)

DORA: When they interviewed me to be a chaperone, I made it clear to Mr. Martins that I would go wherever the ballet company needed me — any city in any country as long as I did not have to go to France. I was born in Paris and had not been back since I was eight.

When the ballet company toured France they usually took Mrs. Phillips. She spoke Italian and usually got along fine with everybody. Then I got the call from Mr. Martins — an overseas call — telling me that Mrs. Phillips had run off with a Sicilian ticket taker who worked at the Opera. I knew he wasn't calling to find out if I'd heard from her. No. He was calling to ask me if I could replace her.

I could have told him no. I didn't need the money. He would have understood, it was last minute. I had a grandchild on the way — two grandchildren actually. Twins run in my family.

But the idea of going to Paris right away, that night, with not enough time to think about the implications or complications did make me slightly giddy. I looked out the window onto Riverside Drive and a limousine was already waiting — apparently for me.

I pack so quickly I forget to bring a book. At the gate I find a *Newsweek* lying on a chair and I take it. As the doors close I read that 25 percent of all French believe that Jews are not normal people. Ten percent believe they should be destroyed. I have three scotches before dinner.

(Lights up on Jitters.)

JITTERS: Are you nervous?

DORA: A little.

JITTERS: Me, too. My mother gave me a Valium and my father gave me a Valium and my Aunt Frances gave me some codeine. This is my first plane flight and I must have fallen asleep during the take off because it feels like we're not even moving and I know we must be because they wouldn't have loaded us onto the plane just to have us stand still, you know? You want a Valium? My mother had it blessed by the priest.

DORA: No thank you.

JITTERS: You ever been to Paris?

DORA: A long time ago.

JITTERS: This is my first time. It's great, right? I'm going to study at the school of the Louvre.

DORA: Really? My mother studied at the École des Beaux Arts.

JITTERS: Never heard of it.

DORA: She was a painter.

JITTERS: Yeah, I tried painting and I pretty much suck at it.

DORA: *(To audience.)* My mother was a gifted painter. My father was her teacher. During the war he hid my mother in his studio outside Paris. When it was over a deranged Frenchman came to my father's town looking for Jews. A woman and two little girls were the first people he saw. First my mother . . .

(SFX: Gun shot.)

DORA: Then my twin sister Pearl . . .

(SFX: Gun shot.)

JITTERS: *(To Dora.)* Hey — are you OK?

DORA: I have to get up.

JITTERS: Yeah, sure.

(Jitters exits.)

DORA: We land in Paris and I am whisked to the Theatre de la Ville where Mr. Martins and the dancers are rehearsing. They are all immensely pleased to see me. When I go to the hotel there are three bottles of Burgundy waiting in my room. A gift from Mr. Martins.

On our day off I go to the Louvre. On the Place Vendome I pass a jewelry store. I glance in the window and there is my sister staring back at me. I blink and she is gone.

I continue to the museum where I come across a portrait of a young girl, a Vermeer called *La dentelliere*. It is *The Lacemaker*. As I look at the portrait, two young people approach me and block my view. I move to get out of their way and they move, too. I step to one side and they step, too. It becomes a kind of game with us. A guard in a grey uniform comes over and asks us what is the matter. The young people look at me and walk off mouthing something. Breathing it as they laugh out of the gallery they call me *"Juive."* It sounds like a curse or a hex or it is something dirty, obscene. *Juive.* And the guard says nothing.

On my way home I pass the jewelry store again — Bucheron — and this time I go in. A necklace catches my eye in one of the glass cases. I attract the attention of a saleswoman who shows me the strand of pearls on a blue velvet cloth.

(A French Saleswoman enters with the pearls.)

FRENCH SALESWOMAN: A beautiful choice, Madame. They are 8740 Francs.

DORA: They're lovely.

FRENCH SALESWOMAN: You are American.

DORA: Yes.

FRENCH SALESWOMAN: These came from California a few months ago. From L.A. From a big big Hollywood movie star. I cannot tell you her name. Would you like to try them on?

DORA: May I?

(She puts them on Dora.)

DORA: *(To audience.)* They are like a kiss on my neck. They are cool and smooth to the touch, like another skin. There is weight to them, but it is comfortable, regular, like an arm around your shoulder, like someone squeezing your hand.

FRENCH SALESWOMAN: They suit you.

DORA: *(To audience.)* But before I can answer her, there is an explosion outside the jewelry store.

(SFX: Loud Explosion. Lights change.)

DORA: The security men rush out into the street. The little saleswoman hides behind her counter.

(The French Saleswoman exits.)

DORA: There is chaos in the store — people are moving toward the exits. I turn away from the counter and I walk out onto the street. There's a huge cloud of smoke and people covered in blood are sitting on the curb. I hear an ambulance and the scream of a child and I see a woman lying in the middle of the street and there is Pearl crying screaming bending over her body and this time I take Pearl's hand and we run, *we run*. My father says I'm quick on my feet. He says I've always been fast . . . Since I was eight . . . standing on the corner . . . me on one side of Mama and Pearl on the other . . .

(Dora opens her palm to reveal the strand of pearls.)

DORA: I have always been fast on my feet.

(Dora exits.)

(Victoria enters and climbs a platform as the lights fade down. SFX: A Splash. Lights up on Victoria as she towels off. It is 1996. She wears the pearl necklace.)

VICTORIA: We move from St. Louis to New York City. We find an apartment on Riverside Drive overlooking the George Washington Bridge. There are ballet posters on every wall. A pink tutu hangs over the bed. There are piles of New York City Ballet programs in the hall. The apartment comes with everything in it. It takes two dumpsters to get it all out.

There is a can of Canada Dry Ginger Ale in the back of the master closet.

When I lift it, it rattles like there's something inside. I try to open it but the pop top is fake. There's no ginger ale in it. It's one of those hollow cans people buy to hide their valuables.

I find a hammer in the hall closet and I smash the can — almost too hard — and a pearl necklace falls out.

I try to contact the previous owner of the apartment but her number in Austria is disconnected. Her lawyer had let slip during the closing that she had run off with a Viennese ticket taker. I get the pearls appraised and they are worth $5400. I wear them. I've earned them. I gave up everything to come here. Everything, everyone, every joy I had in St. Louis.

We have money now. Alexis attends a private girls school. Josh orders cases of expensive wine delivered to the apartment. I walk along the river alone. My friends in St. Louis call me less. I try to drown my loneliness in a glass of wine before Alexis comes home. When I complain to Josh that I'm unhappy, he tells me I don't try hard enough. So the next day I attempt to connect with the mother of a child in Alexis' class.

(Abby enters.)

VICTORIA: Hi!

ABBY: *(Trying to avoid her.)* Hi — I've really got to get to work —

VICTORIA: What are you doing for the holidays? I know Alexis would love to have Chase over.

ABBY: We're spending the first week in Woodstock and then we're going to Rome.

VICTORIA: Rome? How wonderful. I love Rome.

ABBY: We're going to see the pope.

VICTORIA: I love the pope.

ABBY: Up close.

VICTORIA: Really — the pope?

ABBY: We have an audience.

VICTORIA: But aren't you — ?

ABBY: What?

VICTORIA: Aren't you Jewish?

ABBY: I am Jewish. You can be Jewish and still have an audience.

VICTORIA: By why would you — ?

ABBY: Why would I want to see the pope? He's the pope.

(Abby exits.)

VICTORIA: I read in *The New York Times* that there is a team at Mt. Sinai Hospital making a heart from pig guts. That's what I want, a pig heart. The one I have is too soft. But it won't be ready for another fifteen years so I must do with the heart I have for now. I enroll Alexis in a swim program for underprivileged youth in Washington Heights. I fill out the forms — I make Josh an electrician instead of an investment banker and I put us on food stamps. I cannot wait until the program begins. Maybe these are the mothers I belong with. Maybe these will be my people.

(Victoria stands on the platform. Lights down. SFX: A Splash. Lights up on Victoria toweling off.)

VICTORIA: I take Alexis to her first lesson. I gaze at the women clustered on the bleachers. I sit alone, calculating. The timing must be right, I must approach them effortlessly. If I look desperate they will sense it and they won't want me.

(Cheryle enters and sits down near her.)

CHERYLE: I like your pearls.

VICTORIA: I forgot I was wearing them.

CHERYLE: Macy's right? There was a sale last week. I got a string for my mother. They looked exactly like those, except to tell you the truth — I think mine were bigger. Tell me you missed the Macy's sale and I'll just die.

VICTORIA: I missed it, I did.

(Cheryle looks out at the swimmers.)

CHERYLE: Come on Valerie! Go! Go!

VICTORIA: Go! Go!

(Beat.)

CHERYLE: I'm going to the Whitney next week, you want to come?

VICTORIA: Me?

CHERYLE: Unless you're busy —

VICTORIA: I'm not busy.

(To audience.) Her name is Cheryle.

CHERYLE: I figure if you're going to live in the greatest city in the world, you might as well take advantage of it.

VICTORIA: (To audience.) She has little hearts painted on her fingernails and a tattoo on her ankle. Her daughter uses a Playboy bunny towel.

CHERYLE: I like MOMA but lately I've been taking the bus out to Queens to PS 1. I think their collection is improving. Or we can go to the Frick or the Jewish Museum. I can take Mostly Mozart or leave it but I'll stand in line all day for Shakespeare in the Park. As long as I have my *Times* with me. I read *The New York Times* every day cover to cover.

(Cheryle exits.)

VICTORIA: Cultured white trash. Tears well up in my eyes. Thank you God.

(Victoria stands on the platform. Lights down. SFX: A Splash. Lights up on Victoria toweling off.)

VICTORIA: We get our nails done, we go shopping, we go to MOMA. We have coffee with Theresa who has three kids by three different men. We go to a movie with Kyoko whose English is so bad the cashiers at A&P make sport out of overcharging her. I wear T-shirts with logos and dirty beat-up jeans. I change back to my real clothes in the car when I get home. When Josh asks me why Alexis is swimming in Washington Heights, I tell him I want her to be well-rounded. I even give him a picture from one of the meets.

Spring comes and Cheryle and I steal the key to the swimming pool after one of the meets. We start coming down after dinner, after the kids are asleep. We can't get enough of each other.

(Cheryle enters.)

CHERYLE: (Awed.) You did not finish the *Times* crossword puzzle.

VICTORIA: It's Monday. Monday's easy. Try me on Friday — I get four answers.

CHERYLE: I got a date on Friday. Kyoko fixed me up with her brother.

VICTORIA: Her brother!

CHERYLE: She showed me his picture.

VICTORIA: How's he look?

CHERYLE: Japanese.

VICTORIA: What if you don't like him?

CHERYLE: She says she fixes him up with all of her friends. She'll fix him up with you if you want.

VICTORIA: I'm married.

CHERYLE: So?

VICTORIA: You can't go out with Kyoko's brother.

CHERYLE: He makes good money.

VICTORIA: You're crazy.

CHERYLE: You know what I want to do? I want to get married. I want to wear a white dress and stand up in church and go home with the groom. You were smart. You married an electrician. Never out of work. I should have figured out a way to make more money, you know? Tonight Dougie told me he wants to go to college next year and I don't know how I'm gonna do it.

VICTORIA: Can he get a scholarship?

CHERYLE: For what? Dating?

VICTORIA: You said he's smart.

CHERYLE: He doesn't apply himself. He's like me. I didn't blossom 'til I got to Adelphi.

VICTORIA: You'll figure out something. You're smart.

CHERYLE: I don't know why you think I'm so great.

VICTORIA: You are great.

CHERYLE: No I'm not. I'm just a stupid bitch who likes to swim.

VICTORIA: You're great because you're not going to go out with Kyoko's brother because you don't want to hurt her feelings when he ends up being a jerk. You turned her down, didn't you.

CHERYLE: Fuck you — you fucking mind reader! I'll meet you at the car.
(Cheryle exits.)

VICTORIA: Then an article comes out in *The New York Times* about businessmen and their families who support the poor and Josh is in the article. It talks about the job-search project he started for the homeless, and his work for the Parkinson's Unity Walk in Central Park. I'm so proud he's being recognized until it mentions that even his daughter swims with the underprivileged. And there's a picture of Alexis at one of the meets. And then it hits me while I'm reading this that Cheryle is reading it too.
(She removes the necklace. As she says each name, she touches a pearl on the necklace.)

VICTORIA: Cheryle, Theresa, Kyoko and Carla. Juanita and Malva and Sujita.

All the mothers on the swim team — they're all reading it. I take the pearls down to the little park under the George Washington Bridge and I throw them as far as I can into the Hudson.

Then I call Cheryle and I get her machine. Two days go by and she still doesn't call. I go to her house. I sit in her driveway and honk the horn. I call her from my cell phone. I ring the bell. I can hear Pinky, her Jack Russell terrier barking his head off inside.

(Victoria stands on the platform. Lights down. SFX: A splash.)

VICTORIA: I have taken 98 dives. Little by little I chisel the women away from my memory. Their faces are already gone.

(Lights down on Victoria. SFX: A splash. Lights up. She is gone.)

(Abby enters. It is 2000.)

ABBY: We have this farm up near Garrison — twenty-five acres with a stream. Jake loves it because he can take the kids fishing. I tag along one day and I'm the only one who catches a fish — a huge striped bass. Jake offers to cook it for dinner — he's a much better cook than me. Sometime during cocktails I hear him yelling in the kitchen but he won't let me in. He has a surprise for us. So we all sit down to dinner — my sister-in-law and her kids are with us for the weekend — and Jake comes out with this gorgeous platter of striped bass on a bed of spinach, leeks and what do you know — pearls. Apparently when he'd gutted the fish he'd found a strand of pearls inside. How amazing! How incredible! Everybody thinks it's wonderful wonderful — except my mother. She's such a killjoy my mother.

(Gloria enters.)

GLORIA: You're not going to eat that fish are you?

ABBY: It swallowed some pearls so what?

GLORIA: A fish doesn't swallow something foreign unless there's something wrong with it.

ABBY: You want to analyze the fish?

GLORIA: Pass the salad please.

ABBY: Oh give me a break.

GLORIA: Pardon me?

ABBY: Nothing.

GLORIA: *(To an unseen child.)* Sammy put your napkin in your lap and for heaven's sake sit up.

(Gloria exits.)

ABBY: Nobody eats my striped bass after that. Even Jake looks a little nervous. I wrap the pearls in a napkin — the clasp is broken — and stuff it in one of the drawers in the buffet. The next morning I mention to Mom that I'm going to get the necklace fixed. My office is five blocks from the diamond district

(Gloria enters.)

GLORIA: You don't think they're real, do you? They're fake!

ABBY: How do you know?

GLORIA: It's so obvious. They're junk. Why else would they wind up in a fish? Oh, my God Jake — she thinks the pearls are real!

ABBY: *(To audience.)* Now everyone starts to laugh

GLORIA: Abby, wipe your glasses.

ABBY: *(To audience.)* The kids, Jake, my sister-in-law. Everyone's laughing.

GLORIA: Honey, you want pearls go to Mikimoto.

(To the unseen Sammy.) Sammy stand up straight you're slouching.

(Gloria exits.)

ABBY: My mother is so judgmental. She has a comment for everything. Because she's got this ridiculous, highly arbitrary set of standards and precious few things measure up. Precious fucking few.

Five years ago Jake's doing a lot of business in Rome. He pulls some strings and gets us an audience with the pope. I figure this'll shut her up — what could be more impressive, more authentic, than the pope — so I invite her to meet the pope. But she thinks we're kidding. So she doesn't come. We get home, we show her pictures of us with the goddamn pope and she thinks it's hysterical.

(Gloria enters. She is looking at snapshots.)

GLORIA: He's a fake!

ABBY: Mom, I swear to God —

GLORIA: It's an actor. Where'd you get your picture taken? The Piazza Navona?

(Gloria exits.)

ABBY: I show everyone at work and they think it's him. Nobody laughs. I manage 700 million dollars in pension funds. I predicted the market upturn in the fourth quarter last year — and my mother thinks I'm a moron. She makes me give her a key to our apartment.

(Gloria enters.)

GLORIA: In case I'm on the westside and I want to relax.

ABBY: *(To audience.)* She has nothing to do. So she goes to my apartment and moves things around. She goes through my closet. And then she goes through the kids' rooms.

GLORIA: Your daughter dresses like a tramp.

ABBY: *(To audience.)* She hides things she doesn't like.

GLORIA: And your son dresses like a fairy.

ABBY: Ma!

GLORIA: What?

(*Beat.*)

ABBY: Never mind.

(*To audience.*) Then last weekend, she makes us take her up to the country. She loves it up there because the house was built in 1899.

GLORIA: A weekend house should be nineteenth century.

ABBY: (*To audience.*) It's a crystal clear Saturday, the leaves are so green and the water in the stream is deep and blue . . .

GLORIA: I'm going for a swim.

(*Gloria exits. SFX: A Splash.*)

ABBY: And she never comes back. She has a massive heart attack. We have to fish her out of the water. No pearls in her gut.

We wait to tell Chase because she's away at sleepaway camp. But Sammy is with us. He's six. I think we should tell him that Gramma decided to leave her body and become a squirrel. But Jake thinks that's too weird because there are so many squirrels on the property. So I tell him Gramma left her body and became a swan. Gramma became a beautiful white swan and swam down the stream and into the Hudson. And maybe — maybe someday she'll visit us again. Oh, he loves that idea.

I know my mother wants her funeral at Frank E. Campbell in New York — very prestigious, very swank, very Mother.

But I decide no, no — there's a funeral home in Mt. Ivy — a decrepit little place on Main Street. Let's have the funeral here.

(*Abby exits.*)

(*Kyle enters.*)

KYLE: I work at the funeral home. People say it looks like a cocktail lounge with a bunch of caskets in back. But Mr. G pays me cash and he's been flexible about my hours since I started caring for my mother.

I bathe her, I dress her, I carry her up and down two flights of stairs. I shave her legs, brush her teeth, change her diaper. She recognizes my sister when she comes to see her. She can tell you what she had for dinner last night, but for some strange reason, she has no idea who I am. My mother thinks I'm her nurse. Every Friday afternoon she tries to pay me. On Saturdays I take her for iced coffee at Dunkin' Donuts. She remembers that she likes Dunkin' Donuts.

(*Kyle's Mother enters.*)

KYLE'S MOTHER: Buy me a donut.

KYLE: Not 'til you say my name.

KYLE'S MOTHER: That honey glazed one with the pink sprinkles.

KYLE: Go on.

KYLE'S MOTHER: Kyle.

KYLE: That's right. I'm Kyle. I'm your daughter.

KYLE'S MOTHER: If you were my daughter you'd buy me that donut.

KYLE: I'll get you the donut, but we gotta wait in line.

KYLE'S MOTHER: I want it now.

KYLE: Mom, we've got to wait in line just like everybody else —

KYLE'S MOTHER: I don't want to wait.

KYLE: Well, you have to.

KYLE'S MOTHER: Something's running down my leg.

KYLE: Now?

KYLE'S MOTHER: Something's going in my shoe.

KYLE: You just peed in the potty two minutes ago —

KYLE'S MOTHER: My socks are wet —

KYLE: Jesus, Ma.

KYLE'S MOTHER: Miss — you gotta take me home.

    (Kyle's Mother exits.)

KYLE: When I break out in hives on my back and shoulders, Dr. Beckman says it's a reaction to my fatigue. He tells me to check Mom into the nursing home in New City, just for a week so I can get some rest. Where am I going to get the money for that? He gives me ointment for my itch and I go home. But the ointment doesn't work and the hives spread to my face and my neck. I'm so nervous. The more nervous I get, the more I itch. I'm getting less sleep now because Mom's waking up at 5:00 AM. And I'm changing her twice before dinner because she keeps shitting herself — .

KYLE'S MOTHER: *(Offstage.)* Miss!

KYLE: My brother loses one of his jobs so he cuts back on what he sends us —

KYLE'S MOTHER: *(Offstage.)* Miss!

KYLE: We're getting behind on the gas and electric but I make sure she gets clean clothes and her pink donut —

KYLE'S MOTHER: *(Offstage.)* Miss!

KYLE: And she's still calling me miss and this is ten years I'm doing this, ten fucking years. And every night I pray that when I wake up she'll be good and dead —

KYLE'S MOTHER: *(Offstage.)* MISS!

KYLE: So I can get out of here.

(Kyle exits.)
(Abby enters.)

ABBY: Mother needs a suit to wear to her funeral. Even I know that. She has one in a Bergdorf's bag hanging in the back of her closet that she's already bought for the occasion. But I don't really feel like going back to the city. So I go off to Beacon and get a sweet little ensemble at the Salvation Army. Eight bucks. I get her pantyhose at the drugstore in Cold Spring. I find black pumps at Our Lady of Perpetual Help's rummage sale. There's a perfect pair of diamond studs at Woolworth's. Well — they look like diamonds. Then I go home and I lay it all out on the bed and I realize that something isn't right. Something is definitely missing. I fly through the house until I reach the dining room buffet and when I open the little drawer — there they are.

I run into Garrison and beg the owner of this little jewelry store to put a cheap clasp on them for me overnight. She actually does a nice job.

(Jeweler enters. She gives Abby the pearls.)

ABBY: How much?

JEWELER: Twenty-five. Are you sure you didn't want a better clasp on there?

ABBY: No. Thanks.

JEWELER: If you ever want to sell them I could give you a good price.

ABBY: For these? They're fake.

JEWELER: Who told you that? Those are perfectly matched rose pearls.

ABBY: What does that mean?

JEWELER: Spherical, beautiful. High luster.

ABBY: You mean they're real?

JEWELER: You really ought to have a better clasp.

ABBY: Oh my God.

JEWELER: Put them on, I want to see.

(Abby puts them on.)

ABBY: How do they look?

JEWELER: Whoever told you those were fake was crazy.

ABBY: Yeah.

(Jeweler exits.)

ABBY: I go down to the funeral home.

(Lights up on the funeral home.)

(Kyle enters.)

KYLE: Would you like some time alone with her? I'm done.

ABBY: No. Thanks. I want the casket closed.

KYLE: It must be hard to let your mother go.

ABBY: Oh, it's awful. Imagine your own mother dying ten feet from your house.

KYLE: Yeah. That'd just break me to pieces.

ABBY: Thank you.

(She is about to leave then turns back.)

ABBY: Wait a minute.

(She removes the pearls and gives them to Kyle.)

ABBY: These are hers.

(Abby exits.)

(Kyle arranges the pearls on the unseen dead Gloria.)

KYLE: I put the pearls on the deceased. She looks so pretty. That hot pink blouse around her face and hands makes her seem more vivid. And her shoes — you know they're leather by the way they shine. And look at all that fancy jewelry. Expensive stuff. You know that woman loved her mother a lot to be able to give those things up and not take them for herself. It made me ashamed. My mother deserved someone better than me.

(Kyle exits.)

(Lights up on Cindy. There is a large pile of dirt next to her. She holds a cell phone.)

CINDY: *(Into the phone.)* No Mr. Krause, the daughter still hasn't arrived, we've been waiting over an hour. Yes, sir I will but there's a swan out here about half a row down. It's doing this thing where it comes toward me baring it's teeth and then turns around. It's gone back and forth about ten times. What should I do, it keeps getting closer? Yes, sir. Thank you, sir.

(She hangs up.)

CINDY: I fill in the grave and say a quick prayer. There is no one left to bury today and I have already raked the gravel paths. I had looked forward on having lunch with Mrs. Willow, my third grade teacher who died last year — aisle 258, section 96, plot 7 — but it begins to rain so I take the rest of the day off. I dare myself to go to Wendy's. I gaze at the tables of five and six laughing women having lunch with their friends from work. Every night I go to the bookstore and stare at women in the aisles. They turn and flee. I sit in the chairs for browsers and stay until closing. I read the books people have left behind. In the last week, I have read *How To Make Your Own Cannon,* a *Field Guide to Mushrooms, Attila King of the Huns,* and *The Life and Lyrics of Sir Edward Dyer.*

I have a card printed with my name and phone number and that I have dropped it into every Dostoevsky and Faulkner on the shelves. I've left fliers with my name on it in the bathroom at Starbucks. But nobody calls. Not a single person. I am looking for a woman, but no one is looking for me.

I go to O'Donaghue's for a nightcap. Jerry gives me a beer and then I see her down at the end of the bar. What creature sits before me? What soul from heaven has found me on earth? I can not take my eyes off this woman.

(Beth enters.)

BETH: *(To audience.)* I am seventy-four years old and I have never been to a bar by myself. But my granddaughter Amy is still giving me the silent treatment and the television is broken. Six seats down from where I sit there is a woman who weighs at least 300 pounds. She stares at me all night.

CINDY: *(To audience.)* I look at her and miraculously she looks back.

BETH: *(To audience.)* The bartender gives me my Brandy Alexander and says that she is harmless.

CINDY: *(To audience.)* I go to the bathroom quickly quickly!

BETH: *(To audience.)* But it is getting late and I have to go home.

(Beth exits.)

CINDY: When I come back — she is gone. She has left behind a book. It is a book of poems by Sir Edward Dyer. I know this book. I've read this book.

(Beth enters.)

BETH: *(To audience.)* The next night, I take my red dress from Bonwit Teller out of the closet and I go back to O'Donaghue's Tavern. Amy thinks I am at the Piermont library taking a watercolor class. But I am really at a bar in Nyack being ogled by a behemoth.

CINDY: *(To audience.)* She has very blue eyes and small breasts.

BETH: *(To audience.)* Her nose is sunburned. There is a trace of mud on her shoes — but she has a kind intelligent face.

CINDY: *(To audience.)* Jerry gives her back the book of poems. She thanks him. He tells her that I was the one who found it and gave it to him for safe-keeping.

(Beth rises.)

CINDY: *(To audience.)* Oh my God she's getting off her stool. Oh my God she's coming over. She's going to —

BETH: Hello.

CINDY: *(To audience.)* Her elbow grazes my right pinkie. Every pore in my body explodes.

BETH: *(To audience.)* She has nice full lips and smells like chocolate.

CINDY: *(To audience.)* She tells me her name is Beth. She's fifteen years older than me, maybe twenty. Maybe twenty-five. Oh fuck it she's ancient but I don't care.

BETH: *(To audience.)* Cindy's vague about what she does. Something to do with dirt or plantings I think. I tell her about Amy and Kevin and the wedding. I tell her little about myself. What is there to say? The most important thing to happen to me in almost four decades is occurring as we speak. I finish my third Brandy Alexander and I leave. I know Jerry is watering them down and I tip him handsomely.

(Beth exits.)

CINDY: I go to the bookstore and buy the book of Sir Edward Dyer poems. I start memorizing all of them.

(Beth enters.)

BETH: *(To audience.)* I see her at O'Donaghue's again the next night and she's very shy, very sweet. I find her rather refreshing in a big sort of way. She asks me if I want to smoke marijuana.

(To Cindy.) How does it work?

CINDY: You inhale and you keep it in your lungs as long as you can and then you blow it out.

BETH: Then what happens?

CINDY: You feel good for a while.

BETH: How much do you smoke?

CINDY: Quite a lot actually.

BETH: Where do you get it?

CINDY: I grow it. Where I work there's a lot of — land.

BETH: They let you grow it there?

CINDY: Who?

BETH: The people you work with.

CINDY: The people there — ?

BETH: Yeah.

CINDY: They're pretty quiet about it.

BETH: *(To audience.)* She takes me to her car and we smoke the marijuana. I let her touch my breasts. What do I care? It feels good. I am having a wonderful time.

CINDY: "Seas have their sources and so have shallow springs;

And love is love —

BETH: "—in beggars as in kings." I love that poem.

CINDY: Really?

BETH: Sir Edward Dyer. 1543–

CINDY: To 1607.

(Beth exits.)

CINDY: I am drowning in fireworks. I am giddy at gravesites, I have lost all
decorum.

(Cindy returns to the cemetery.)

CINDY: Mrs. Willow: I have a love! And she's alive!

(Kyle enters.)

CINDY: *(To audience.)* I meet my friend Kyle for dinner. She has hives all over
her arms and bags under her eyes.

    (To Kyle.) Are you OK?

KYLE: Tired.

CINDY: Kyle, have you ever been in love?

KYLE: I'm not sure.

CINDY: Plato said: "Love is the joy of the good, the wonder of the wise, the
amazement of the gods."

KYLE: No, I'd remember that.

(Kyle removes a box from her pocket.)

KYLE: I'm selling a string of pearls. You know anybody who'd be interested?

CINDY: Where'd you get them?

KYLE: They just sort of . . . came to me.

CINDY: How come you're selling them?

KYLE: So I can put my mom in a nursing home in New City and take a vaca-
tion.

KYLE: Where are you going?

KYLE: To sleep.

CINDY: I could buy them. I could give my love a token of my affection. How
much?

KYLE: Seven hundred.

CINDY: That's a lot.

KYLE: OK, $650.

CINDY: $675.

KYLE: Cindy. Don't be an idiot.

(Kyle gives her the box.)

CINDY: *(To audience.)* I go to the bank and take the money from my savings
account and I give it to Kyle. The Grand Canyon of Hope has no bot-
tom.

(Cindy exits.)

KYLE: I take the money and I put my mom in a nursing home and I go to
sleep for a week. When it's time to pick her up, she's waiting for me at

the front door with a young man, an orderly. The minute she sees me she grabs his arm and says,

That's her. That's my daughter. Kyle. I pick up her suitcase and lead her to the car; I've got a honey glazed donut with pink sprinkles waiting for her in the back seat. And we go home.

(Kyle exits.)

(Beth and Cindy enter.)

CINDY: I have something for you.

BETH: *(To audience.)* A gift?

CINDY: *(To audience.)* My heart is thudding in my chest —

BETH: *(To audience.)* She's half my age.

CINDY: *(To audience.)* Sweat is running down my armpits —

BETH: *(To audience.)* I have no gift for her.

CINDY: *(To audience.)* She opens the box.

(Beth lifts the pearls out.)

BETH: *(To audience.)* Is it possible? No. Once love is gone it doesn't come back. But they are so flawlessly round and so perfectly white. Suddenly I am so sure that these are my pearls.

CINDY: *(To audience.)* That's all she says.

BETH: *(To audience.)* I know these are my pearls.

CINDY: *(To audience.)* And then she begins to cry.

BETH: *(To audience.)* I know that if I tell my granddaughter Amy, she will think I am crazy. But I am so sure. And as I sink deeper into the person I forgot I was, there is Cindy sitting next to me . . . After so many years, could this be . . . ?

CINDY: *(To audience.)* She is speechless.

BETH: *(To audience.)* Love?

CINDY: *(To audience.)* And she is so beautiful and soft I make love to her.

BETH: *(To audience.)* And I let her.

(Cindy puts the pearls on Beth and exits.)

BETH: I toy with the idea of keeping them. The next night, I take off all my clothes and I get into bed with only the pearls. But there is no thunder, no earth shakes below me. Ethan doesn't come to me in the middle of the night. In fact, I have a very odd dream; I dream that Amy and Kevin have a baby which is silly because I know they have no intention of having children. I take the silence and the dream together as a sign and the next morning I knock very softly on Amy's door.

(Amy enters. Beth puts the pearls on her.)

AMY: *(To audience.)* I am getting married.

BETH: *(To audience.)* She is wearing my pearls.

AMY: *(To audience.)* Gramma thinks they're Mom's pearls — her pearls.

BETH: *(To audience.)* She doesn't believe me.

   (Beth exits.)

AMY: I want to believe her. She is so sure. Does it matter? I wear them with my wedding dress — which I finish the night before —

   (Beth enters with Cindy.)

   And I marry Kevin, though I am certain as I walk down the aisle that all eyes are not on me, but on Gramma who is on the arm of a very large and much younger woman.

   (Cindy exits.)

   Kevin and I spend a week in Maine and then it's back to work. I am instantly pregnant and — we are overjoyed. Delirious.

   (Amy exits.)

BETH: Cindy and I babysit for my great-granddaughter, Lily. We play hide-and-seek. For years we play.

   And then one day I see Lily in the kitchen holding a cookie in one hand and the string of pearls in the other and I want to tell her to be careful. I want to tell her that she is holding something very precious in her hand. But she will only think that I am talking about the cookie.

   Then before I can says a word, she waves at me, sails out the door and is gone.

   (Lights down.)

END OF PLAY